Jill Vedebrand was born in London but business as a Production Manager and Line F with Roger Corman and continuing with othe feature films starring Ron Howard, Oliver George Kennedy and many others. In the m ... met a Swedish sea captain and made the choice to join him at sea, where she was to spend the next ten years on a variety of cargo ships and oil tankers. Jill discovered that life at sea had quite a lot in common with the film business.

'When you work on a film set or on a ship, it's generally considered that you are living a very glamorous life. It can be, as in both situations you have extraordinary experiences and see wonderful places, but there will be many days and nights with little rest or sleep and you will constantly be driven to mental and physical extremes-Financial decisions are made by others, hundreds of miles away, arriving out of the blue by telex or e mail, changing the port of call, cutting the art budget in half, leaving the crew to make it work, somehow. Your family and old friends seem to be living on another planet, you cannot relate to any news that they tell you. You miss them, you try to sound interested but their world is so removed from yours. People in the film business are fond of saying, "Hey, the train has left the station," too late to change your mind, get on with it, don't think about anything else but the job. When the ship leaves port it's the same for the sailors. In our fast paced automatic world, where cargo is unloaded in hours not days, crews have few opportunities to fulfil what is suspected or envied by those ashore, and on a film you have to be obsessed with detail to ensure nothing goes wrong, if you relax, then it surely will. The good part, the most fun, is feeling one of the team; you share it all with your companions in arms, your shipmates. At sea, if you are not crew, you are listed, as I was, as a 'supernumerary' or in excess to requirements, but there are compensations. There was a hammock slung up on deck in the sunshine, a book to read out on the bridge wing, a typewriter in the spare cabin with no telephones ringing, the changing beauty of the sea and sky, the cast of friendly characters on board and the captain, always a complete entertainment in himself'.

When Jill and Tomas were not at sea they lived on a small farm in a remote Scottish glen where they kept geese, ducks and chickens, dug a pond, planted trees, cut endless grass and patched up the old stone farmhouse.

Tomas is now a Deep Sea Pilot working in the English Channel and the North Sea. In addition to TRAVELS WITH MY SEA CAPTAIN, Jill has written a novel, TWO SAILORS, a dramatic sea story set in the 1950's.

Also by Jill Vedebrand

TWO SAILORS

TRAVELS WITH MY SEA CAPTAIN

Jill Vedebrand

1, 2 (page 76)
    Extracts from UNDER MILK WOOD by Dylan
Thomas, copyright ©1952 by Dylan Thomas.
Reprinted by permission of David Higham Associates
Limited for English language worldwide and New
Directions Publishing Corp. (U.S. rights).

Printed in Victoria, Canada

Note for Librarians: a cataloguing record for this book that includes Dewey
Classification and US Library of Congress numbers is available from the
National Library of Canada. The complete cataloguing record can be obtained
from the National Library's online database at:
www.nlc-bnc.ca/amicus/index-e.html
ISBN 1-4120-2091-3

TRAFFORD

This book was published on-demand in cooperation with Trafford Publishing.
On-demand publishing is a unique process and service of making a book available for retail
sale to the public taking advantage of on-demand manufacturing and Internet marketing.
On-demand publishing includes promotions, retail sales, manufacturing, order fulfilment,
accounting and collecting royalties on behalf of the author.

Suite 6E, 2333 Government St., Victoria, B.C. V8T 4P4, CANADA
Phone 250-383-6864 Toll-free 1-888-232-4444 (Canada & US)
Fax 250-383-6804 E-mail sales@trafford.com Web site www.trafford.com
TRAFFORD PUBLISHING IS A DIVISION OF TRAFFORD HOLDINGS LTD.
Trafford Catalogue #04-0015 www.trafford.com/robots/04-0015.html

10   9   8   7   6   5   4   3   2   1

To Tomas

Many thanks to Peter Allam for editing the manuscript, to Mary Downing for inspiring me to write this book, and to all my friends for their encouragement and support.

CONTENTS

CHAPTER 1

ONE THING LEADING TO ANOTHER

Full of anticipation, I stood at the upstairs window of the silent house looking out into the night, waiting for headlights to appear on the road between the dark hills. I ran my mind over the many items squeezed into the bulging suitcases that waited down in the hall. Had I forgotten anything? I checked the tickets and passport in my handbag for the hundredth time then ran back upstairs to the window, this time looking at the horizon in the direction of the village.

Moniaive was six miles away and hidden from view behind the mountain, but if a car took the twisting glen road, the beams from the headlights would flash and reflect up into the night sky, appearing, disappearing, reappearing all the way up to the house. If you were busy with other things, it was cat and mouse to catch the moment when you were sure, as every minute the glen could become inky black again. You would say, "I think I see them coming" but take the pan off the stove in case, not to spoil dinner. Just as your back was turned, the lights could flash cheekily from behind a hill. You would look back, but already they may have disappeared behind a bend. You could only be certain on the last stretch, the part we called the 'river run', where the road curved along the edge of the Dalwhat Water and the valley flattened out into the fields that surrounded the house. Then the car lights would blaze full in at the house windows and the pot could safely be returned to the stove.

The only lights in the glen now were at the kitchen window and stable yard at Glenjaan, a farm two miles away on the opposite hill. Brilliant security lights shone across their yard. Dick worrying about his prize bantams; and the fox.

One or two stars popped out between the thin clouds and the shadowy moon. The wind tossed the branches of the rowan tree that

1

stood by the gate, scattering berries onto the path. Still no lights appeared to signal that Jock was on his way. What if I missed the plane? I could miss the ship. There was such a distance and so many possible delays between our house at the top of that remote Scottish glen and the port of Singapore, it seemed impossible I would arrive in time, that I would actually find myself stepping onto the ship and into Tomas' arms at the right hour of the right day when the ship was due to stop briefly in port.

It was autumn 1989. Tomas was a merchant sea captain who had been at sea since he was fifteen. I had been on one large ship, the France, on a crossing from Cannes to New York many years ago, but apart from that, and the occasional ferry, sailing and the sea was a mystery and the harsh world of a working cargo ship unknown to me at that time. When Tomas was at home he liked to leave that world behind. Our old stone farmhouse in Dumfriesshire and the surrounding seven acres became his full time job. Weeding and scything under the big sky of the glen, planting and seeing things grow, digging and smelling the earth, this was my sailor's dream after weeks at sea.

Now I was going to enter his world. I had been alone at the farmhouse for fifteen weeks. The prospect of being apart from Tomas for seven months on the day he left had prompted an outpouring of grief that had caught me by surprise. "After all, you knew he was a sea captain for goodness sake," I said to myself as I made mooing noises all the way home from the airport. I had enjoyed being alone in the wild glen before. I had our beloved geese, ducks and chickens, the passing wildlife, two jolly border terrier sisters, the wonderful peace of the great outdoors, good friends. But when I arrived back I sat at the kitchen table and looked at the remains of his breakfast on the table and could not begin to think about seven whole months stretching ahead of me. Wandering around the house I noted the usually irritating sights of underpants on the floor, male pee unflushed in the loo, no top on the toothpaste, drawers hanging open ready to bruise my shin, papers strewn about and greeted everything with a misty eyed smile. Already the heart growing fonder.

The possibility of joining him on the ship on that day was very remote. It was a new company and the ship and crew had problems. "Maybe on the next voyage out," Tomas had said as we parted, meaning the end of the next year.

Slowly, I returned to the pleasure of creating my own rhythm, to the advantages of being alone, to being able to change my mind without too much consideration. When you put your emotions on hold in this way the adjustment can be brutal when the time comes to share again. Questions about where to hang a picture can turn into a crisis. Discussions on who said they would do what become screaming matches in seconds as the resentment at being separated comes tumbling out and you look at each other and say "How did we get into this?"

Someone who had experience of this was Elna who lived not half a mile away up the glen in a modest bungalow with her husband Charles, a retired colonel. Both Scots born in Glasgow, they had returned to enjoy the peace of the glen. Charles' platoon was now a small group of extremely spoilt black faced sheep. Elna had created nineteen different temporary homes in several countries. In every place she heard similar stories from the soldiers' wives and families. Stories that would be reflected in the conversations I would have with seamen on board ship. Love is a complex emotion that needs constant nourishment to survive.

It was easy to feel a flash of jealousy at someone's cheery question about a 'sailor's life' at a party, usually followed by a slightly leering "What port is he in now?" A wistful question perhaps and not meant to be malicious. Unfortunately, it would produce a sudden stabbing effect in the heart.

It was often weeks before our letters reached each other and a fortune to talk over the ship's satellite phone in those days before mobile phones became a worldwide thing. Sometimes Tomas would use the ship's agent's phone in a dockside office but the stiff exchange of "How are you's" with people listening was not a lot of comfort to either of us.

"Say something nice then."

"I'm phoning you aren't I?"

His postcards with their Swedish accent were different. When they came I smiled all day.

San Jose – Costa Rica

Please receive my warmest greetings which is sent to your heart. I will by all means try to keep myself alive that I can meet you soon. Tomas

Huang Po – China

Banana plants and sugar cane mix with huge oil tanks and farmers working with their irrigation system between. Please do not dream stupid dreams. I am yours to one hundred percent. Your Tomas.

About half way through the seven months, the red post van came over the hill with a letter from Tomas written on board the rusting 37,000 ton oil tanker he had been assigned to in May.

South China Sea   August 24th 1989

Dear Jilly

We are now approaching Huang Po once again. The weather fine, fair wind on port quarter and sun is shining rather bright today. All on board I expect feel rather relaxed after a hectic upstart of this voyage. The ship was in a very depressed condition when I took over. The old crew was pissed off, only four renewed their contracts with us. It took some time to clear the ship of dust and poor organisation. Previous captain had a different style to me which is now washed and ventilated away. We also received seven new walkie talkies rather necessary during berthing and topping up of tanks.
Engine department has had their difficulties. The compressors broke down again the other day. On the same morning we found that the Chief Engineer, a Norwegian, was missing. After searching the ship in and out for an hour we came to the conclusion that he had gone overboard twelve hours earlier when the cook had seen him leaning on the rail, fifty nautical miles south of

the Anambas Islands. Sent a man overboard message to the Coast Radio Station in case he was one of those lucky ones who find turtles, dolphins or a big drifting tree. Message sent to ships in the area to keep a sharp look out.

When in Singapore the case was finalised and I wrote a letter to his Japanese wife and twelve year old daughter. I also arranged with the Seamen's Mission to include him in their next Sunday service. As he was new to me, the crew let it be known that he was drinking heavily and did not eat. The engine crew told me they were always worried when he came down to the engine room, that he would fall down the iron steps.

Now I have a Philippino Engineer and just now I am very relaxed and thought I would write to my Jilly to say thank you for all wonderful letters, photos and information about the vegetable field. Please never stop to write to me. I read the letters over and over. My heart is in Benbuie with you. When I come back to Singapore I hope to find you waiting. I am sending some papers so you can join the ship. You are welcome on board!

My love Tomas

As I was reading the last part of this letter with mounting excitement Jock had arrived for a cup of tea carrying a jar of homemade jam and two very dead rabbits. Jock was a large part of our life at Benbuie. I had known him for many years when I had lived in the area before. He was a wonderful character and a good friend. He lived in one of the original cottages in Moniaive, famous for being covered with spectacular roses in the summer. "Never touch 'em" he would tell the passing tourists who stopped to take a photo. "Just shovel on some muck now and then." A short man with a bent back and often in pain with arthritis, he kept himself strong with hard work and his great sense of humour. Then in his late seventies and showing no sign of slowing up he would demonstrate how to lift a giant stone that had fallen off a dry stone wall by first rolling it onto a sack before heaving it back into place. "Aye, you have to know how to do these things" he would say with satisfaction before whizzing off again around the surrounding villages in one of his succession of battered old cars. Intrepid Jock, he worked every day. Mole, rabbit and rat catcher, dry stone wall builder, fisherman and local historian, he always had a joke and a tale to tell.

Now as I waited for him, an arc of light appeared far down the glen, sending my heart racing. Jock had offered to take me to the airport but it wasn't without some risk. His cars, bargains all, were full of characteristics, leaving visiting cards of pools of oil on the driveway and making grating sounds when starting up. A free wheeling running start down the drive was the normal thing when Jock left after a visit. He kept tools and strange equipment in the back and on seats, along with fish bait, last week's lunch, the odd dog or two, mysterious things in smelly old sacks, pots of paint and in season buckets of rhubarb or windfall apples.

I went outside the house, locking the door behind me, watching as the headlights made the river run. The car stopped at the distant gate and Jock's figure crossed in front of the lights to open it. I looked back at the house, at the three tall dark chimneys outlined against the pale night sky, hoping all would be well while I was far away.

Out on the pond the geese on their homemade island muttered to each other and the island swung on its sea anchor as they shuffled about. The oldest gander, George, let out a screech as Jock's car continued down the driveway towards the house. I smiled into the headlights, my suitcases at my side. Normally the two border terriers, Feisty and Fiona, would run to greet him in great excitement but they were away at the boarding kennels in Dumfries. It had been the toughest thing to leave them there. A small compensation I had, and hoped they had too, was that they were sharing a large kennel and were probably curled up, belly to belly as they were every night. Rose, another neighbour in the glen, would be coming to feed the geese, chickens and ducks each day.

"Something wrong with the car?" I couldn't help asking. He was half an hour later than we had arranged.

"Distributor, but nay problem." Jock opened up the back of the car and displayed the unusual sight of empty space lined with a neatly folded blanket. Only the strange smell remained as evidence of the previous contents.

6

"That's kind of you Jock."

"Just as well with this lot" said Jock, displaying his strength and hurling the suitcases inside. The car sank by two feet.

We trundled up the driveway, then the winding road, crossing cattle grids with a disconcerting crash. The hem of my new coat and shoes gathered the usual splashes of mud and cow poo as I opened and closed gates. It was starting to rain quite hard and the car tyres were squeaking on the wet road as we rounded corners.

Four miles from the village Jock stopped the car and switched off the lights. A wall of darkness surrounded us.

"What is it?" I whispered.

"Saw him in the headlight," Jock wheezed, grinding down the window and slipping his gun out into the night.

"I'll miss my plane!"

Rain poured in at the window. Jock suddenly switched on the headlights and fired the gun. The car was filled with the sound of the explosion as the shot went wildly into the air. "And that's something else that needs fixing" was all he said as he started up the car again.

At Glasgow airport, his smiley old face under the grubby hat at the car window made me suddenly sad to leave.

We balanced the suitcases on the trolley and gave each other a hug.

"You be careful now. It's a long ways away."

Glasgow to Amsterdam. Then a disappointing wait under the sign JAKARTA VIA SINGAPORE DELAYED. I tried not to think about what effect this would have on my timing. I watched the world walking by, careful not to nod off on the handle of the baggage cart in case the plane left without me. Here I was. On my way to join an oil tanker in South East Asia. Looking back it was amazing how things had changed over the last three years.

In 1986 I was a production manager in the film business with a fair to middling career, living in West Hollywood and working all over the States where I had been living for many years.

In the December of that year, my mother asked me to go home to London for Christmas. I was divorced from my American husband. My two English born daughters had now returned to go to college and launch careers in Europe after many years in Los Angeles and I missed them. All summer long and into the autumn I had been working in a blazing hot Dallas. I had planned to go back to Scotland where I used to live. At some point I was thinking to retire there in the distant future. I would take a plane onto Scotland for a day or two, put a deposit on a dream house and return to London for Christmas. Christmas in the cool air.

It was not cool, but dingy, hot and smoggy the day I left Los Angeles for that Christmas holiday. One of those days when everyone is irritable. The Santa Anna winds were blowing smog from the valley out to sea and it gathered like impending doom about a mile off shore in a thick orange and brown band. As your hair fizzed on end from the static electricity, small mistakes could become reasons for all out war, for jumping off bridges, for changing your will, for telling your boss the truth.

It was on such a day that I met Tomas.

At the airport, he and I, unknown to each other and delayed by separate events out of our control, converged at the check in desk behind a group of men who were in the middle of a fierce argument with the clerk behind the counter.

"What is going on here?" Tomas demanded to know in a loud voice. Was he addressing me?

"Who knows," I said, glancing at him. He looked angry, his curly light brown hair was a bit dishevelled and there was a faint aroma of whisky.

"You're not American are you?" he said in an almost accusing tone.

I stared back at him. "No. I'm not."

He had a strong accent, perhaps German or Dutch. His dark blue suit looked European. He was carrying a guitar case stuck with labels from many countries.

He stared back unflinchingly with slightly blood shot hazel eyes. Quite nice looking but a bit of a handful I suspected. Was he drunk?

I turned my attention back to the noise going on at the counter and looked at my watch.

"I will fix this," said Tomas and strode up to the counter and bellowed at the clerk.

"Are we going to get checked in today!? Are you going to make us miss our plane!?"

The group of arguing passengers were transferred to another counter.

I checked in and after going through security Tomas spoke loudly to me again as I was heading for the boarding gate.

"Are you going to London? I will only be passing through. I am going on to Sweden but I am not looking forward to it as my wife has asked me for a divorce!"

"Sorry to hear that," I muttered, not without irony and in a low voice, hoping to set an example.

"I have been nine days on the ship from Ecuador to Los Angeles thinking about it," said Tomas.

I was tired from weeks of work. My daughter had leant me her fake fur coat to keep me warm in London. I was wearing the coat to save the weight in the suitcase and I was hot and uncomfortable. No time to put make up on, I was looking forward to fixing myself up on the plane and getting some sleep.

We moved forward into the corridor leading to the plane and he told me he had three sons.

"It is Christmas," I said. "If the divorce is going to happen your sons will need you there more than ever." I showed my boarding pass to the stewardess.

"I think you are a wise woman and I will come to speak to you after the traditional meal!" Tomas announced to almost everyone on board the plane.

Traditional meal? What did he mean?

It was not as if he was flirting. Up to that point he had not smiled once. I felt as if I had just received some sort of instruction and was mildly irritated. I had always been reluctant to have long conversations with people on planes after I had been working hard as it was the one time when the phone wouldn't ring and I could have my thoughts to myself. I had been working fourteen hour days, for

9

weeks.

As it was December 17th the usual rush of Brits going home for Christmas had already begun and the plane was bustling with people trying to stuff grand pianos into the overhead lockers and crates under the seats.

At last the door was locked and we started to take off. To my amazement, the two seats next to me in a three seater by the window had remained unoccupied, although the plane was crowded. Someone had missed the plane and sealed my fate.

I was not thinking of Tomas at that moment but rather a large brandy followed by a good sleep in the wonderful space beside me.

I ate the strange tasting plastic dinner. The 'traditional meal' I found myself thinking.

I saw him pass by with a glance at the two empty seats, then appear minutes later carrying a tray with two glasses of whisky and two cups of coffee. Although we were both in economy he must have gone to first class as he had glass and china instead of plastic and there were macaroony biscuit things as well. He sat down in the aisle seat leaving a space between us.

"I seem to have two of everything," he announced to no one in particular.

"OK," I said, by now amused "But I am rather tired so I can't talk for long."

"I am tired too," he said emphatically as if that wiped out the reason for not speaking as long as he wished.

He moved into the centre seat and passed me a glass of whisky.

The stewardess came along with earphones for the film at that moment.

"We don't need those," said Tomas firmly "We are talking."

"I might want to watch a movie" I protested but the stewardess had moved on.

Tomas wanted to tell his story. He and his wife had had four sons and for much of their childhood she had managed alone while Tomas was at sea. Tomas said he hated airports and railways stations where the family had said goodbye so often. Regretting the career he had chosen, he found as many sailors do, that it was not easy to fit in

10

ashore. Tomas had missed so many days of his son's experiences, times of happiness or conflict. He would return home on leave to find that he was almost an intruder as he tried to catch up, be Dad and take control. "No continuity. Too much change," he explained.

A few months ago his seventeen year old son had been killed in an accident on a nearby farm. The relationship between Tomas and his wife had been difficult in recent months but instead of bringing the family together, it made things even worse. Tomas had been home at the time, but then had to return to work half way across the world. The family were left to grieve without him and Tomas to bear his pain alone.

His wife had told him she wanted a divorce by telephone when he was in port in South America. Now he was going home to see what he could do.

We changed the subject and I told him a little of my life working in production in the film business. It was fun to talk to someone from another world and experience. Tomas has a very direct way of speaking as I discovered from the beginning but he was also humorous. Our ways of life were so different and we were very amused by each other's misconceptions of the life at sea or filmmaking.

He was also very masculine. I liked his broad hands and the way he laughed. I felt then that he was incapable of hiding what he was thinking. His candid opinions came tumbling out, uncensored and with no concern as to what impact they might have on me. His laugh, like his voice, was also loud and I glanced at the occupant in the seat behind us. It was strangely enough an elderly woman who had been close to us when we spoke in the checking in line. I had noticed her because she was holding a piece of crochet that she worked on as she was waiting. She was working on it again and glanced up over the flying needle and caught my eye between the gap in the seats.

One of the things we discovered was that we had both been delayed by things out of our control and we hated to be late. For Tomas it had been a pre-Christmas party at his shipping agency in Long Beach where they had asked him to play guitar and had taken photographs. The photographs were meant to be shown to the head office in Stockholm and Tomas was asked to wait while someone took them to be developed.

My delay was caused by a key. An art director friend and his wife were to house sit while I was away. I drove us all to the airport in my car and at that point was in good time. After being in the line for a few minutes they returned to find me. They had accidentally put the key for the boot into the ignition and it was stuck. Out I went to the kerb, fiddling away with the key while the voice overhead intoned about temporary parking for loading and unloading passengers only and the police were quickly on the scene. I must have managed to get it free just as Tomas was arriving in his taxi.

Somewhere over Greenland the moon shone in at the plane window and I woke up to find my head resting on the edge of Tomas' broad shoulder. I had a peek at him. He was asleep with his face turned to me. As I studied his face he opened his eyes and looked at me.

I had been thinking how good he smelt, like a new book, so quickly turned away to the window to point out the land far below us. The night was very clear and the icy mountain and glaciers were shining in the moonlight.

He leant across to my window to see out, our faces were very close.

"I am sorry, but I have to kiss you now" he said, and did, very thoroughly.

I was completely flustered by it. I have gone mad, I thought, and wondered if the lady behind us was crocheting faster than ever at this soap opera unfolding in the seats in front.

The kiss made us laugh. It was so ridiculous. We dozed off to sleep again.

When the plane landed he got up, straightened his waistcoat and said earnestly, "Do I look fat now I have stood up?" I found this endearing. I was thinking that he wanted to look his best for his wife who had another person in her life now, someone who would not be going away to sea perhaps.

"Is your wife meeting you at the airport?" I asked him.

"I suppose so" he replied.

On the people mover we politely exchanged business cards. Tomas took off at the transit passenger sign and I to the baggage collection. I didn't expect to see him again.

Within two weeks of being back home in Los Angeles, now January 1987, I returned from a shopping trip to find that Tomas had left several messages on my answering machine.

I was with Annie, an Australian friend and script supervisor and we had flopped down onto my bed, side by side, to listen to the messages. We were both waiting for news of the same film getting the green light and hoped the number indicating several calls was a good sign.

"Hello hello. Do you remember me from the plane? I am again in Long Beach but I leave tomorrow...beep"

"Hello again. This is me. Tomas. My phone here is..wait..I get the number. Beep."

"Now I have it. No this is wrong, wait..I am leaving for Panama. Please call. Beep."

"I cannot find the bloody number. I am at the Hyatt. Hyatt hotel. Please call me."

Annie laughed. "Who's that?" I explained.

I phoned the Hyatt and Tomas asked me to have dinner with him that evening.

"You are not going to drive all the way down to Long Beach to have dinner with some guy you met on an aeroplane are you?" Annie was incredulous, watching me quickly change into a dress.

"He has no idea it will take me an hour and a half to get there. He's Swedish."

"It's raining and the rush hour. It'll be a nightmare."

"I don't want to let him down. He doesn't have a car here. He's a sea captain."

"How'd you manage to meet a sea captain on an aeroplane?"

"Don't ask. And what's more he's never even heard of Warren Beatty."

Driving along the San Diego Freeway that night in heavy rain, I was tempted to turn back. What was I doing going to all this trouble to meet someone who was working and living in another part of the world? As I pulled up at the hotel I saw him immediately. He was not waiting at reception, or at the bar, or worse in his room but pacing up and down under the awning.

As I got out of the car he came over swiftly and gave me a bear hug like a long lost friend. "I am so pleased you came," he said as we went into the foyer. "I want you to meet my Peruvian girlfriend, she has no legs."

I was immediately thrown. What was this? He reached behind a pillar and took out a guitar. "You remember her?" He played a few chords like an expert. My goodness, how romantic and rather funny. People strolling by looked to see if we were some kind of entertainment.

When we went into the restaurant there were few people dining. The waiter sat us at either end of a huge table which Tomas rejected immediately and started to move his own knives and forks. "I do not want to sit here!" He announced to the waiter. "I am not having dinner by myself. I am having dinner with her!" The waiter was good-natured and we all laughed including the three other people at the back of the room.

We spent the night together. It was impossible not to. At four in the morning the telephone rang to alert him for the car that would take him to the airport. "I am not needing it now," he said into the phone "I have someone else who is taking me."

"Where to, Panama?" I asked.

"The airport. That's OK?"

I stood at the window of Tomas' hotel room looking down at the Queen Mary lit up below us in the harbour. I had just spent the night with a sailor. What next?

As we crossed the reception area Tomas must have sensed what I was thinking.

He gripped my arm. "We did the right thing Jill," he reassured me. "The right thing."

We sang songs and sipped brandy all the way to the airport. What was I doing now? I'll get arrested. ("Is that an open bottle of brandy and a sea captain you have in your car Ma'am? Kindly step out of the car and place your hands on the roof.")

We hugged and parted reluctantly at the airport where we had met just a month ago. A week later a slim letter on thin paper arrived from Panama with his schedule and a note.

Holiday Inn – Panama

Dear Jill
You, your hands, eyes and voice are very very present, near, to me. Looking forward to see you again my dear travelling friend. Leaving for Armuelles 0945.
Tomas

CHAPTER 2

ECUADOR, HOLLYWOOD AND SCOTLAND

We were not to see each other again for several weeks. Then in a mad moment we decided to meet in Guayaquil in Ecuador in early March. Tomas had five days off and I was to fly down. Friends warned me of finding myself stranded. I had never been to South America and was very excited. Their doubts made me book a hotel room for the day I was to arrive. "He may not turn up," said one of my friends. "Why not?" I was sure he would be there. We had exchanged many phone calls since the night in Long Beach. I would not have been so sure if I had known then how shipping times can change. The airline schedules were not so reliable either and Ecuadorian Airlines had altered the times twice already.

I looked into the guide book. Guayaquil. In the sixteenth century there was a Prince Guayas and a Princess Quil. When the Spanish came to conquer the area they committed suicide and the city is named in their memory.

A major port, a crowded city with a wild nightlife said the guide.

It also advised that there would be armed guards at the hotel doors and to be glad of them. There were warnings about not walking far from the city centre, especially if alone. Of course Tomas would be there to meet me. Wouldn't he?

Coming into land from Miami, over flooded fields, a wide river and the sea, I felt the crazy, caution-to-the-wind flame in the heart thrill of adventure.

You could smell the swampy humid air as the plane door was opened. It enveloped the air conditioned passengers as we descended the steps and in minutes we were all glistening and steaming.

I was glad to be wearing a floaty peachy muslin dress but was now insecure about the turquoise and silver jewellery (glamour over caution in spite of reading the guide).

The airport security guards in uniform with gun holsters were accompanied by other men in khaki with bands of bullets strapped across their chests and pistols tucked into the waistbands of their trousers.

I was thrilled to see both suitcases turn up and then the pale face of Tomas in an even paler shirt, easy to spot as he was several inches taller than the brown faced smiling Ecuadorians also waiting at the barrier. We looked at each other, suddenly shy.

Out into the noisy street and into the waiting taxi, a big old sixties American Ford with squashy seats. I told Tomas about the hotel I had booked. He had intended us to go to the house owned by his Swedish shipping company so I said I would cancel the reservation.

We were driving through narrow streets passing old crumbling houses at the time.

"Maybe its better at the hotel" he said. "Not so much furniture at the house."

Not so much furniture? I looked out of the window at the houses.

We checked in at the Hotel Oro Verde ('Green Gold, named for Ecuador's biggest export, bananas) and then went down to the bar. Sitting on the stools under the whooshing ceiling fans drinking Pisco Sour I felt completely free. I was forty seven and felt twenty at that moment. Tomas was forty three. The feeling between us was light, happy, unstoppable.

We were never to forget that moment at the bar in that hotel.

In the morning I was to discover why Tomas had looked so pale at the airport as I hung out of our hotel window and he continued to suffer in the bathroom. Within two days I was to endure the same condition. Pizarro's revenge.

At breakfast in the dining room, a waiter appeared with an ice sculpture of the Statue of Liberty on a trolley. It was a bit lopsided. Several people appeared, mainly elderly, and gathered round to admire it. They were Americans and about to take a trip to the Galapagos Islands, a place Tomas and I had thought about for a visit.

We looked at each other. We didn't want to be a part of a crowd.

"We can take a jeep up into the Andes," Tomas suggested.

It sounded great to me until we came from the car hire place and Tomas handed me the keys.

"You drive," he announced, "I am not so used to cars."

He had never been further inland than the banana plantations although his ships had called at the port many times over the years. Someone had told him about Cuenca, a city up in the mountains. We were going to see it together for the first time.

Driving out into Guayaquil's chaotic traffic was a bit of a nightmare. Only for love I said to myself, feeling a bit resentful at having to drive.

Out on the highway away from the city, the fields were flooded on either side. In the distance, houses were several feet under. Banana plants and palm trees poked up out of the ochre coloured water.

Far up in the sky over the sea, sculptured black shapes turned slowly in the wind.

"Frigate birds," said Tomas. "Their wings can grow to more than two metres."

"They're called pirate birds aren't they?"

"For good reason. They steal the food from the other birds' mouths."

I was so busy looking I nearly ran into the dead mule in the road. I spun across to the other side and to add to the scare, several vultures rose up from the carcass, screaming.

Further along the road, the snow covered Andes rising in the distance, Tomas bought two coconuts with their tops cut off from a roadside stall. As I gratefully sucked the coconut milk through a straw I handed him back the car keys.

It was just as well. We hadn't gone very far when a bamboo barrier was lowered across the road and soldiers held up their hands to signal us to stop.

As I could not speak Spanish I had no idea what it was about.

They were very serious and spoke angrily. Tomas spoke just as angrily back to them. "They want to see your passport," said Tomas and I handed it over with slightly trembling fingers.

After several minutes of an exchange in rapid Spanish we were allowed to go on our way.

"The President was kidnapped yesterday," Tomas explained.

"The President?!"

"This sort of thing happens all the time here. A political opponent, something like that."

On the journey up into the mountains the landscape was constantly changing. Fields of vegetables gave way to jungle, then rocky sandy plateaus sweeping away into distant jagged peaks on the horizon.

We stopped by a mountain stream to wash the mangoes we had bought at the roadside stall. The perfumed mangoes were luscious and still smelling of the flower. Huge blue butterflies flapped in and out of the trees.

As the landscape changed so did the hats that the people wore. From village to village, from altitude to the next, the style of hat changed. We passed people wearing a pork pie weave, and everyone in the same style, from toddlers to grannies. Then further on it would be a type of sombrero and again everyone in that village or region wearing the same kind of hat. Hats being the thing in Ecuador it seems a shame that their most famous hat is called a panama. It should have been called an Ecuadorian or something but President Roosevelt wore one to open the Panama Canal and the wrong country got the credit.

Tomas told me about the famous 'fino' and the 'fino fino' which is even finer. It can take four months to make one of the very finest weave as the hat is worked on under water to keep the special grass supple. The weaving can be so close it can feel as smooth as silk. Most 'panama' hats for sale are rougher imitations. They can be rolled up and kept in the pocket but do not have the flexibility or lasting quality of the true 'fino fino'. At that time in 1987, a 'fino' coast over two hundred American dollars. In Ecuador.

Tomas enquired about buying a fino at a small store at the next village.

"Ah," said the man, naming someone.

"What did he say?" I asked Tomas.

"He said he thought that a man was making one but it would take us two days to walk there through the mountains."

We drove into and through clouds that would suddenly clear to reveal a woman weaving by the side of the road, or children walking by themselves in a group, carrying tiny babies in tightly wrapped bundles. The people had bright rosy cheeks from the lack of oxygen in the thin mountain air. They looked sturdy and strong. I liked Tomas so much for not stopping the car to look or take a photograph.

Cuenca is beautiful. We stayed in the old colonial centre in a tasteful brown roofed hotel on the banks of the Rio Tomebamba, a fierce, tumbling mountain river where the women washed clothes and left them to dry in a kaleidoscope of colour on the grassy banks. The hotel was small but had wonderful wooden panelling, a carved wooden staircase and great coffee.

Our room was 'en suite' but the bathroom door had a two foot gap at the bottom and the top, rather like a saloon door in a western. As we were both embarrassed by now with Pizzaro's revenge we took it in turns to 'disappear' when the other was indisposed.

A wonderful place to go in such a small hotel was the flat roof where you could look out on the rooftops of the city, at the blue domed and golden cathedral and the mountains beyond.

The day after we arrived we walked slowly through the streets and came to the cathedral just before a service was to begin. A choir was singing softly and many candles glowed just inside the entrance. We stood to one side on the steps as many mountain people were arriving in colourful cloaks and skirts, their strong bare feet making soft sounds on the marble as they removed their sandals and shoes and filed down the aisle.

A small child stood waiting at the cathedral door, carrying what I thought was her doll. She looked up at me with beautiful dark eyes and then proudly down at the bundle in her arms. She was about three years old and her 'doll' was a newly born baby.

The men removed their hats as they entered, revealing long thick black hair woven into a plait that hung down their backs.

It was Sunday and the day for church and for the market. The Otavalo Indian people are the main sellers and manufacturers of the lush wool garments and rolls of dazzling materials on display. There were baskets of colourful flowers, and rows of pottery.

The jewellery, woven carpets and ponchos were all tempting. I bought chunky sweaters for Tomas' sons and my daughters in a mad moment (how on earth was I going to add five large sweaters to my baggage home) and a creamy soft woollen shawl.

The weavers who made the clothes came to the market to buy their brilliantly hued aniline dyes. They filled jars of kerosene from a large barrel to light their homes in the mountains where there was no electricity supply. The women, swathed in heavy swinging skirts and shawls, often with a contented baby on their back, shopped and stopped to talk in groups around the stands selling fruit juices, their bright eyes and serene faces were so lovely it was difficult not to stare.

The hotel owner told us that after mass many Indian men go to the tavern to drink sugar cane rum. They pass a small brimming cup from one to another. The women drink only a little. 'Chicha, the old Indian drink of fermented corn, makes men laugh and sing. But aguardiente, the distilled fire water rum, makes men weep and fight.' Ancient rivalries flare into bloody blows so they say.

Whisky has been known to do the same thing to us Brits and Aquavit, I was to discover later, can have a similar effect on Scandinavians.

Something I thought I would never eat was raw fish. I turned Sushi down when offered it in California and then in Cuenca I found myself eating ceviche and loving it.

Ceviche is raw seafood, usually corvina (sea bass) marinated in lime juice, lemon and onions. You eat it with plain popcorn. The other tasty thing was llapingachos, potato and cheese pancake. The name comes from the sound it makes when you mash them. Potatoes were first cultivated in the Andes before the rest of the world. We had seen many fields on our journey.

We seemed to float through those few days together in Ecuador.

21

When we drove back down from the mountains we were floating as well as driving through the streets of Guayaquil as the rains had caused the river to flood even more.

It was scary for awhile. Tomas found his way through the unfamiliar back streets that were not flooded, taking his reference from two points. One he called 'Jesus under repair' which was a statue in the cemetery surrounded by scaffolding, and the other, another statue of a well known historical figure striding manfully forward with arm raised that locals called 'the man catching the bus'.

The water lapped around the car and we stopped at the shipping agents office near the port to find out the local news and situation.

The agent was a man with a wicked smile and a revolver flamboyantly displayed on his belt buckle. Tomas told me he had seventeen daughters and was used to having jokes made about the difficulties he would have to get them all married off and therefore not dependent on him anymore.

They spent some of the time laughing and talking and slapping each other on the back before having a short serious conversation. No matter what was going on, the back slapping and jokes seemed to be standard greeting between Tomas and anyone he knew there, mostly Ecuadorian shipping officials. I got the impression that it was five minutes of joking and then 'sorry but your dog died' or 'your ship just sank out in the bay." With all the guns at the ready, perhaps the jolly overtures were a reassurance. To start off with a serious expression could be misinterpreted and set guns blazing.

We stopped at Tomas' company house which was a smart house that had once been a consulate. Tomas' concern about "not much furniture" was that the large rooms had one sofa or simply a coffee table and a chair. There was a double bed upstairs in one of the rooms but no double sheets I was told. Tomas had slept the night before meeting me in one of the single bedrooms.

"I had no time to buy sheets," Tomas explained.

"I understand now. I thought it was the place and you didn't want to bring me here."

"Why would I not want to bring you here?" Tomas asked sounding cross.

"Perhaps its a language problem."

"I have no problem" Tomas glared at me. It was the first flash of a quick temper that was to become familiar.

"What did the agent say?" I asked to change the subject.

We drove down to Puerto Bolivar south of Guayaquil and close to the border with Peru. Tomas had to talk to another captain on board one of the company ships which would be in dock the next day.

We stayed in a hotel that had only one colour along the corridors and in all the rooms. A vivid blue. It reminded me of Antonioni's film The Passenger, with Jack Nicholson, who played a man who takes on someone else's identity only to discover that the man is a gunrunner.

There were several gunshots in the night, echoing around the streets.

"Don't look out' was Tomas' sleepy advice from the bed as I got up to go to the bathroom. The window was long and narrow and high up. I could understand why.

The agent had told Tomas that there had been an earthquake the day before. Part of the Pan American Highway that we had travelled had collapsed and sixty people had been killed. A major oil supply pipeline was also broken and oil was gushing down the mountain. Fuel was going to be rationed. There were tremendous floods in the banana plantations and the supply to the ships would be considerably delayed.

Real life was intruding into our romance in all kinds of ways. I had to get back to Los Angeles and to a considerable workload. I was flying back the next day.

We had lunch at the bar. "This barman will remember me. I spent five hundred dollars on this bar phone." Tomas repeated what he had said in Spanish to the barman. The barman laughed and set up our drinks, not knowing the reason for it.

It had been the day Tomas had heard about the divorce. He had then sailed from Puerto Bolivar to Los Angeles to take the plane home and had met me.

Tomas came to California at the end of April, staying at my house in West Hollywood. I was between movies and was able to show him my favourite places. We toured through the Mojave Desert and up into the snow of the Sierra Nevada and had a joyous time. I threw a party in my garden above Sunset Boulevard and friends came to meet the Swedish sea captain. Tomas played host, serving drinks and then entertained on his guitar of course, singing Mexican and Spanish songs (popular) and long verses of Swedish songs (interesting but tending to send people glassy eyed at the tenth verse)

We had several severe arguments. One went on for two days when Tomas decided that a friend and I were making fun of him. He reacted by getting very drunk. I had never been with someone who fed their anger by drinking and even when he went to sleep, to my great relief, he woke up half an hour later and started shouting and drinking all over again. After two days of that I was furious.

I thought he was under a lot of strain, upset to lose his family and his house in Sweden of which he was very proud.

He was, but Tomas, funny, generous and loveable, had a dark side. He could switch his mood and become difficult in the extreme, sometimes it came out of a clear blue sky.

It made me pause to think about this aspect of his character.

He had reason to think about my less attractive side as well. I was a production manager and used to working with fast talking, fast thinking people and this sent my mind into overdrive even when arrangements were being made for leisure or social reasons. I was used to solving complicated problems fast. I had to. It was my job. When it came to making plans with my very masculine man who was also used to being in charge in his own world, a man whose English was not one hundred percent at that time, the sparks would fly. I was certainly too bossy by half. I loved to surprise him and have fun things for us to do. He appreciated that. However, he did not like to be 'controlled' as he termed it.

"You cannot push me," he would say as a first warning. This could be in response to a sweet suggestion of co-operation on his part or to giving him a direct order. You never knew.

Woe betide you if you told him he was about to run a red light.

You could find yourself suddenly sitting in the car on your own.

I was often in floods of tears in those early days of our relationship, a certain percentage from my own making. It was always easy to make it up in the end but I used to describe us as the two warrior lovers.

We found it difficult to give in to each other except when making love. We also had the language and cultural differences, particularly humour. The British enjoy the wry, dry remark, the 'bon mot', but Swedish people have a different humour.

They say "Ja?" and wait for you to explain just what was funny. If you try, then the joke as anyone knows, gets killed in the explaining. On the other hand they think to repeat a joke, not just the next day or the next week, but immediately after the first telling, is quite hysterical. A Brits response would be an irritated "You just told me that" but a Swede would listen avidly, knowing the punchline, and laugh louder than ever when it came to the end.

Later only bits of the joke are mentioned. "The old man eh?" or "his underpants" and they will all roll about. Something that would produce wide eyed boredom in a Brit. Americans are not so snooty about humour and will smile congenially at anyone who is having a good time finding something, anything, funny, but I think humour is a unique country by country thing. We had music, political inclinations, 'the nature' as Tomas called it, the same taste in movies, books and plays, and we had love.

Seven months to the calendar day since we met, on July 17th, Tomas phoned to say he was coming to California.

"How long are you coming for?" I asked.

I hadn't spoken to him for some days. He was in Sweden again, agonising over what to do. We hadn't seen each other since May.

"For the rest of my life if you'll have me," came the astounding reply. I was stunned, thrilled, confused.

I went to the airport to meet him. He arrived tipsy with very little luggage. I wondered about his words on the telephone. "Are you sure?"

"Are you sure?" he said, looking hard into my face.

Tomas took a ship to New Zealand that next month and then gave up his job having been promised a new ship with better money. It was not to be. The company had to deal with strikes in the shipyard where the ship was being built and the waiting, for Tomas, went on for weeks. I on the other hand started the first of three back to back productions that were to last until the end of 1988. Tomas took an interest in all that was going on and helped out on all three films. His three sons came to visit us for six weeks and were on the set with us every day. They were a joy and still are.

In November 1988 at the end of months of hectic work, we found ourselves in Arkansas. I had completed the last of the three productions and could be free for awhile. I was exhausted. Tomas suggested we drive slowly home to California across the States instead of taking the plane. He knew when I got home it would be more phone calls and messages.

On that journey back we decided to move to Scotland to a house I had bought on that Christmas trip in 1986. "The movie business is not my style" Tomas would say. One of our careers had to go or we would never be together. I was ready to be in Scotland again, in the fresh air, marking the seasons. I would miss America and my American friends and it was difficult to be away from my youngest daughter Nicola who by now had returned from four years at Art College in Brighton and was once again living in Santa Monica and making her reputation there as an artist. I missed my eldest daughter Claire too. She was a successful fashion model living in Paris, travelling the world doing the collections. They had their lives but I wasn't sure what mine was meant to be. Tomas and I had wild ideas that we would make some kind of business at the place in Scotland.

We had seen it once together on a very fleeting visit sandwiched in between the film productions when we flew over to Scotland for ten days. Lit by golden evening summer light and overgrown with forget-me-nots and buttercups, we stood by the chattering river and dreamed impossible dreams. Seeing it in summer was different to living there in the middle of winter.

The house at Benbuie was two cottages joined together. It had two staircases, three large rooms and a bathroom upstairs and three large rooms downstairs. It had a stream running down from the mountain, stables and buildings at the back. It had not been repaired for years and years. I had bought it on a dark December afternoon. The mood I had been in was one where the further up the glen I went from civilisation, the more excited I became at living in whatever lay at the end of the road.

It was a mad but lovely decision. Without knowing it I had found a house and met the man who was to live in it with me, all within twenty four hours. I had bought the house for my retirement or could afford to stop working. I had thought then that I would be living there alone.

The property had the most glorious unspoilt views but when Tomas and I arrived to actually move in it was January 1989 and in the middle of a storm. Charles, the retired colonel, who had written to me asking to keep some of his sheep on the paddock in front of the house appeared out of the gloom and extended his hand in greeting. "Terribly sorry," he said, "but I think your barn is blowing away." Great shards of sheeting were flying across the fields and the main structure was leaning over in its final death throws.

Tomas refused to undress that night and lay on the make shift bed (furniture still to arrive from California) with hat and gloves on saying over and over again as the loose tiles rattled on the roof and the wind whistled through the single glazing, "You have bought a barn. This is not a house, it's a barn. I cannot live in a barn!"

We poured money into the place, working round the clock alongside carpenters, plasterers and of course Jock, who came regularly to help and give advice (not always welcomed by Tomas) and to build the chicken house. A JCB arrived to dig a huge pit and Tomas made a giant pond fed by the running stream. I sowed wild flowers. Frogs, butterflies, bees and birds arrived. We worked like mad, fighting over the details and exhausting ourselves lifting earth and giant stones, but Tomas and I turned it into a wonderful home. Tomas removed tons of rubbish that had been buried over the years, made a huge vegetable field that produced carrots and peas that tasted like no others, planted trees, dug ditches and drains and crowned the newly painted house with three tall chimney pots that he lifted onto the roof and cemented himself.

By that June 1989 we realised that we had spent far too much money and Tomas said it was time for him to go back to sea to bring in some income.

When his contract came, it was for seven months.

"You go Jakarta?"

I was jerked out of my day dreaming by a tall Indonesian man carrying a bagful of Barbie dolls.

"You go Jakarta?" he demanded to know.

"No, Singapore. But I think it's the same plane." I pointed up at the sign.

I looked at my watch, I had been sitting there for three hours.

Travelling alone meant not being able to potter around the shops especially with my heavy 'carry on' bag searing my shoulder. My bag was more a drag-behind-you but I was trying to give the impression that it only weighed a kilo or two.

The Indonesian man sat down, sighed and said "Jakarta" to himself and to his bevy of blue eyed dolls who all stared up at him from various angles of repose and indifference.

On the other side of me a dignified Indian Sikh was snoring into his beard. Then a mad scramble as it was apparent we were boarding at last. "Sorry for the delay," said the boarding clerk every minute as we filed by and down the slope. "Sorry for the delay, sorry for the delay," echoed behind me. I was trying not to panic.

What would this delay mean? That I would have to take off for the next port if I missed the ship and where would that be, China? Probably I would just have to return home. I would not allow myself to be depressed before knowing. I knew one thing, that Tomas was somewhere out on the South China Sea heading for Singapore and that he was thinking of me as I was of him. Somehow we would be together soon.

I was on my way now and nothing was going to stop me from finding a way to get on board that ship.

CHAPTER 3

SINGAPORE

Changi Airport, Singapore. Super modern, efficient, glamorous and sparkling in the sunshine. Two tiny Malaysian women in bright red blazers and matching lipstick were holding a sign with the name VODIBIN. I walked by, then returned. "I'm Jill Vedebrand," I said. "Are you looking for me?" I was not Vedebrand but Griffith at that time but Tomas' name was close enough and no one else was laying claim to it.

"Yes, yes," they said almost in unison. "We official airport greeters." They took a pre prepared sticky label with VODIBIN on it and stuck it to my jacket.

"I am actually Griffith," I said but they marched ahead. The shipping agency? As we were still to go through immigration I thought the conflict of passport name and label would be a problem. I reached to remove it.

The smiles disappeared "Oh. Do not remove label please!"

The immigration officer did not even glance at my label but made serious business with my passport photo and the checking of the dishevelled but slightly look alike self in front of him.

The ladies and I moved into the baggage collection area.

They were smiling once again. "Please to give bag ticket we will take care of bags."

They had no idea. My suitcases would give them a permanent injury. I had a quick vision of both of them lying on the floor, each with one of my suitcases on top of them.

As the dreaded bulging bags came swaying along the carousel I leant to swing them away from their outstretched arms. Like two iron anchors, one on each hand, the suitcases propelled me into an elderly Chinese gentleman. For a moment he buckled alarmingly at the knees.

I struggled to place the suitcases onto a cart. I was being observed by a young Singaporean man in a short sleeved tee shirt that displayed his muscular, sailor like arms.

He was staring at my label but when he spoke he pronounced the name correctly.

"You Vedebrand for Dai Ichi Hotel." It was a statement more than a question.

"Harbour Hotel," I corrected anxiously as he swept up the suitcases as if they were matchboxes and strolled ahead. I turned to say goodbye to the 'greeters' but they were gone. I had so enjoyed being met but I never found out who sent them.

I followed my suitcases out to the car, still bleating "Harbour Hotel?" which was the name of the hotel on my papers that Tomas had sent to me. It was where I was to be picked up to be taken to the ship. After the plane had arrived so late, the last thing I wanted was to be taken to the wrong hotel. I started to feel very anxious.

The suitcases were now being loaded into the car. I held out my papers.

"Harbour Hotel?" I said again as perspiration trickled between my breasts. The sun was fierce.

"You wife Captain Vedebrand?" he asked suspiciously. Truth was on my tongue but if that was what he expected I would only confuse him by telling him we were not married.

He opened the car door and I got in. I decided he must be one of the crew.

Inside, the car smelt of frangipani and cool air slid over my flushed face like melted ice cream. Bushes ablaze with bright flowers whizzed by the window and the glittering towers of modern Singapore rose up in the distance. It was all lovely and I was going to see Tomas, wasn't I?

As we pulled up at the hotel I looked out at the brass lettering on the wall. THE DAI ICHI HARBOUR HOTEL. Muscles and I looked at each other in triumph.

He carried the suitcases over to the reception. "Oh I'm not checking in," I said.

He spoke to the man at the reception in Chinese who reached for a key.

"Ship come tomorrow."

"Why? Is anything wrong?"

"Ship delayed. The agency will call you. Goodbye."

I let myself into the room feeling dubious. I suppose it was alright. The phone started ringing.

"This is agent. I speak with your husband. We come for you 09:30. OK?" He sounded cross.

"The ship won't be in port until the morning then?" I asked.

"The ship is at sea," he said, unnecessarily I thought.

I was standing by the window looking out on the container port. The sky and sea were blue but on the horizon there were thick dark clouds. Tomas was somewhere out there, perhaps in a storm. Was this why he was delayed? I tried to put that thought out of my mind as I did when I was at home and switched on the radio to hear "This is a gale warning to all shipping."

I looked in the mirror. I was not looking my best. The long flight and lack of sleep on the previous night. My neck felt as if it had been bolted into place by a zealous welder.

My eye fell on the hotel directory. The Delight Health Centre was on the ground floor. I would have a massage.

The gimlet eyed receptionist demanded 'money up front' which was a new one. What did people do? Have a massage and rush out the door without paying? A version of dine and dash? Two brawny Australian men were chatting to each other and lolling on the counter. They turned to look at me and gave me knowing smiles. I asked for a woman masseur.

"You are number seven," said the receptionist after I had paid. "Down corridor."

Number seven was a large square room decorated in purple with a double mattress on the floor and a shower cubicle in one corner. The only lights were candles. Smoke from incense wafted in swirls around the room. Not exactly what I had expected. Strange atmosphere.

A large athletic oriental woman entered the room behind me. She was wearing a lot of make up, a bra and shorts. She pointed at the cubicle, and like the receptionist, failed to smile.

"You wash."

Inside the shower, I twiddled with unfamiliar knobs, forgot to put a shower cap on and blasted myself in freezing cold water.

Outside the masseur became chatty. "Many girl here no like massage woman but I no mind." What did she mean? Was she promoting herself for a good tip or advertising her sexual preferences. The truth slowly dawned. Was this a 'massage parlour'? What an idiot I was.

I had recovered from my controlled scream from the icy water and found my voice.

"I'm here to join my husband who is arriving in port tomorrow."

"You here for good time?"

I was unnerved by that one. If I said yes what would happen? Would she leap at me with a vibrating dildo or would the wall roll back and ten male nude dancers come high stepping into the room?

I reflected on the grim receptionist, the money up front, the smiling Australians.

What should I do? Should I leave?

I emerged and wrapped the towel firmly under my armpits.

"It's my neck and shoulders," I said looking her in the eye.

"OK." She pointed at the mattress. I thought, I can just dress and leave but by now I was feeling stubborn. My back was so stiff. I needed that massage. The one I had come for.

I laid down firmly on my front.

"You husband sailor?" she asked as she swept away the towel. "We have many sailor come here."

"It's mainly my neck," I said rather coldly, now feeling depressed.

"You no like anything else?"

"I walk your back, OK?"

Crunch, crunch, crunch, she marched up and down. She seemed to know what she was doing. My face was being pushed into the mattress by her efforts and I was trying not to breathe in.

She wedged her bare feet between my shoulder blades and rocked back and forth.

After ten minutes she stepped off and I staggered to my feet. "Thank you," I said.

(We British, polite to the end) I should have said, "What a pain! I want my money back!"

The following morning I looked at my back in the bathroom mirror. I was covered in bruises.

What would Tomas say? The good thing was, I had slept all night like a log.

At 09.30 Muscles arrived and drove me down to the dockside where I craned my neck to see the name of my Tomas' ship. Nowhere to be seen. The rain was coming down monsoon fashion. I tried to stay centre of the umbrella and peered out like a stone statue from a fountain. Through the waterspouts, two Singaporean men introduced themselves in an off hand kind of way, then resumed their long conversation in Chinese. We did not appear to be going anywhere at that moment. I waited as patiently as I could, watching the fishing boats and launches bob against the rickety wooden jetties. I knew Tomas' ship was 37,000 tons. This place was too small.

A noisy launch arrived. A driver, no one else on board. Tough and greasy looking, the boat was surrounded by tyres, like a tugboat. My suitcases were loaded on board and I looked in at the dirty seats.

"Where are we going?" I shouted above the din of the motor.

"To join your husban' ship"

"Oh?"

In my technicolour dreams I had imagined the moment when I would join the ship. The sun would be shining and as I ascended the gangway, Tomas would smile from the top of the steps. I would be looking my best of course and to surprise him, slim, and in my dreams, several years younger.

My hair had been destroyed in the massage parlour, I had a large nervous pimple but I was wearing my favourite dress. I scooped it around me to avoid the tar and oil as I climbed aboard. We roared off. The noise was incredible. Blue fumes filled the small wheelhouse. The two Singaporeans conducted a conversation at scream pitch and the driver joined in with the odd word, turning from the wheel and showing red stained teeth when he laughed.

After about twenty minutes when we had passed many tankers docked at various jetties and looked as if we were starting out to sea, I stood on wavering feet and tried to make myself heard.

"ARE WE NEARLY THERE?"

"FORTY MINUTE OUT. FORTY MINUTE."

Forty minutes? Was the ship in Malaysia?

I checked the black flecks on my face and tried to comb my hair as the launch hit deeper water and we rolled and bounced from side to side. Another twenty minutes of this?

Now I scanned the horizon. Far away, ships on the sea but apparently not moving. What I later learnt was, 'On the roads'. Trouble was, no road. Or dockside for that matter. What was it the agent had said? 'The ship is at sea.'

The city and shoreline had become a blur behind the rain.

Six miles out, my heart skipped a beat as I saw the name of the ship, but how on earth was I meant to get on board?

We got closer. The ship loomed above us like the side of a ten-storey building.

The sea slapped and swirled against the great ship's sides. Everything was in motion. The ship went side to side, the sea went up and down, the launch was backing up and tossing to and fro, and my knees were moving like concertinas.

Then I saw the staircase. Metal steps descending from the ship down to the water but not actually ending up in the water but about two metres above the surface. There was a single banister through which an elephant could have been hoisted up the ship's side, and lots of air between each step. The whole thing ended in a kind of platform which had no banister at all and kept submerging into the swirling waves as the ship rolled.

I could not believe that I was meant to jump onto this platform like a trained athlete.

"Yump! Yump!" shouted the Chinese boatman at the wheel, chewing furiously on his damp cigarette and waving impatiently.

He gunned the engine and we roared backwards as he tried to keep alongside without actually smashing up his boat. I saw the reason for all the tyres.

What was I meant to hang onto? I looked up at the wall of dripping steel.

The two Singaporeans timed their jump and hauled my suitcases up the steps. I felt guiltier than ever at their weight. Stupid me to bring so much. Now I would really pay for it. They will probably tumble down and knock me into the sea. ("So sorry Captain, wife fall into sea with suitcases. Very sorry Captain.")

The ship lurched and the anchor creaked. The platform was level with my head, then my feet, then my head again.

The boatman looked purposeful as if he meant to give me a push.

I jumped. As I landed, the platform dipped and my knees gave way. I found myself in a crouch, like a large frog. Why did I wear a dress? I heard the launch roar away as I climbed the steps with trembling legs.

And where was Tomas? Certainly not at the top of the steps.

Far above me I could see someone ready to take my hand. A large man with a big smile. This was Rolando, the third mate as I was to discover. (Later on, ever famous to me for his answer to my question, "What will you do if pirates get on board?" which was "Hide in engine room ma'am." He was serious.)

He greeted me as if I was not soaked to the skin, or terrified, but rather as if I was a first class passenger on the QE2 and directed me across the puddles between the oil piping that covered the deck, as if I was picking my way through deck chairs. I was so glad of his strong hands and warm welcome. To me it was nothing short of a miracle that I was on board.

Inside the ship now, humming from the generators, the smell of oil, male perspiration, fish frying somewhere.

Rolando turned another corner and we nearly bumped into a man in his underpants, who was mortified and adopted a kind of crouching karate position, hands stiff, elbows tucked in. He hurried by avoiding our eyes while Rolando muttered his apology.

As we climbed to the top I heard Tomas' voice before I saw him and my smile returned.

Tomas clamped me to his chest. He was as wet as I was.

35

"I have been standing out on the bridge wing for the last hour!" he roared in my ear.

"When did you come on board? It's the bloody cook. He was drunk last night and stole the ship's mascot so I had to tell him a thing or two."

"Mascot?"

Tomas pointed to a Japanese china doll in a glass case. "This is always across from me at my place at the table." Tomas rocked with laughter. "I was bound to miss it."

"How did you find it?"

"I just told them all no shore leave until I get it back. The cook was found singing to it in his cabin. Swore to me that he hadn't stolen it. Just borrowed it for decoration.

In the ship's office I saw a small Philippino man sitting in a hunched position.

"The cook?" I whispered.

As I walked in I saw that tears were flowing down his cheeks.

"OK, OK, go and sleep it off. We will talk more on this later." Tomas gave him a friendly pat.

The cook left.

"So no dinner tonight?"

"We can have that ashore."

"Ashore?"

"We are going into dry dock for repairs. Should be leaving in about thirty minutes. That was the agent who came aboard with you."

"You mean to tell me I risk my life climbing on board in the middle of the ocean and you are now going to dock when I could have joined the ship by taxi?"

"We're going to the other side of the island, opposite Malaysia. Selat Johor. And not so easy to come aboard in dry dock. You will see. Come up on the bridge and watch us take off."

The bridge is the floor above our cabin and office. A place full of mysterious instruments, a bench with charts and a radar that looks like a giant video game. At each end of the long room, the sliding doors open out to the bridge wings, where you step out into the open air and can see the length of the ship far below and all the sea and sky surrounding you.

It must be everyone's favourite place, and it quickly became mine.

The sky around was piled high with clouds and dazzling patches of blue. The rain had stopped and I could see the twinkling skyscrapers of Singapore on the horizon. High above the sea, a gentle breeze was blowing. It was only then that I remembered my hair was plastered to my head.

The ship, a motor tanker that had seen better days, was in need of a face-lift and other surgery. First time on a tanker, I realised that the one hundred and eighty five metres of ship stretching before my eyes was simply a long tin can.

On the bridge wing, I was standing on the only recognisable bit of ship that was a ship to me, a kind of apartment building mounted on the back end. This was where everyone slept and worked, the rest of the ship was for the cargo. The deck was covered with fat pipes, pumps and valves, no place for a sunset stroll. You would end up with a fat toe or slide unceremoniously overboard on the greasy deck as the ship changed course. I strolled around the back of the bridge windows where I could see Tomas and the Chief Officer preparing to leave and was confronted by the huge ship's funnel, growing out of the deck in front of me, throbbing and belching smoke. To one side of the funnel, a fiercesome yawning chasm led down into the engine room far below. It was like looking down into the very pit of hell.

Heat as if from a hundred ovens and the roar of pounding machinery made my stomach lurch and wonder that men were actually down there, working, when suddenly, we were moving.

I ran to the bridge wing and leant on the metal wall that came up to my chin, looking forward, then to the side, as we gained speed and the water swept by in long lovely swirls. Then up at the sky at the puffy clouds moving overhead.

It was like standing in the road with the whole street taking off under your feet. I looked across through the open door to the bridge. How could Tomas do this? Hurtling through the water with this great lump of steel that takes twenty minutes to slow down or whatever. So easy to, well, bump into something.

As we approached Sambawang Dry Dockyard, far north of the city, the shoreline became less commercial. On the Malaysian side, fragile jetties, fishing poles, nets and rickety huts. Slim boats skimmed over the water and the western world was left behind. We were heading along, dead slow, about two knots, as two jaunty tugboats, SEA CHEETAH and SEA LEOPARD came nuzzling up to the side of the ship to guide us up to the lock.

Once we were inside and the giant wooden gates were closed, balanced somehow on blocks that ran along the underbelly of the ship, the water started to drain away.

When it was gone, I looked down into the huge well of the dry dock below us. We were perched in the middle, like a great beast mounted for display, empty space all around and below.

"How will we get ashore?" I asked Tomas

"They will rig something," was all he said as he hurried to the office.

I was to learn that as soon as we came to a halt anywhere, 'on the roads', or in port, Officials, Salesmen, Chandlers, Immigration, Agents, Port State Control, Loading Masters, Company Representatives, Health Officials, Crew with toothache wanting to go ashore, Federal Express with the Mail and Engine parts, would soon come swarming into the office, all requiring the Captain's attention and his signature. They would all need cold soft drinks or coffee, and as the ship had only one steward, which is standard on cargo ships, I found there was something I could do.

I was to learn that even if Tomas had been up all night on the bridge, guiding the ship through rough weather, there was no falling into bed once the ship had docked, as the routine of all of the above would begin as soon as the accommodation ladder (my mid ocean bête noire) was cranked down.

The parade of people would continue for hours. I had imagined that I would be sailing along with my love's undivided attention as soon as I came on board, but this was the reality.

Dry Dock

I sloped off to inspect our cabin, happy to see a shower/WC off to the side but a bit amazed at the size of the bed. At home we have a king size, this was not even a double but a single for a large person. Tomas stuck his head in at the door. "OK?"

"Bed's a bit small for two isn't it?"

"Made for Japanese," laughed Tomas. Of course, the ship had been built in Kudamatsu. I had read the brass plaque along the passageway.

"We will fix something," said Tomas, disappearing again. I could see future nights spent with my face pressed up against the wall. We were both on the large side from eating all that good country food at Benbuie.

My giant suitcases had been left in the cabin and took up almost all of the floor space. As I started to unpack I became conscious that my eyeballs were starting to simmer in their sockets. My hands were wet and my clothes still clung to me. There was a temperature gauge on the wall. Thirty degrees! Centigrade? I felt the air vent in the ceiling. Nothing. Better not ask at that moment. I opened the small closet and stared in at Tomas' clothes. There were two hangers and about six inches of space left to one side. I opened the drawers under the bed. Life jackets. I opened the small drawers out in the sitting room. Ship's papers, iron bolts, forgotten diaries from years back, hideous gift mugs, an old T shirt, paper clips, and definitely no room. I sat down. I would have to use another, perhaps a spare cabin for my clothes. I looked around the sitting room. Two chairs broken and lashed with cord. The cloth on the table looked dingy and the artwork on the walls was really ghastly.

There was a curtain partition between this room and the office where I could smell smoke from the many cigarettes and hear papers being shuffled.

The curtains parted and a hand appeared with a tall glass full of ice cubes and something liquid and delicious.

I stood up and took it gratefully as Tomas popped his head in briefly and kissed me quickly on the lips and disappeared once again.

I laughed to myself, looking out of the porthole at the clanging noisy world of the rusty shipyard and took a large swig from the glass. Vodka and orange fizz.

I was still very glad to be there I said to myself just before the tremendous crashing began. BANG BANG BANG BANG BANG. It was like being inside the thing as it was being built.

I took my drink outside onto the small deck outside the bedroom.

Trucks had arrived along the dockside and people were jumping out. An iron plate segmented gangway was being rigged from ship to dock wall. Suspended over the scary space fifty feet below, covered with sticky black grease, it looked like a jungle bridge and just as swingy and swayey as any in an Indiana Jones movie.

I will never cross that! I said to myself.

The people on the dockside were swathed in cloth as if they were about to cross the desert. These were the sandblasters.

There were women as well as men and before too long they were swinging on ropes and trestles against the ship's side, looking like a scene from Gulliver's Travels, tiny figures swarming over a monster. Old paint and rust flew through the hot sticky air as they worked their dozens of drills. The noise was insane. I went back inside, ashamed to be standing there with a cool drink.

The crashing inside the ship had increased if anything.

I took a face cloth from my suitcase and placed a few ice cubes in it and lay on the bony sofa in the sitting room. After a few minutes I felt someone squidge in beside me.

"No room" I muttered, pretending to be sleeping.

"The work stops at six. Then we can go ashore if you like."

"Not crossing the bridge," I said crossly as if I was eight years old.

"You might want to. We'll be here for ten days."

I whipped off the face cloth. "Ten days!"

The banging changed its tune. BANG CRASH BING BANG CRASH BOOM BOOM BANG CRASH BING BANG CRASH BOOM.

"Help," I said.

Tomas laughed. "Aren't you glad to see me?"

We didn't get ashore that evening. There were barely two minutes between one knock on the door and the next. Customs wanted to search the ship for drugs and Immigration for stowaways. After the longed for letters were read, several crew wanted to use the telephone, now rigged from ashore but in the Captain's office. A line of smiling Philippino crew waited at the door for an advance on their wages to go into the city and the third mate kept coming in and out with telexes.

Hours later we squeezed ourselves into the Japanese bed, and promptly, fell asleep.

"Good morning Tony," I said, fanning myself with a newspaper. "Hot isn't it?"

Tony was the steward. Young, uncertain and shy, with too much to do as he also assisted the cook. I was not able to communicate too well with him.

At least I could never get him to understand me and I noticed that the other Philippinos in the crew had the same problem, whether they spoke to him in English or Tagalog.

"You like me take paper?" he asked, as I continued to flap about, as if he suspected that my hand had become glued to it and I needed assistance. The air conditioning or lack of it was part of the grand scheme of the ongoing list of repairs. Everyone staggered about soaked in sweat, like castaways that had been flung into a Turkish dungeon, their shirts open and hair over their face, staring ahead with boiled eyes to some distant paradise (like Alaska) as they passed along the passageways.

"Humidity ninety eight percent," said the Chief Engineer, emerging from his fiery hellhole to take a breath of what he hoped was cooler air. We stood outside, breathing in iron filings and fumes, our damp faces held high to catch a passing zephyr, but no luck.

The new Chief Engineer was now a Croatian, a man in his late forties. He was grey in appearance, partly due to the fact that he refused to use the ship washing machine and washed all his faded T shirts himself, hanging them in a long line in his cabin to collect the smoke from the five hundred cigarettes he seemed to smoke every day. I called him Eeyore privately as he was so negative.

I started to find his gloomy views a bit difficult at dinner each day.

"Dinner was early today."

The Friendly Philippinos

"That's why the meat's half raw."

"I might go ashore and do some shopping this afternoon."

"Too expensive."

"The parts you were waiting for arrived a day early."

"That gives me time to send them back, half of them will be wrong."

"The new First Assistant Engineer will be here today."

"He'll be worse than the last the one that just left"

He didn't seem to have any political views and appeared not to have any idea what was going on in his country. He hadn't been home for a long time and spent his time ashore on the other side of the world.

Tomas asked him to join us to watch a video in our sitting room one evening; a film we thought might cheer him up. A comedy, What About Bob, with Bill Murray.

He sat in silence while we rolled about, and when it was over, thanked us and said, with the same serious face, "That was quite funny." I suppose I would have been a bit gloomy if I had to had to work in the terrible heat and noise of the engine room. I asked him if he would show me the engine room one day.

He gave me a kind of smile. "When we are at sea. Then you can come."

I didn't argue. I had planned to go ashore and escape the heat in the luxury of one of the cool shopping malls in the city.

After three days I had given up on Tomas being able to come ashore with me. "There is always something," he would say, and there was.

I had yet to cross the swinging bridge and Tomas came to see me off, shouting after me every few seconds, just to remind me how dangerous it was.

"Don't look down!" "Take it easy!" "Don't go too fast!" "Hold on to the rail!"

Feet sloping, hands groping, and not wishing to make a fool of myself, I slithered along and arrived on the dock with relief, only to realise that I would have to make the crossing in reverse as soon as I got back.

As I crossed the bridge I saw women sweeping up the piles of paint filings on the floor of the dry dock far below me in the sweaty heat and I realised how fortunate I was.

A frangipani smelling cool taxi was waiting. Bliss. I could have ridden around in it all day. The taxi was decorated with tiny golden Buddhas and coloured lights along the dashboard which flashed on and off to the sound of a musical jingle. The driver smiled in the mirror.

"I collec' money" he said. (Who else? The conductor?)

"Right."

"You Englis'?"

"From Scotland."

"Oh. Swisserlan'. I know."

He passed an album over to me as he drove along. Page upon page of bank notes from many different countries. I got it.

When he dropped me off at Orchard Road I paid him in his currency and then added a Scottish pound note as a tip.

He waved his hand, nodding his head. "Tank you, tank you. I not have one from Swisserlan."

As everyone knows, Singapore has changed from the mysterious, dangerous and very Asian port into a modern metropolis, and any of the old wicked charm is hard to find.

What is has, it has in abundance. Shops and Restaurants galore.

Carpets, souvenirs, wickerwork, Chinese dragons and lions (lots of those) pewter, watches, cameras, antiques, vases (tons of those) fabrics, jewellery (enough to make a mountain) all in a dizzy display from the ritz of the Raffles Centre to the exotic jumble of the Handicraft market.

I tried to haggle with an Indian trader over three cotton shirts for Tomas but I am always bad at it, preferring to pay too much and creep away.

There were real orchids everywhere and thousands of orchid brooches in many colours.

I bought a large paper butterfly from a cross-eyed street trader who also sold wonderful kites in the shape of fish and dragons.

It started to rain a little, and fearing for my butterfly, I popped into a shop selling umbrellas.

Once inside, I saw that they were all made from bamboo and waxed paper. The Chinese shopkeeper smiled in welcome and I pointed at the rain, turning to leave, but quick as lightning she opened up one after another and displayed them around me.

They were wonderful. Not one of them the same. I was dazzled.

"They're very beautiful," I said.

"Only six Singapore dollar." She twirled one for effect.

"OK for rain" she assured me, but in any case I was sold. I had to have one. I walked off up the street with a ring of golden birds and red orchids over my head. She was right too. Not a drop of rain came through the wax and varnished paper.

When I got back to the ship, Tomas was trying to sleep, perspiration rolling down his forehead.

I stood in front of him twirling my umbrella and he opened his eyes and smiled. "Not too tired to go back tonight? I'll just take a shower. The car will be here at seven."

The largest Chinese group in Singapore speak the Hokkien dialect.

'Yau Kui' in Hokkien, means, 'one who loves to eat' and it certainly applied to us. Hokkien Mee: Thick yellow noodles mixed with rice vermicelli, prawns, squid, beansprouts lime and red chillies. Hmmm I'll think about it. Char Kway Teow: Noodles, egg, cockles, black sauce. Hmm. Cockles? Nasi Padang Assam Kepala Ikan: Fish head in a sour, hot, tamarind and spice gravy. Uh. Otak-Otak: Bundles of mixed spices, coconut milk and cuttlefish wrapped in coconut leaves and barbecued over charcoal.

When a Scandinavian takes you out to dinner, you can be certain that if there is fresh fish to be had, that is what you will eat, and along the East Coast Parkway, Singapore has the finest seafood.

We sat at a little table out in the breezy air, drinking ice cold beer and eating Chilli Crabs and Har Loke (fresh prawns fried in their shells in soya and spices). We had washed the shipyard from our armpits and feet and we looked at each other in our fresh clothes and smiled a lot. We also smiled at everyone as they walked by our table, a dazzling parade of nationalities, colourful dresses, men groomed to the hilt. Couples strolled along the shore in the lights from the restaurants. It felt wonderful to sit there in a cool silk dress in just the right temperature. Romantic. I was just breathing another sigh of contentment when I noticed Tomas was standing up ready to go. He paid the bill quickly. "Have to get back," he said, looking around for a taxi. This, I was to discover, was how it was to be. There was no peace for the Captain.

Back on the ship, as we turned to take the steps up to our cabin, I saw the edge of a blue frilly skirt disappear around the corner. It hadn't escaped Tomas' notice either.

"THIRD!" He shouted in at the officer's mess, then continued up the stairs.

Rolando came puffing up behind us.

"How many women on board?" Tomas barked.

Rolando smiled nervously, looking from Tomas to me and back again.

I feigned disinterest and started to make some coffee.

"Mario have birthday tonight. Some cousins..."

"Tell Mario to come and see me. And get someone to stand in for the watchman and get him up here as well."

"Yes Sir. Right away." Rolando's back stiffened. Then he rushed off.

"See what happens if I go ashore?" Tomas said crossly.

I tried to be neutral "Aren't they allowed to have, er, visitors?"

Mario had already arrived, having picked up that Tomas was back on board, or heard his bellow. Tomas could be loud on occasions like this.

Mario was looking very festive in a bright yellow shirt and bow tie. As Chief Officer he was in a slightly better position to defend himself. A handsome Philippino with a clipped rakish moustache and a flashing smile, he could be a bit of a charmer, but this was not the moment. The watchman was right behind. Employed by the dockyard, the watchman was not one of the ship's crew.

"You let people on board this ship without permission?" Tomas asked him angrily. The man opened his mouth but nothing came out. He looked at Mario.

"You have a list? Show it to me! You like to keep your job?" Tomas was so fearsome I crept away into the sitting room, to listen avidly behind the curtain divide.

Mario spoke next. "Sorry sir, but I know these four ladies sir, they friends of mine and it's my birthday party sir. I will have them sign sir."

"You will not only have them sign, you will be personally responsible for them. If there is anything missing from this ship, ANYTHING, you will not only pay for it but you will probably go ashore yourself. Understand? And they leave by seven hundred. Understood?!"

"Yes Sir. Thank you sir" said Mario brightening up slightly that the women would be allowed to stay. The Indian watchman, encouraged by this, started to mutter something.

"And YOU will not, I repeat NOT, EVER, let anyone on board this ship without my permission in the future, or I will get you fired!" said Tomas in a voice like thunder.

I heard them bow and scrape away. I popped my head around the curtain.

"THIRD!" Tomas yelled again, and Rolando appeared like a genie out of nowhere.

"How much have you sold to the crew tonight?"

I gathered Rolando was in charge of the bonded store. More eye rolling.

"Just some beer sir, two bottle Johnny Walker and one Vodka sir."

"Then that's enough. If I catch anyone who is on duty drinking you can tell them from me. Birthday party or no birthday party. Have Tony take two crates of soft drinks."

I passed Tomas a cup of coffee just as Mario reappeared. Mario's smile was back. "You honour me sir if you and ma'am would come to my party."

Tomas' expression was interesting.

After he had gone, we had a brandy with our coffee. It was a little cooler in the night and at least no one was trying to rebuild the ship for the moment.

"Times have changed," Tomas said moodily. "Years ago many women came on board when we were in port and rarely was there a problem. Now it's a question of security. They can plant drugs, steal, and that's not to mention Aids. Its a whole other world." He stared out of the window at the dockside. "There were enough crew on board that some could even play football during the loading. If anyone got drunk or stayed ashore for a night, it was ok. The work got done and the companies were happy. They made more money than they do today."

"Should we go down to Mario's party?"

"They would probably like it. But we won't stay long. I never do."

"Cramps their style?"

"No. Well, probably. It's the Karaoke. Fifteen minutes and I've had enough."

There was an enormous cheer as we walked into the crew mess. Undeserved, I felt. The four brightly dressed 'light footed women' (Tomas' term) cheered and waved at us along with the rest. In full skirts, tight waists and provocative make up, they sat together in a row, like friends in the fifties waiting for the next quick step at the local dance hall. The Second Engineer was yowling 'MY WAY' in front of a large Karaoke screen, and although he was hysterically off note, he received tremendous applause as if he had been Frank.

Mario rushed forward to pour us a tumbler of Vodka and Pepsi Cola. Not a drink of choice but his enthusiasm was hard to resist.

There was a highly decorated bar at one end, and a drum set and small stage. Except for Tomas and the Chief Engineer (who was not there) the crew were all Philippino on board. They were in high spirits, dancing around and joking.

Mario grabbed the microphone. "I like to dedicate this to my beloved Captain and his lovely wife, and to my family on this my thirties birthday"

He launched into "HELP ME MAKE IT THROUGH THE NIGHT". With four eager volunteers I didn't think he would have a problem. I was agog. He made extravagant gestures with his arms in our direction and also in the direction of the women and my smile became fixed as I tried not to giggle.

As soon as the cheering and clapping stopped, another got up and also dedicated his song, this time to a long list of people that was touching and funny at the same time.

"To Alec, and to my grandmother who is eight five last week, and to my sister Delia and to my friend Ernesto and to my wife Rosarita... etc etc."

While this was being said, someone was being helpful with the karaoke, stopping and starting, fast-forwarding and reversing, the sentimental images of waving lovers, mountain tops and crashing surf whizzing to and fro. There was a pregnant pause. The would-be singer had finished his introduction but his usual song was not in place. There was a discussion, and for a moment I thought they were going to start in with the drums, someone was tinkering with them back there on the stage, when the screen lurched into life and sweeping strings.

"DON'T CRY FOR ME ARGENTINA" crooned the singer to his far away family in the Philippines. Don't cry for me Argentina?

After the fourth performance we got up to leave but Mario gave Tomas a Spanish guitar.

Mario knew what I knew. Tomas could not resist the guitar.

Tomas rattled off MALAGENA and ZAMBA DE MI ESPERANZA both of which he also sung dramatically in Spanish. To louder than ever cheers, we made our way unsteadily back up the stairs.

"We still have not resolved this stupid bed," I said, gazing down on the four inches of space he had left me at his side. Tomas was very comfortably propped up, reading a magazine. "At least you know I'm not able to get four women in here with me."

In the early hours of the morning, restless in the heat and not really sleeping, I heard giggling and shooshing coming from outside, as the 'cousins' made their way across the greasy metal jungle bridge to a taxi purring on the dockside. There was a great deal of goodbyeing, catcalling and whistles from the ship side. All four taxi doors slammed at least twice before they roared away.

I lay smiling in the half light.

Philippinos make up the majority of seafarers today. There are about 450,000 seamen and 8,000 officers working world-wide and their numbers are increasing as freight prices become more competitive and European sailors and their unions a luxury that few shipping companies can afford anymore.

The Philippino salary has increased to match their ever increasing skill. The salary is less than a British sailor would expect, but the cost of living in their country means they are among the highest paid there. A teacher in the Philippines may earn 200 USD per month where a Second Officer on a merchant ship may earn 1,200 USD and, as one officer told me, someone to help their wife and a driver as well (imagine that in Newcastle-upon-Tyne).

A few years ago, Philippino crews' reputation was tarnished by a few sub standard Maritime Schools and the possibility of buying a certificate before being fully trained, but that situation has improved. They are required by law to send eighty percent of their salary home, tax free. Their contribution to the Philippine economy is considerable.

In addition they are gregarious and loyal to each other. They can cope with the isolation and boredom and are far less likely to complain about small details.

I had worked in the Philippines some years before and liked the people enormously. They were endlessly cheerful and good company, but their loyalty did (and can) present a problem.

I had been asked to employ someone who was not up to the job, but in spite of all evidence that he was a handicap to everyone, no one complained, so I had to be the bad guy in the end and fire him. Philippino colleagues involved with his department had had to carry his mistakes but not a word was said. The comical side to this was that he returned two weeks later, applying for another position. Having shaved his beard off, he gave me a false name. I found myself pretending I didn't know who he was.

Tomas had a similar experience once when a new Chief Officer came on board in India. Ship Management companies sometimes employ crew they have not interviewed themselves but have been recommended, in this case by the Manning Agency in the Philippines. Tomas was not impressed when the man came on board, but he became alarmed when he realised that the Chief Officer could not calculate the loading or the ship's draft.

Had the other deck officers known him before? Only when the new Chief Officer left the ship in the next port of call, 'suffering from arthritis' (terrified of Tomas and his questions that he was unable to answer) they said that they 'were surprised that an Able Seaman' (one position higher than an Ordinary Seaman) was 'on board as a Chief Officer'. The more serious side to this, that it could have compromised the ship and the safety of the crew, was not so important as keeping quiet and not losing the man his job.

The Ship Management company became defensive on being informed and said that the man had been interviewed by an 'executive of the company'. This did not help Tomas' mood that day. "Ridiculous!" he kept muttering to himself.

Almost all the Philippinos I met were practising Roman Catholics and although their faith was important to them, I don't believe it was this alone that made them so loyal to each other. Nearly all I spoke to supported an extended family, meaning friends of friends as well as their own immediate people. When they went home for the two months out of the year, they were looked upon as the great providers, often staggering home with boxes of stereo equipment, video machines and cameras. If they were able to get through their custom officers without paying inflated import taxes they might arrive in their small town the hero of all the nephews and nieces eagerly awaiting their return. They knew what it would mean to them if they let them down.

One day I saw the helmsman re reading a letter, agonising over something. Eventually he asked Tomas if he could extend his work contract a further six months. He had already been on board for ten. Tomas advised against it but the man was adamant. When Tomas was not in the room he decided to confide in me. "My brother in law's house burnt down" he explained. I wondered sometimes if the families knew what they were asking. Another six months without shore leave?

Twenty years ago there were twice as many crew on board ship as there are today. There was flexibility and someone to cover for you if you needed time off. There were no air conditioned cabins, but no closed doors either. There was a greater sense of community and time to be sociable. With fewer people to run the ship, the work is harder and crew spend time off sleeping and with the changes of hours and shift work they can find themselves eating alone.

They might get a day ashore, but the busiest and most expensive time for a ship is when it's in port. They worry about their families and can do nothing about being with them if someone is ill or dies. If it happens, chances are they are in the middle of the ocean and days or weeks from the next port.

The ship is an island, and the men marooned on it. The crew will travel thousands of miles but their environment remains the same. When they arrive home and tell friends they have been to Europe, they can enjoy the looks of envy as everyone conjures up a kind of holiday scene with their friend walking along with a girl on each arm.

Seamen can become withdrawn if they spend too long at sea, and adjusting to life when they do get home is more difficult the longer they are away.

I began to understand why it was so important that the Captain maintains his position and that the crew hold him somewhat in awe. As friendly as the crew may be, underlying problems, or sadness hidden from view, can cause tempers to flare and a knife fight to erupt in seconds.

At the same time, a balance has to be struck, so at other moments, Nelson has to turn a blind eye and allow the crew time to let off steam.

There was a Captain who took over from Tomas once, who soon came into a bad relationship with the crew. It came to a head when someone wrote on the notice board, that if the Captain did not mend his ways he would not reach the next port. As Tomas' experience with the crew had been without incident, although Tomas had been quite tough with them on occasion, he wondered what the problem had been. Apparently the new Captain had rationed the time they could spend watching video films and locked the films away in the ship's office. He had decided that they were using too much soap powder and limited the use of the washing machines. When they became angry at these petty concerns, he cancelled the Saturday evening barbecue. Out of such decisions, mutinies are born.

The Saturday barbecue seems to be a ritual on most ships. A chance for the various ways of cooking to be discussed and demonstrated. Traditionally the barbecue is set up on the stern deck, fashioned from two empty oil drums cut into two lengthwise and with the Boson's co-operation in the invention of a roasting spit. The huge fire is lit mid afternoon and the barbecue begins about 1800 hours. Louder-than-you-can-stand-it music is played to drown the sound of the throbbing engine and everyone makes a fool of themselves dancing around.

Thundering along with the sea rolling by on all sides, chewing on half cooked lumps of meat, and simultaneously having your ears blasted, while men who would be deemed too old to be allowed into any disco, leap about in a frenzy in the semi-darkness, is to experience a ship's barbecue. No one, to my knowledge, fell overboard on these occasions, even when the seas were rough and we were rolling enough to warrant the barbecue contraption being lashed to anything that would stop it disappearing into the next wave. Sometimes half a lamb or a small pig would be turned on the spit. It was a lot of fun and everyone looked forward to it.

Before I came on board, the ship had been in China. Passing Mario's room one day, Tomas saw that he had a chubby little dog with him. Wanting to be tolerant and at the same time not wishing the dog to interfere with the ship's work, Tomas volunteered to take care of it, as they were underway and it could not now be put ashore. He became quite fond of it. It used to like to sleep under the washing machine in the officer's laundry room on the same deck, its little tail sticking out the only evidence it was there.

One day the dog was no longer to be found. Tomas asked Tony, the steward, to look in the laundry room, which he did, in what seemed an off hand and disinterested way. Soon the whole crew were sent around to look for the dog.

After some time Tony came back, looking guilty. He reported that the dog had fallen overboard. How was he so sure? "I sure. Dog fell overboard" Tony kept repeating. Tomas remembered where he had seen similar dogs, displayed in the Shanghai market. The stallholder was holding dogs up for inspection while prospective buyers were feeling how plump they were.

Tomas felt suddenly depressed.

He didn't say anything, but he didn't go to the barbecue that particular Saturday.

Tomas brought me a bright new boiler suit and rubber boots from the storeroom. We were going down into the dry dock to view the ship from the fish eye point of view. In crisp white, I felt like a nuclear technician in the wrong factory. We descended the steps to the dock wall and paddled across the dock floor. I glanced anxiously at the giant wooden doors where the sea water trickled through.

Feeling meek and small looking up at the ship, with an inclination to run back up the steps, I waved to a team of cheerful workers polishing the enormous brass propeller. To be finished off with a coating of fish oil apparently. Were they pulling my leg as they had done before? The difference in the ship's performance after painting and cleaning saves tons of fuel and is the main reason for going into dry dock regularly.

The ship was a Brontosaurus. All belly. The anchor chain and anchor were fascinating. Huge of course, and tremendously heavy looking, draped down the ship side like a curtain pull for the Giant in the Jack and the Beanstalk story. We walked along to the bow. Above our heads two painters were perched on a simple wooden plank, suspended by ropes against the side of the ship, forming the new letters. Even the name was being repainted. It was all looking very smart. The ship's funnel, blue with a red stripe, (said to be in honour of the original owner's wife's nightgown) was also being repainted.

When we returned to the ship, the cook was waiting to see Tomas with a note. It said: 'I have to leave from ship or I cannot be responsible for what I will do'. Tomas read it and handed it back in a rough way. "Go and change this," he ordered, "Otherwise I have to arrest you. Ernesto!" Tomas shouted in the direction of the Second Mate as he was passing by. "Go and help cook write a better letter," he instructed him. "Ridiculous," Tomas muttered angrily. "Giving notice like that. Just when we are about to leave."

The cook's contract actually expired about the time we would arrive at the next port, which was to be in the Gulf. Not the easiest place to leave the ship and the Philippino men had extra reason to be reluctant to do so. They often knew female relatives who worked there and the stories of exploitation were hair raising. There was a degree of hostility between the Philippino and the Gulf States. Tomas knew this and was considering the cook's request from this angle. "He doesn't want to leave from the Gulf," he explained to me. "I can understand that."

Ten minutes later Ernesto came back with another note. This time it made Tomas laugh. Ernesto had taken down the cook's words for him he said. This time the note read: 'I have been on board ten month and I have to go home as my wife is about to give birth.'

"To kill the boyfriend?" I asked

Ernesto had no expression. The cook was nowhere in sight.

"Tell cook I will think about it. You know we are leaving tomorrow?"

"Yes sir," said Ernesto

"We cannot get a replacement on this short notice. Tell Allonzo to come and see me."

Allonzo was the Assistant Cook, a pleasant enough man but not terribly experienced. He appeared, unsmiling, with a premonition of what was in store for him.

"I will help you," Tomas explained "I will do the ordering and deal with the Chandler until we can get a replacement. Do you think you can manage? I will see you get the same as the cook's pay while you are temporarily in charge."

The cook's job was horrendous. He never seemed to get any time off. He was up at five and had to provide three meals a day for a crew of twenty six at regular hours as well as meals for others working shifts. When the ship docked, which was often in the middle of the night or late evening after dinner was over, he had to provide food for the working crew who were loading or unloading the ship. Just to keep track of the ship's stores was a job in itself. Food had to be stored sometimes for weeks on end as companies requested that the main purchases were bought in a less expensive place than in Europe.   Then as everybody knows, there are always critics. Complaining about the food was a release for some people (like the Chief Engineer).   They may be hating the weather or missing their girlfriend but instead of mentioning it, the soup at lunch would get their full venom. And speaking of the weather. How about balancing yourself in a swinging ship while you try to create something to please them all? Huge steaming pots would slosh alarmingly within the rails that surrounded the hotplates. Just try chopping things up in a force nine gale.   A suitable apprenticeship would be to create a dinner for four while riding on the Colossus at Blackpool.

Allonzo brightened at the prospect of the extra pay. Whether he could actually cook or not was not discussed. We were all to find that out.

We were leaving in the morning and the ship took on a different atmosphere as everything was checked and ears bent to listen to the newly tuned engine.

The cook arrived looking combed and happy, carrying a cake he had made. Tony walked behind him with a giant platter of fruit. Offerings to the Potentate.

"How is Allonzo?" Tomas asked him, purely for the exercise, he knew he would be reassured otherwise the cook would lose his chance to go home.

"Oh he is very good sir. He can even make bread," replied the cook enthusiastically.

"I have sent the office a telex about you. The agent will be on board at 0400 tomorrow and you will be ready. He will take you to the airport."

"Do you think it wise to send him home in the circumstances?" I joked to Tomas after they had left.

"Who knows?" Tomas laughed. "Even if the story about his wife is true, they often accept it.

Ten months is a long bloody time. A lot can happen."

Again I felt lucky to be on board. It was not a cruise ship and far from that comfortable. But we were together. In all future voyages on board several ships, no one expressed the slightest resentment that I was there and their wives and girlfriends far away. Of course many were a lot younger than me and had small children to look after.

One Able Seaman told me he had thirteen children at home. "Thirteen? Your wife must be very busy!" I replied, thinking at the same time of the huge expense on his salary.

"Oh she have aunties and sisters and parents close by. They all together," he said, looking remarkably proud of his virility. His wife became pregnant every time he went home. Then he had to be off again and the new one would be a month old when he returned.

A cynic would say that this was one way of keeping things tidy.

CHAPTER 4

MALACCA STRAITS   BAY OF BENGAL   ARABIAN SEA

Five thirty in the morning and dark outside. We had left the dry dock at last and were waiting for the pilot. I saw the red mast light in the distance and then the see-all lamp swept the ship's newly painted sides.

Leaning out from our porthole in our bedroom I watched the pilot climb the ladder, an even more horrible way to get on the ship than the metal steps I had climbed ten days ago.

The pilot ladder is a concertina of wooden steps joined by rope that is let down and then hauled up. The ladder was flapping against the ship's side in the wind. I watched the now familiar routine of the small boat trying not to get crushed by the big one. The pilot leant out from the ship's rail to wave that he was safely onboard. Minutes later I heard his footsteps passing on the way up to the bridge.

Quiet seas as we travelled the Strait of Malacca, Sumatra on the port side, Malaysia on starboard.

Distant blue grey hills. Smoke rose up from hidden fires, spreading a veil. Mile upon mile of burnt out forests, torn stubs and jagged tree trunks.

Through binoculars on the bridge wing I followed the depressing shoreline, then panned with a slim fishing boat, its arched cabin painted jade green and dragon red. Small thin brown men balanced on the deck on bare feet and stared at us as they went by.

"Looking out for pirates?" Tomas asked as he joined me from the bridge.

The skies were pearly and the sea to match. As pearly as an oyster shell. Tomas said it was a quality he had noticed before in the Malacca Straits. I was feeling elated and excited to be on the way somewhere. Puffy clouds rose up in pompadour grandeur all around.

We were now bound for the Gulf to load with oil and rode high in the water. When ships are loaded and barely skim the surface, it' s easy for pirates to board the ship.

This area is notorious for attacks from fast moving boats. They use grappling hooks or hydraulic ladders, matching the speed of the ship and getting on board in seconds.

Running along the deck with a machine gun in a place where weapons are not allowed, they are in charge of the situation.

Ship management companies send out circulars that Captains should take the necessary precautions, but what exactly?

You can have four people on nightwatch and all they can report is that ten men with guns are on board. What then?

Doors to the accommodation can be locked at night, but men are working, sometimes cleaning the tanks to be ready in time and moving to and fro.

I had read of a tanker, boarded by armed men off Hong Kong's Lantau Island and forced to sail to China where the crew were killed. The ship's cargo was taken, the ship renamed and repainted. In the shipping business they are then called 'ghost ships'.

At times the pirates are uniformed men in official looking patrol boats, scanning the vessel with arc lamps as if they are customs officers, then robbing everyone when the vessel stops for them to board.

"I stop for no one," said Tomas, handing me a cup of coffee and the first of Allonzo's buns.

"Thirty armed pirates got on board this ship from a patrol boat and locked up the crew for two days in the engine room. Then they set them adrift in the lifeboats. They were lucky."

"Gosh," I said, sounding like a heroine in an old movie. But that was what it felt like. Pirates?

"They don't wear large hats with ostrich feathers," said Tomas, "but no one ever did. You could never have kept it on your head."

Rolando was listening. "What would you do Rolando, if pirates got on board?" I asked. Rolando blinked. This was a serious question.

"Hide in engine room ma'am," he said, without the trace of a smile.

Tomas was warming up on the subject.

"There was a certain Captain who liked to have a few too many each evening. The crew were used to him not appearing before lunchtime and ran the ship anyway, without him. When he did not appear after lunch, they decided to investigate his cabin. There he was, gagged and tied to the chair, the ship's safe door open and the money gone. Men had boarded in the night and then simply left again. As you know, the ship has to carry a lot of cash to pay for parts or supplies in the next port. Not everyone wants to wait for a company cheque coming from Glasgow all the way to Puerto Bolivar in the wrong currency."

"And always American dollars" I had noticed Tomas counting money in the cabin.

"Shipping runs on the dollar," said Tomas, noticing for the first time that the bun he was eating tasted rather strange. "What *IS* this?"

I laughed. Having taken a nibble of mine, I had lain it aside.

"Too much bicarbonate of soda, I think, I hope. It tastes a bit like Polystyrene."

"Well if this is a sample of what's to come."

"We can always invite any pirates who come on board to stay for lunch and kill them all off."

"I'll have to have a word with him."

"Give him a chance. He's just started. In any case, the crew will give him a hard enough time."

"I am now not looking forward to my lunch."

"I think it's a perfect situation. A new way to diet."

Not far from the ship I saw a fin cut through the water.

"Shark!" I yelled, very excited.

"More like a dolphin," said Tomas and passed a pair of binoculars to me. "Look further out."

I could see heads bobbing in the water a few hundred metres away.

"One came to check us out. They hear the ship's engine, and then come to jump over the wake, especially when the seas are calm like this."

Four appeared at first, leaping in unison over the bow wave. Then a dozen more.

I ran through the bridge from one wing to the other. We were surrounded by them.

Silvery grey arcs jumping side by side. One got up on its tail fin and skipped backwards. It looked up at us with its mouth wide. It really looked as if it was laughing.

"I always thought they trained them to do that."

"Its one of their own tricks. I've seen them do it many times."

Down on the deck three crew had stopped work to look over the side at them, and on the next deck down, Renalto the Electrician was leaning on the rail.

Thrilling and funny, the dolphins entertained us for some time, then sped away from the ship like torpedoes, streaks of churning water just under the surface, and were gone.

The Strait of Malacca is a kind of tanker motorway. We passed many ships, and there were ships in front and behind us. Because of the curve of the earth, they looked as if we would collide with them. I got tempted to be a back seat driver as yet another monster loomed ahead, for all the world looking as if it was bound to hit us dead on.

"What about that one?"

"Passing west of us."

"And that?"

"They are changing course."

I stopped asking after a while as I realised I had no idea. Knowing what ships are going to do and observing their heading is a skill like anything else and you need training.

Tomas was patient with me as I was so green.

Speaking of being green, seasickness was not something that had come into my head.

I didn't know how I would react in rough water. A cargo ship doesn't have stabilisers like a passenger ship. When empty, the ship is 'in ballast' meaning that it takes in sea water in its tanks to a degree, to stop the ship from rolling too much. It still moves differently. In a swell coming from a distant storm it can pitch and sway quite a bit.

When people ashore ask Tomas how many storms he has been in, he regards it as an insulting question. They want to hear exciting stories of course, but Tomas will always say that it's his business to AVOID storms. "If I am caught in a storm I have made a mistake" he will say, but ship's schedules and pressure from the office to be in port while the price is right can cause captains to take chances. When ships had sails and relied totally on the weather it was not so easy to change course. Now there are constant weather reports coming in, a Weatherfax that prints out a map with all the millibars, but experience, looking at the sky, observing the direction of the wind are just as important.

We went down to lunch with a sense of foreboding. As the cook had left there was bound to be criticism of anyone new until they had established themselves, but looking at the pile of greasy chicken wings and the grey soup, we avoided catching anyone's eye.

"That's OK" said Tomas, which he always seems to say when it very much isn't and he is in fact rather cross about something.

It was almost inedible. "Very nice" Tomas called out to Allonzo as we passed him sweating away in the kitchen. We had carefully thrown most of our lunch away.

"See I told you. We can lose weight."

"Well we have to find a way to help him. There's no replacement until we get back to Singapore in a couple of weeks or so. He is obviously not a cook," said Tomas helping himself to a large chunk of cheese from our refrigerator in the cabin.

The Chief Engineer put his head in at the door. "What was that we had for the lunch? Will someone kindly tell me?"

Tomas told me a story about a 'crazy cook' on another ship, who would always refuse a drink, even a beer at Christmas with a loud "No thank you!" and as he was mildly eccentric in appearance and ways, this was accepted without thought. He was also a first class cook, in fact a chef.

One day when they were thirty miles from the Swedish shore he asked to use the telephone.

He came up to the bridge and made a short call. "I haven't spoken to my wife for five years and what do you think was the first thing she said to me? Are you still drunk?!" said the cook, marching off, indignant and angry.

The ship docked and the usual representatives came on board. The cook appeared.

He was carrying a tray on upturned fingers and whooshed around the officials seated in the ship's office. "Coffee anyone?" He said, setting the cups down with exaggeration.

"And something beside?" he added, placing a glass of schnapps in front of each surprised customs officer and port official. It was eight o'clock in the morning.

Tomas looked up at the cook. He was a little red in the face, that's all.

The work and discussion continued around the table for a few minutes. The cook hovered. "Ah, I see you don't want it" he said, stopping at the first one at the table. The cook picked up the glass and tossed down the lot. Trying to ignore his behaviour and not wanting to bring attention to it, Tomas continued with the business at hand.

"Oh you don't want yours either," said the cook, swigging down the next persons glass.

Everyone stopped and stared. "I'll just take the rest away," said the cook, gathering the still full glasses back on to the tray. "Maybe you don't like it?" he continued in a sweet voice.

"I think we are alright now thank you," Tomas said, in a tone that said don't come back.

When everyone had left Tomas thought about the cook and decided "I will talk to him"

The cook came up. He was now quite drunk.

Tomas gave him coffee and tried to listen to his problems but as always the ship business kept intervening. However, the cook left saying he felt better and would go to sleep it off and promised to go 'back on the wagon', as Tomas now realised he had been before.

Within seconds of feeling rather good about helping him, Tomas heard a loud scream and rushed out into the passage. The ship had a female radio officer. She came running out from her room holding her rear end. The cook's loud cackle could be heard as he ran down the stairs. "He came into my room while I was making my bed and pinched my bottom" she complained loudly.

Mayhem ensued in the cook's wake. One step ahead of Tomas he doubled back along the passageways and shot up and down the gangway steps, turning things over and swinging from the door frames like a monkey.

"Close the doors! Don't let him into the kitchen!" Tomas shouted at passing crew.

"Who? What?" They asked at Tomas' flying figure. Two other officers took up the chase, the pathway of the cook's journey through the ship evident by scattered items on the floor, people emerging and shouting indignantly from their cabin doorways.

"He stole my shaving cream!" cried the third engineer, holding a razor in one hand.

Sleepy naked sailors poked their heads out of doors.

"Ah hah, ah hah!" yelled the cook bounding ahead. Then silence.

Tomas and the officers looked at each other.

They crept along to some storage cupboards and discussed in mime how they would tackle him once the door was opened. The officer pulled the door open. Nothing.

They split up. There were no sounds to guide them now.

Tomas rounded a corner and was confronted by a strange sight. He didn't immediately recognise that it was the cook who was standing at the end of the passage looking back at Tomas, his face simply covered with the third engineer's shaving lather. The foam was smothered over his hair and around his chin in a large white beard like Santa Claus.

He opened his mouth to speak and large globs of foam fell onto his chest.

"Take it easy now," said Tomas, guiding the cook firmly into the cook's room.

After he had locked him in, he heard a lot of noise from inside. The cook was breaking the place up.

Tomas sent for a taxi. He didn't want to get the Police involved.

65

Five of the burliest crew took the cook between them, packed his belongings and struggled down the gangway with him to the waiting taxi.

The taxi driver looked up at the group and his intended passenger in alarm.

Used to the docks and the occasional drunken sailor, he was not pleased to see what was coming. The cook had now become somewhat violent.

The Boson was sizing up the cook's chin, his fist at the ready while the others were trying to hold the cook and get the taxi doors open. The shouting and commotion had everyone's attention on the dock and ship.

The cook was Swedish and in his hometown. Tomas had made a quick judgement and knew he would be better off there than anywhere. The next port of call was in West Africa.

The cook saw the look in the Boson's eye and calmed down.

The crew managed to jam the cook and his belongings into the taxi; the driver was given the address and extra money for his trouble.

Tomas watched from the bridge wing in relief but no sooner had the taxi driven away, then it came to a screeching halt further along the dockside and the cook jumped out, heading once more for the ship.

The five crew who had taken him off were just at the top of the gangway. They rushed back down. This time the Boson hit his mark.

He looked up at Tomas on the bridge wing as the others carried the cook back into the taxi.

"Sorry sir. It wasn't too hard a knock. It'll just keep him a bit quiet until he gets there."

Bosons are always interesting people on ships. As the foreman over the Ordinary and Able Seamen, he has to be tough and knowledgeable to keep things cracking along. Our Boson this time was allegedly a part owner in a ship which had apparently collided and sunk somewhere in the Mediterranean. It was 'in the hands of the insurers' and he was only working until he got his money back, so he said.

This gave him a certain status among the men as a 'ship owner' and a reputation that he didn't have to start to prove. Bosons always have a certain style, a little bit lofty, even if they are clonking around in greasy overalls with a wrench in one hand.

You may spend weeks on the ship and never know his name unless you look on the crew list in the office. Out on the deck, in the mess room or ashore, I have yet to hear any of them called Gerry, or Alf or Eduardo.

He is only ever known as 'Boson'

As the key person in charge of anchors, cables and rigging, he has his work cut out as they say, on this ship.

Although we had been in dry dock for maintenance so recently, we now have a problem with the windlass and when anchoring 'not enough steam' which I suspect is serious and am rather glad to be ignorant of just how serious.

Tomas muttered about flags of convenience and old ships, known in the trade as 'rust buckets'.

I am to learn that there are many more on the ocean and the idea is frightening.

Tomas went down to the kitchen in the afternoon to have a meeting with Allonzo and Tony.

He was not encouraged by it and came back feeling extremely sorry he had let the cook leave in Singapore.

"This is what happens if you try to be kind," Tomas grumbled.

"What's on the menu for tonight?" I asked

"Steamed cod with boiled potatoes and white sauce."

"Oh, very Swedish"

"I know. I am the one who is cooking it."

We took two days and nights to travel the Malacca Straits to the Great Channel at the top of Sumatra before we turned west into the Bay of Bengal.

Flecks of foam were kicking up the sea and lightning flashed on the dark horizon as I took the stairs.

Tomas was on the bridge. It was about four in the morning and with the increased movement of the ship, I couldn't sleep.

My dressing gown flew in the warm wind that whipped at the curtains around the chart table, curtains that separated the rest of the bridge from the lights overhead, keeping the main part of the room in darkness. Those on duty could then see out into the night and pick out the lights of passing ships. I pushed open the curtains and closed them behind me.

Silhouettes at the windows, and beyond, the dark expanse of the ocean with green lights and red lights suspended in mid air, shadows of ships between, close by and on the horizon.

The radar spun its circle in dark blue and gold, and smudges and crossed circles moved as we moved, and passing ships travelled on.

Two lighthouses, one on the main land, the other on the island of Sabang, swept their beams across the water. A soft light from the moon behind clouds.

I drank tea and looked out into the night.

Back in bed again I rolled from side to side (at least I had the whole thing to myself). It was a drowsy, sensuous movement. The cups rattled in the next room and the bathroom door swung and creaked. The clothes in the closet joined into the swing and there was a new movement, a kind of jerk in the upswing, that gave an edge to things.

I fell into a how deep is the ocean kind of sleep.

Dawn appeared, thin and watery, and rain pattered on the windows.

Things in the next room were beginning to slide and some to clatter to the floor.

I got up and staggered about like a drunk, trying to be inventive about stowing things away.

We were now in the Great Channel. To the north, the Nicobar Islands and the Andaman Islands. I read about the islands in the Mariner's handbook.

The Andaman Islands were a penal settlement used by the Indian Government until 1942 when the Japanese turned up. The original inhabitants were two distinct tribes, the Jarawas and the Sentenese.

The Jarawas had a reputation of killing anyone on sight, but both groups were said to be hostile. The Onges, on the other hand, were coastal dwellers, and 'friendly again'.

So if you were unfortunate enough to be convicted of a crime in 1941 and shipped to the Andaman Islands, and managed to avoid the Jarawas and possibly made a friend or two among the Onges, you would have been mightily dismayed when the Japanese arrived.

We continued into the Bay of Bengal where we began to swing and sway in earnest. Dipping movements, deep into a trough and up again, we roll on the fringe of waves before falling down. Down and up, down and up, side to side and down and up.

"Sleeping again?" enquired Tomas, his head around the door. I smiled dreamily back like a sated courtesan from her boudoir.

After more snoozing and nodding I sat up on the bed and looked out. Our bedroom window looked forward over the deck.

A small brown bird came cheeping in, out of the grey sky, and circumnavigated the ship several times before flying away.

Something plopped onto the deck, and wriggled about. Then another. Fish?

Yes they were. They were flying fish!

"Flying fish Tomas!" I called out. I could hear him at the computer in the office.

"Quite good eating," he shouted back.

Right in the middle of the Bay of Bengal, after many hours without seeing another ship, we had a near collision.

I was making coffee in our sitting room, looking idly out of the windows waiting for the water to boil when another ship popped up on the horizon, identical in size to our own, almost a mirror image.

I glanced at it from time to time, and knowing my poor judgement on direction was not concerned until I felt…surely not!

I went up the stairs to the bridge where I could hear the radio officer calling on the VHF, on Channel Sixteen, the emergency frequency that ships are supposed to keep tuned to, more so then, which was before the introduction of GMDSS (Global Maritime Distress and Safety System)

There was a calm but tense atmosphere. Both Tomas and the Chief Officer were there with binoculars glued to their eyes.

The mirror image ship was very close. There was nothing else to be seen in a wide expanse of sea on either side.

"They are still not answering sir," said the radio officer.

"OK. Keep trying. Hard starboard."

I saw there was a helmsman at the wheel. We had come off the automatic pilot then.

I stood silently out of the way, my heart beating.

The other ship's behaviour was curious. Like a heat-seeking missile it seemed determined to cross into our path no matter what direction we took to avoid her.

Pirates? But it was a tanker, just like ours. A curious ghost ship? A mirage even?

Tomas went out onto the bridge wing as we managed to swing out of her way and read the name on her bow.

How did it nearly happen? I was burning to ask.

Suddenly an Indian accent crackled over the VHF.

"We are having problem with our steering. Please take evasive action. Over."

Everyone on the bridge laughed. It broke the tension. "Now they tell us!"

I went out onto the bridge wing and watched as the other ship headed away from us, making a wavy line in her wake, almost turning pirouettes.

"Why doesn't the idiot stop then?" said Tomas.

"With so much ocean, why did they have to come so close to us?" I dared to ask.

"We are both following shipping lanes. The fastest course between two points."

"Like a car coming from the other direction on the motorway and crossing the divide?"

"Exactly. Wouldn't have been a problem if they had answered our calls. We started to call them a long time ago. Better not to change course in those circumstances without communication. You can often make things worse by guessing what the other one will do."

Tomas was very calm.

I had to laugh again as I looked behind us at the ship still weaving around, at least well out of our way. "Who could guess what THEY are going to do."

"Put out a SECURITE message. Give her position and course." Tomas told the Radio Officer.

"If they can't monitor the VHF in those circumstances they may not do it themselves."

"What's a SECURITE?"

"A warning to other ships. MAYDAY is when you are certainly going to have a disaster; PAN PAN is when you might. SECURITE is a general warning to ships in the area."

Tomas gave my hand a quick squeeze. "OK? I saw you come up. You were quite calm in the circumstances."

"There was nothing I could do." I answered cheerfully feeling a little proud that I had managed not to get excited. My nerves must be quite good, I thought, but carrying coffee, the cups clanked like mad on the saucers.

Letters to be mailed at the next port were left in a tray by the office door. The pumpman, Carlo, who had seemed an unpleasant character, and was always snapping at the crew, had written to his wife who was working in Libya. He caught my eye as he placed the letter on the pile and suddenly started to tell me about her. That she was working in difficult circumstances and that she 'couldn't leave'. He shrugged when I asked him why not, and a tear was in his eye as he turned away and went back to his cabin.

I glanced at the letter which he had decorated with kisses and wondered if she would receive it. No wonder he was bitter.

Tomas told me he would not send the mail off in the Gulf port but put it away and quietly send it off when we returned to Singapore, to make sure it arrived.

"They have a mail system don't they?"

All Tomas said was 'they can object to things'. I looked at the sad pile of letters. What a world.

Passing the second mate's open door your eye was caught by the photographs covering the walls surrounded by cut out pink paper hearts. He hadn't seen his family for eighteen months.

His father had died and left many local debts. This was Ernesto's inheritance. He wrote several times a week and received many back. Not all bills I hoped.

The Second Officer, in this case it was Ernesto, was also the medical officer on board. The Second Officer was supposed to have received training, at least in First Aid, but in Ernesto's case I had doubts.

I had seen him dress a wound, cigarette dangling from his mouth. Not something to give you confidence. Neither was his knowledge of medicines. When I asked him for an anti fungal cream for athletes' foot (an ongoing hazard on ships) I went back to the 'hospital' where he was still counting for a forthcoming inventory.

"This cream is for piles," I objected. Most of the creams and pills were in generic packaging and the label required careful scrutiny.

"Same thing" he said. "No. Not really" I replied, as gently as I could. He shrugged.

Perhaps he knew something I didn't know. Perhaps cream for piles did work on feet.

"Do you have any anti fungal cream for athletes foot?" I enquired again.

"Have" he said. This was his standard answer to any question. It meant absolutely nothing. I peeped into an open drawer and seeing Penicillin impregnated gauze four years out of date decided not to pursue the matter and buy my foot cream in port.

Sometime after we left the ship, Tomas and I would still joke when one asked the other if this or that was in the refrigerator or cupboard at home. "Have" we would say, which we knew could mean yes, or no.

I looked into the bathroom attached. It looked very grungy. Someone had hung up washing.

I questioned Tomas about the state of things in the 'hospital', a shambolic room that looked like a ward from the turn of the century, with iron beds and very little comfort. It didn't look all that clean either and the medicine cabinets!

We had quite a row. "That's his job," Tomas said. "That's what he is doing now. He has to list everything and report back. And I've asked Tony to clean in there but you can see how little time he has to do anything extra. Anyway, people don't get ill on ships."

"Oh really? Well all I can say is, if I am taken ill, don't take me in there as I would certainly end up having to be buried at sea."

"This is not your business," said Tomas sharply.

The row escalated. I was trying to tell him 'how to run the ship' and I should keep my nose out of things otherwise I should go ashore, Tomas was shouting.

"Well you can put arsehole cream on your feet and potassium permanganate up your nose and die of blood poisoning when you have a blister and he advances on you with his nicotine fingers but not me!" I yelled back.

"You mind your own business! No one tells me how to run my ship!" Tomas yelled back.

I stomped out on my peeling feet and went for a walk between the pipes out on deck.

It was a bit scary but exhilarating. The sun was setting but not in a blaze of splendour, simply slipping behind dark clouds. The sea was a seething mass, it suited my mood, a gunmetal coloured moving blanket tearing along on either side, sweeping off and finishing in a churning tail foaming out from under the stern.

The pistons juddered and thundered underfoot as I passed over the engine room below. I circled around and looked in at the Boson's storeroom up under the windlass.

There was a honk from the ship's funnel. I stepped back from the storeroom and looked up at the bridge. In the rapidly failing light I could just see Tomas at the windows.

FLAM FLAM it went again and made me chuckle, but I was still very angry at what had been said. Go ashore indeed. Maybe I would do just that. I strolled nonchalantly up the deck.

When I reached our cabin Tomas was not there but two tall drinks stood waiting. I ignored them and went into the bathroom to take a shower. As I passed the bed, I saw a large new tube of cream lying on the cover. 'For The Prevention, Protection and Cure of Athletes Foot"

When I paddled out after my shower, my smeared feet encased in clean white socks, Tomas told me a story about when he was second mate and one of the fitters got a piece of solder in his eye. The problem of the tubes and boxes all looking alike had arisen at that time too. "The fitter was screaming like hell so I grabbed what I thought was something to wash out the eye and gave a hearty blast of it right into his eyeball. Well, he nearly took off like a rocket, screaming louder than ever.

I took a quick look at what I had used. It was not eyewash but EAR wash. Good Lord, I thought. I took up a kind of basting thing and drew up ordinary water and grabbed him and gave his eye another gigantic blast. He quietened down a bit. Then I found the eye wash and gave him a final blast with that, all the time I am almost fighting with him to hold him down. He drooped off, almost crying and I was rather concerned I can tell you. His eye was like a fireball. I had dressed it a bit with a clean bandage and in the morning thought of him immediately. He came up to me in the mess. No bandage on and smiling, the eye was a little reddish, but looked good. "Very good treatment!" he said shaking my hand. Whatever I had done, it had certainly removed the piece of solder alright."

I had not realised when I joined the ship that people became ill and even died perhaps in the middle of the Atlantic and not much could be done about it until you reached shore.

You can get advice from a doctor over the telephone but what if it's too late?

"What do you do if someone dies? Do you bury them at sea?"

"Put them in the cold store," Tomas explained. "I was on a ship when that happened and we cleared out the fish freezer and put him in there. The crew wouldn't eat fish for weeks after that, even when it had been scrubbed out. These days you have insurance and all kind of officials involved. Bury someone at sea and it could be considered suspicious. People get lost at sea of course, and not only when ships go down."

I remembered Tomas' letter about the Norwegian Chief Engineer.

As we rounded the tip of India, off the Coromandel Coast, things started to move across the cabin with a purpose. Chairs and tables were already attached to their loops by chains to the floor but I was quickly to discover many loose things about the place. The relative calm seas of the voyage so far, had lulled me into thinking that that was how it would be all the way. But various items, coffee cups on trays, files and papers had not been STOWED, except in a token way, placed on 'sticky' mats that held in normal circumstances.

I was curled up in the chair reading when the first LURCH, SHIFT and LIFT movement happened and I found myself trying to grab things and hold on at the same time.

Plant pots wedged into the window sills, leant precariously and everything on any surface rolled or crashed to the floor. A wandering sugar bowl can make a great deal of mess for a start.

It would have been comical to watch me. I was trying to hold up a house and contents in the middle of an earthquake.

As fast as I gathered up papers with my legs spread wide, bent from the waist, the ship gave a lurch in the opposite direction and I was on my knees in the sugar and coffee dribble and earth from plant pot mixture.

I could hear my shampoo and various cosmetics holding a roller skating contest in the bathroom, smashing ominously up against the metal towel rail and the steps to the shower.

The door wrenched open and Tomas marched across the room to pick up something from the office desk.

"Just changed course."

"I discovered that."

"You have to stow things properly."

"That too."

"Look at my files! What a mess!

"This is MY fault?"

"Well you have nothing else to do."

Lucky for him he departed. I was about to reach for the soggy toilet roll that had just entered from the bathroom.

After considerable swearing I managed to clean up the place and change my clothes.

It's surprising how cross you can get with the movement, as if an unseen hand is deliberately trying to annoy you, pushing you this way and that.

My legs and arms ached from the tension. I flopped down on the bed, exhausted.

I knelt up after a few minutes to look out at the weather. Blue skies, not a cloud.

Now things were not falling around I could quite enjoy the ride, and I realised something else. I did NOT feel sick. Perhaps I would be one of the lucky ones.

The waves were actually green. As green as glass.

What sea beasts were
In the wavery green
When you were my master?

I'll tell you the truth.
Seas barking like seals,
Blue seas and green,
Seas covered with eels
And mermen and whales. [1]

Lie down lie easy,
Let me shipwreck in your thighs. [2]

Now we were really whacking down in the water. The waves broke into white spray twenty metres high and then rolled along the deck.

[1,2] Under Milk Wood – by Dylan Thomas copyright © 1952

The house phone rang.

"Won't last for long. Have to head up for a bit until we get lee" bawled Tomas down the phone as if he was speaking to the moon. "Come up and have coffee."

"I'm not dealing with coffee in this."

"You only have to drink it. Third mate has already made it."

Up on the bridge there are tall, swivel chairs like bar stools that are fun to sit in at the windows and keep you in place even when the ship is moving about a lot. I sat in one and looked through the binoculars at the Indian shore, misty blue, with white palaces, pillars and domes. Magical.

The rough ride became fun, the weather was sunny and dry and Renalto the electrician came up on the bridge to visit and told us a story. Telling stories are what you do between ports.

Renalto was always smiling. It was a roguish Clark Gable-Gone-with the-Wind kind of grin. Renalto was Brazilian. In his late forties, he had spent all his working life at sea.

"You know this very nice place," he said indicating the Malabar Coast, now off our starboard side. " I come here when I was very young sailor. You see the churches. This was Portuguese settlement."

"Vasco de Gama."

"He was buried there. But I think they take him back to Portugal now."

He leant on the window sill, one hand on his hip. Ernesto was on duty and looked bored. He had probably heard it before. Tomas could stand repetition and would rather enjoy it, adding bits you might have forgotten, that he remembered from the previous telling, with a 'don't forget this or that', and reminding you, infuriating at times, of whether it was a Thursday or a Friday when it happened

Renalto launched into his story.

"This was the time after they have independence from Portugal. It was Easter 1963. We were to load eleven thousand tonnes of ore for Poland. When we arrive, we discover the authorities (ortoratees) have plan to build cranes in the port, and consequently (conseeckently) the women, hundreds of women, would lose their jobs."

"Where was this?"

"Goa. And you ask why the women? They were the one who carry the ore from the railway wagons to the ship side, in a big basin on top of the head, you understand. You can believe how long this take. But was very pretty for sailors to see the ladies coming along in long line very graceful with this horrible stuff on their head." He picked up a book and strolled around the swaying deck to demonstrate.

"So there was a big strike," he continued. "And many many ship coming into the port from all over and lined up waiting out on the roads. So we were waiting with all the others and when nothing was happening for sometime, the crew was allowed to go ashore by launch. It was a holiday, Easter, so only the Captain and watchmen stayed. When we get ashore it is more like carnival than strike as all sailors from the ships are also ashore from about forty ships and there was a lot of ladies who were not working. It was a kind of a paradise." Renalto sighed looking away at the shore several miles away.

"We were swimming and eating lobster. We had also got ourselves a little established before the others came, lodging in beach huts along the beach. We were eating lobsters with new baked bread and Hercules XX Rum. Then we had to start to fight off the Greeks and the Norwegians who were also looking for paradise, so we also have this excitement, but it was a kind of comical warfare you know? Not so violent. We play joke on each other. We blow snuff in their face or wrestle on the sand. One or two had a nose broken."

"How long did the strike last?"

"Thirty days. Thirty days of sailor's dream. The Captain sent launches for us to get back to the ship and we would run into the jungle and hide. Then the strike included the drivers of the launches so we were stuck ashore. This was excellent news. I was twenty and I really think I had gone to heaven. When I go back from that trip I had been at sea for fifteen months and my brothers used to go through my bags when I arrive, looking for exotic artefact or present, and they find two pair of lacy underwears from this time. My mother was not so happy even when I told her they did not belong to me!"

It was Tomas' turn with a story, also about India. This was about the time his ship was in Calcutta. A Swedish ship and all Swedes on board, including an exceptionally handsome blonde third mate who looked like a film star and turned heads wherever he went. What the crew knew and others didn't was that he was well known for making mistakes and was often 'on the wrong tack', but because he was so good looking, he managed to get by.

Lars went ashore and found himself a girlfriend. She was also very beautiful, gracefully dressed and they made a dazzling couple. Lars talked about her all the time, including to the Captain. That she was from a very high family and well up in the society, so much so, that when the Captain held a dinner on board for the Swedish Ambassador and executives from the shipping company, the Captain thought it would be pleasant to have a beautiful elegant woman at the table and asked Lars to invite her.

At the dinner, where Swedish aquavit and beer (a deadly combination) was served with the fish, she became very happy and when others were talking and telling stories could not resist telling one of her own.

"You know last week I met this man but he was too fat and could not do anything but yesterday I met two very nice men and I got ten rupees as well."

Silence fell. Shortly after this, Lars took her home. He decided instead to concentrate on taking a driving test which was possible to do at that time, for an international licence. He had not managed to pass the test in Sweden and it was suspected that he had not practised at all in between. Lars took one of the Able Seamen with him for company and he brought back the story of the test to the ship.

There were two examiners; one sat in the back next to the Able Seaman.

The examiners had been very gracious to Lars, impressed with this tall golden God. There were many 'after you's' as everyone got into the car, which had been hired for the occasion.

As Lars took off, he immediately backed into another car.

"I can see sir," said the Indian examiner, "that you are not used to the automatic clutch. Just drive on."

After a few hair raising incidents through the crowded streets of Calcutta, Lars drove into a cyclist, catching the front wheel and knocking him to the ground.

"Just drive on, drive on. It was his fault," said the examiner

Needless to say, Lars passed the test and was released into the unsuspecting driving world.

So it goes for the beautiful people.

Swinging to and fro in a high chair on the bridge and watching the hypnotic rise and fall of the waves through the windows and listening to stories were the most delightful times on board ship.

Many days from shore and days to go to the next port and your spirit started to lark about. This was the heady freedom feeling, the what care I and what can I do about it sailor's life that is missed when the sailor goes ashore and like the rest of us, is subject to the constant nags of everyday life. There is the ship, and there is the weather, and the tasks at hand resolved by the few immediate people on board.

This is not to say that there were not disputes on the ship, but they were short and swift as a rule. If there was a serious troublemaker, they were sent ashore at the next port with an air ticket home.

"You shore people make too much of everything," said the Chief Engineer, who had joined us and was complaining about many things.

As he stared out of the windows at the horizon, inhaling deeply on his cigarette, I noticed that Ernesto the Second Mate was looking at him with a curiously mischievous expression.

Late afternoon in the Arabian Sea. Beautiful. More pearly than the Malacca Straits and as calm as a lake. As we skimmed along, barely making a wave, small brown snakes with yellow stripes wriggled in the water and huge jellyfish flumped along just under the surface.

It was all Arabian Nights and Sinbad. The smell of roasting lamb lifted my nostrils.

We had continued to have seriously poor food and this had taken off as the main discussion on board. Allonzo had become defiant and proud as every kind of suggestion came his way.

He had been dropped into it after all. He was doing his best.

It was another Saturday. The Chief Engineer was in charge of the evening's barbecue. Woe betide anyone who complained to him.

He was making a whole stuffed lamb, something the Philippinos were not at all keen on, pork or beef was their meat of choice.

The Chief Engineer had been talking about it for days, ever since he had hauled it out of the cold store.

He was going to make it 'Yugoslavian style' stuffed with rice and herbs. It sounded great to me, but his emotions and tensions about the whole business took the edge off expectations.

He was always angry that the salad oil on board was not real olive oil but generic stuff out of a large can. This would be mentioned as the reason why he wouldn't have any salad each day, which was something Allonzo could do, creating a lovely display with artistic flare.

He needed good olive oil for the basting, he said, several times. Alas, no Sainsburys in the Arabian Sea.

Tomas had purchased a few bottles of red wine from the bonded store to complement the dish.

I went to take a shower and change for the evening. It made me smile to look into my vast wardrobe that I now kept in a spare cabin along the passageway. There were so many things that were unsuitable for this ship, where rust and grease seemed to leap onto your clothes as you passed by, even if you walked like a surgeon going from the scrub up to the operating table.

Out on the rear deck, crew were arriving, all in whiter than white tee shirts and smiling in a conspiratorial way as the Chief Engineer battled with his revolving lamb.

Our wine bottles were opened and I gave him a glass. "Cannot take that now!" he said crossly from behind a cloud of fumes. He had just splashed water onto the coals to calm it down.

Allonzo arrived with plates of salad and his famous bread. There was a large plate of cold meats which the Philippinos descended upon. There was a roar from the 'cook'.

"You are going to have lamb! What for you think I am working all afternoon!"

They were cowed and retreated from the serving table and sat at the empty tables to wait. One switched on the cassette player.

"And we not have this jungle music. We have some real music!" yelled the Chief Engineer. It was changed to a Strauss waltz.

Boson gave the Chief Engineer a glass of what looked like orange juice. They had an argument about whether he wanted it or not, then he wiped his brow and downed it in a gulp.

"What a fabulous evening" I said to Ernesto. He didn't reply. Everyone was watching the Chief Engineer, who was slicing the lamb and actually starting to smile. Success! I thought, he's enjoying himself. He started to chuckle and almost skip around.

Afterwards I thought of the possible connection between Ernesto and the medicine cabinet, but said nothing to Tomas. The Chief Engineer was passing out his plates of lamb and actually singing.

The lamb was delicious. We ate too much and I drank several glasses of wine.

The last I saw of the Chief Engineer that evening, he had jumped with feet together, up on to the seat of a chair and was dancing energetically on the spot.

The Strauss Waltzes had been abandoned in favour of the Eurythmics.

Tomas and I went up to the bridge. Tomas to check on the third mate Rolando who was on duty, and I to look at the sunset.

No clouds, a perfect canvas. A pale blue wash and a ball of crimson sinking into a navy blue sea.

I leant on my elbows and stared at the sun as it slipped from view.

As the last tiny piece of the rim disappeared from view, an amazing thing happened.

A brilliant emerald green light glowed on the horizon just where the sun had sunk into the sea.

The light increased. It was like a gigantic jewel, a glass spaceship beaming across the water.

"Look! Look!" I yelled, pointing.

Tomas turned just as the last of the intense green light was vanishing.

"It was the 'green flash'," he said excitedly. "You saw the 'green flash'. All the years I have been at sea I have looked for it and never seen it."

Something that happens if the conditions are right, and the sky is clear, spoken about but rarely seen to that intensity.

My evening of the 'green flash' turned into a night of stars.

Somewhere down below I heard someone singing softly as they climbed the outside steps to the next deck.

The ship's funnel swung gently, tilting like a tall hat against the Milky Way.

CHAPTER 5

STRAITS OF HORMUZ PERSIAN GULF AL JUBAYL OMAN

In the Strait of Hormuz the *shamal* was blowing. It added to the new tension on board.

We had passed through the Gulf of Oman and were now in comparatively narrow waters, off the Musandam Peninsular, with the vast land of Iran on the distant shore. The wind played with us as we negotiated our way through the oil rigs.

The chart was covered with purple signs. Oil platforms and pipelines.

Ernesto told me that three years ago, many seamen had died in the area, as during the Iran/Iraq war, merchant ships had been fired upon indiscriminately. Companies had paid double salary for the days spent in the area, but any insurance was invalid when in a 'war zone' so it hardly made up for loosing a leg or an eye, especially on Philippino salary.

We were observing the twelve mile offshore war time limit, although at that time no one was firing at anyone, the situation could change overnight. There were also mines.

Arabic music warbled from the little radio propped against the window on the bridge.

There were new signs around the ship.

> 'All liquor to be locked into the bonded store before entering Saudi Arabian ports. Crew are reminded that they are subject to all local laws. All nude or semi nude photographs/calendars to be taken down and destroyed. When filling in crew declaration form, be accurate.'

The crew hate to be in the Persian Gulf. Not only are they unable to go ashore, they are made fearful by the sometimes arbitrary whims of the visitors who they tell me, ask an unsuspecting seaman for 'a beer', then when it is brought, the visitor would pour it onto the deck and fine the poor man one thousand dollars for his kindness.

Photographs of sweethearts or wives in bikinis or sleeveless dresses are treated like pornography and ripped from the walls of cabins. They can be arrested for such infringements.

What is not so amusing to Tomas is that the Captain can also be arrested for the crew member's indiscretion. (Tomas spoke about China, where neighbours who live either side of a matricidal lunatic, can also be executed for 'failing to notice a problem'. You would spend a great deal of your time listening at the walls.)

Tomas checked all the cabins personally.

We juddered and twisted about in the fierce waves.

The Persian Gulf is surprisingly shallow, less than ninety metres overall, and deep draught tankers have to navigate with care. There are also complex currents and tidal streams which add to the close watch that has to be made on the bridge, avoiding the oil rigs that are all around.

Sharks, not dolphins, in the water this time, skimming along the side of the ship.

The humidity had dropped. Smalls left on the line in the bathroom, dried in no time in the desert air. The wind continued to play with us. Tomas sent a telex to the port, Al Jubayl, to say we would be delayed.

A telex came back by return to say WOULD we be delayed, as several ships had slowed due to the wind and that there was now a 'queue'.

If we are to anchor off shore, the crew say they will fish for squid.

An American naval ship called over the VHF to check who we were. The laconic tones of one of the Southern States were a startling intrusion, booming out over the voice of the Arabic singer on the radio.

Al Jubayl was once a small fishing village where they also dived for pearls. Now it has steel mills, smelter works, petrol plants and refineries. There is a large artificial harbour and a naval base. I learnt this from the pilot book, not from going ashore, which is not allowed for women (and an unveiled woman at that)

We hoisted the appropriate flag. Green with a text in Arabic which means 'THERE IS NO GOD BUT ALLAH AND MOHAMMED IS THE PROPHET'. A sabre is underneath.

Failure to fly this flag means imprisonment, for someone, probably Tomas.

"What if you find that you don't have one?" I asked.

"They probably say too bad! And still arrest you."

We anchored off shore. Outside, a Hockney painting of Beverly Hills. All ochre, blue and white, sparkling water and no trees, geometric shapes and miles of concrete under a glaring sky.

The fish were still there in spite of the oil factories. Long fierce looking fish like pike or gar. Cuttlefish swam close to the ship's sides. The crew were warned not to fish. Not even the men who worked in the port were allowed to fish, it was a port regulation.

The terminals ashore were like huge soda fountain machines but instead of flavours their signs read: NAPTHA, KEROSENE, JET FUEL, HEAVY OIL, DIESAL.

We were there to load with thousands of tons of kerosene.

A Yorkshire accent came over the VHF, the warm vowels making me homesick for a second.

He was the all important Loading Master ashore. When he heard there was a Brit on board he promised to bring a present.

When he arrived, he brought a precious English newspaper and six McVities Digestive Biscuits.

Later, when I opened up the newspaper it was like Origami. It was full of holes. I thought he had played a joke on me until I realised that the holes were caused by the cutting out of several photographs. Even the Queen had not escaped token execution. Must have been wearing a sleeveless dress.

The Yorkshire man told me that his wife had come to stay with him at one time but had since returned to England.

Women are not allowed to drive and certainly cannot go to the beach in the company of men, even their husbands.

The money was good, he told me, but I thought secretly how boring it was for him and may not be worth it, especially if the waiting wife back in the UK decided she was bored too.

A Saudi Man accompanied anyone who came on board. The shipping agent was Indian and he never came alone, one or two Saudis were with him, dressed in long white jalabas and red and white chequered head scarf. The Saudi men spoke mainly to each other or to the agent, rarely to anyone else on board. I was unsure if this was a policy or simply a language problem.

The first item of business was the ship's bonded store that contained all the alcohol on board including the cooking sherry from the ship's galley, plus sundry items kept to sell to the crew, like after shave and shampoo.

The ship's office suddenly became empty of officials. Rolando had escorted them to the bonded store where the alcohol had been locked away and unlocked the padlocks.

Several people were required for this apparently important inspection and were left to 'inspect' unhindered. After the inspection the seal would be reapplied.

I had been reading in the bedroom, out of sight to avoid possible controversy and resigned at not going ashore at my first port of call, when I heard a sound at the sitting room door.

The snub of a machine gun appeared, followed by a tall young soldier in brown uniform, smiling away at me as if he had just enjoyed a good joke. My stomach turned over.

He strolled across the room and sank down into an armchair, slouching one leg over the arm and balancing the gun across the other knee. About twenty years old, with brown curly hair and hazel eyes, he had a confident air that was no doubt partly due to the gun he was holding.

"You have nice time today?" he began, as an opening gambit.

"Yes thank you," then, "I am the wife of the Captain," I explained.

"Oh, wife," he said grinning more than ever as if I had said something funny.

"You have beer?"

"Sorry. Only tea." I reached to switch on the kettle and set up the cups thinking he was not going to get me on that one.

He rolled his eyes and laughed, throwing his head back and barking like a small dog. Then he leant forward, shifting the gun.

"Chivas Regal Number One!"

"Do you take milk and sugar?" I asked, feeling like a character in a Pinter play.

"You know? Chivas Regal? Whisky?" he said, looking a little less harmless and staring at me with some candour.

"Oh yes," I said facing him and forcing myself to smile, "But I don't have any. Its all in the bonded store. Locked up." I pantomimed the turning of a key.

He swung the gun to and fro on his knee, looking me up and down, with a smirk.

"You been Bangkok? Bangkok Number One."

I poured the tea, with a strong desire to say 'Sorry, no booze or sex, just Earl Grey.'

As I passed the cup over, I said, "Are you guarding the port?" and offered him one of my precious McVities digestives.

He ignored the tea and biscuit and started to prowl around the room, looking on shelves and tipping open cupboard doors with the tip of his army boot.

I sat on the sofa and drank my tea, my heart beating.

Unable to find a beer or a naked woman anywhere he sat down and moodily took up his cup of tea, suddenly looking like a disappointed small boy.

We sat for some minutes. I picked up a book and started to read. The soldier started to hum, keeping time by tapping on the gun. Many minutes ticked by. It seemed he was hoping to wear me down by sitting it out, that I might weaken and a bottle appear.

Tony the steward appeared at the door with the vacuum cleaner, stared in with round eyes then disappeared quickly like a frightened rabbit.

A few minutes later Tomas came in. "Coming down to lunch?" He looked at me and then at the soldier without surprise. Tony had passed the word.

The soldier shifted his position but didn't stand up.

"I see you have a Heckler and Koch" said Tomas, crossing to the soldier and looking down at him. Tomas asked him a lot of technical questions about the gun, how many bullets and when and where it was made and the young soldier, unwilling or unable to answer, got up and left.

"Must be one of the guards from the gate" said Tomas reaching for his radio. "I may have to go along with their rules but I'm not having people coming on board with guns without a bloody good reason and permission from me."

The Indian agent came in and apologised with a lot of head shaking but the Saudi Man at his side looked suspicious. He muttered to the agent, his glittering eyes on me.

"I am asked if you wish to make a complaint about something?" said the Indian Agent looking sweaty and nervous. Before anyone could answer, a breathless Chief Engineer had arrived at the door accompanied by two Saudi officials.

"Now we have trouble!" He announced loudly, ignoring any conversation that may have been taking place. "They arrest replacement first assistant engineer." He said dramatically, glaring at his companions and then at Tomas.

"What for?"

"I not know. I can't make out what is problem. I not go to move from this port without new engineer with this windlass and other problem I need to do for voyage!"

Tomas looked at the Indian agent who spread his hands in apology. "Know anything about this? We are expecting a crew member. Morales. Garcia Morales."

One of the Saudi officials spoke in English "We are detaining him for questions at the moment."

"What for? What has he done?" Tomas asked. They looked

sternly at each other, eye ball to eyeball. "Where is he being held?"

"I not leave port…" The Chief Engineer began again but Tomas held up his hand.

"What has he done?" Tomas repeated.

"It seems we get report this afternoon" said the Indian Agent. "Meanwhile we also have problem of oil on deck."

This created a small uproar. The oil was about a tea cup full but if it should slide down the side of the ship it would be considered serious pollution. Everyone went out onto the deck, my own small drama completely forgotten.

I went to lunch.

After lunch, a snooze due to the heat, interrupted by voices out on deck. I hung out of the bathroom porthole just in time to see the Boson rip the film from a camera, one that obviously belonged to Renalto the electrician who was shouting his protest.

"I only take photo of FEESH you idiot! In the water! What the hell matter wid you!"

The Boson didn't bother to reply, simply handed the camera back and went on his way.

"HEY YOU SON OF BITCH!" screamed Renalto, examining the exposed negative in one hand and the camera in the other. I toddled back to the bedroom and explained what was happening to the slumbering heap on the bed.

It was about a zillion degrees in the room.

"That's all we need, the electrician getting himself arrested."

Photography, even of the David Attenborough variety, was strictly forbidden anywhere in the port.

During the evening Garcia, the new First Assistant Engineer, a Philippino, turned up, looking pale and angry. He had been rescued by the Indian shipping agent.

Garcia had been detained because customs had found his Bible in his suitcase. They confiscated it and it was this that had made the row. Garcia, a devout Catholic, refused to part with it.

"My father gave to me before he died," he kept repeating, urging

Tomas to try to get it back for him, which Tomas said was unlikely, even if he made an official protest.

"They not like me to go from airport to ship with my bible, they tell me. They take from me," he said, almost in tears. "My father gave to me."

In the end they had threatened Garcia with imprisonment so he had to leave without it.

Tomas was more exasperated than sympathetic and said to no one in particular after he had gone, "You would think they had never been to sea before!"

The Chief Engineer, who had previously announced he was a total atheist, smiled a rare smile upon seeing the new assistant arrive and barely listened to Garcia's story. "He can pray without it! Especially when he see problem in engine room he have something else to think about."

I went up on the bridge feeling cross with both of them. It may have been a small thing to them, but not to Garcia. I looked out on the naked desert world beyond the ship's windows.

Rolando was there, correcting the charts, an ongoing job for the Third Officer, who received the 'Notice to Mariners' regularly in the mail.

"What are you doing?" I asked him, and he showed me the small corrections he was making.

A buoy moved from a previous position, a new shipwreck, a new sandbank emerged, hazards and warnings, and all of this information coming from the Hydrographic Office in the UK. "This job never end," said Rolando.

Rolando's ambition was to stay at home and work with his wife in the small family shop. He missed the gradual growing up of his children, as they all did, seeing them now and then, each time a few inches taller, new ideas on their minds, talking of friends their fathers had never met.

Unlike the Europeans, who worked for an average of four months before going on leave, the Philippinos and other Asian seamen worked for most of the months of the year. It was an unimaginable hardship for those ashore as well as at sea. After the first elation of

91

making the grade and getting the job, the realisation of the long separations must sink in. So much living spent apart. So many moments unshared.

As I was thinking of this, two Able Seamen came onto the bridge asking Rolando's permission to make a phone call. This was, of course, over the satellite phone. There was no mobile phone or radio connection there to the Philippines. Had to be an emergency, it was so expensive. One of them signed the book. The cost of the call to be deducted from his salary. There was a long discussion in Tagalog before the call was made. I understood from Rolando that one of the men was going to speak to the other one's wife on his behalf. Pleading his case? A dog eared letter was consulted by all three and conflicting ideas exchanged.

I would have felt embarrassed to be hovering around except that they knew I could not understand a word they were saying. I went out onto the bridge wing but the sun gave me such a blow over the head I rushed back into the air conditioning.

The friend was now shouting into the telephone. The reception was poor and the wife at the other end was having to shout as well. Whatever subtleties and persuasions were intended, the conversation was reduced to a shouting match with all tenderness gone. My heart ached for them. I slipped away back down the stairs.

CRACK CRACK CRACK CRICKETY CRACK CRACK CRACK CRICKETY CRACK.

We were again at sea, fully loaded and on our way back to Singapore.

It was early morning and the infernal noise over head had woken me up. I pulled on a dressing gown and went up the outside stairs to the bridge wing.

There they were. Four smiling faces, heads swathed in cloths, little hammers raised.

Chipping. That infernal job that I came to loathe. Chipping away the rusty paint from the deck, making it ready for a new coat. A truly terrible racket.

I appeal to Boson. "But it's such a beautiful day."

"Yes Ma'am and we need to paint when weather is fine."

I groan and go to search for the earplugs I wear on the aeroplane sometimes.

I meet Mario the Chief Officer who laughs at my discomfort. "No one like the chipping," he says.

"You surprise me."

Mario added to the din by shouting a story at me through the noise overhead and my earplugs. He held onto my arm.

"I have Captain no like the chipping." he bawled into my padded ears. "He English person also" He laughed, as if believing this was a particular English eccentricity.

"When he hear men working, he come out, like this." He mimicked someone rather pompous, walking with stiff knees and head in the air. "He say nothing. He walk up to the men working, like this. He bend down" Mario mimicked someone bending stiffly from the waist. "He pick up the hammers, one by one, like this, then he throw them overboard into the sea. He still say nothing. He walk back to his cabin. Anyone start again, he do the same. Ship never having new paint on deck. Not when he was on board." I laughed at the idea, and told Mario I would like to do the same.

"That Captain drinking too much" he said by way of explanation as he walked away.

Of course. With a hangover it would be really unbearable.

Ernesto had been listening, leaning at his open cabin door.

"I had English Captain who paint everything grey. He paint deck, doors, everything. Same grey colour. Grey chair. Grey table."

"Perhaps it reminded him of his old battleship" I said.

"No," said Ernesto seriously, not understanding my quip. "He just buy a lot of cheap paint."

It was too bad. A lovely calm day with blue sea and sky and bedlam going on all around. I went up to the bow, then to the very point by the jackstaff, looking down at the azure water below and the ghostly outline of the bulb of the ship as it ploughed along.

I had a sudden pang of shame, moaning about the noise. At least I didn't have to DO the wretched chipping, but I had started to look for quiet places to write each day where I would not be in the way or disturbed. I still had an agent in Los Angeles, and began to delve into the impossible, to try to sell an original screenplay. Heaven knows I had read enough turkeys when I had worked on breaking down and budgeting scripts in between actual productions. This fact made me hopeful and foolhardy.

The ship seemed to be a good environment to write. The phone, if it rang, was not for me. I was not required to shop or cook, but there were many days when the typewriter would keep sliding away from my fingers, or my chair rock back and forth in an irritating and distracting way. When the ship was in port, the bustle and action invaded even into any corner I had found, so what was left was some precious days of tranquillity when conditions were right and I could fantasise to my heart's content. I was to write ten screenplays over the years at sea and needless to say did not sell one, but my lovely agent Lew Weitzman continued to receive them and make encouraging noises and I had the fun of writing them.

It was superb to feel the breeze again. We had been in mind warping heat for days when you think your eyes are frying like two eggs in a hot pan. You send your tongue hanging out in search of icy limy drinks but will settle quickly for just plain old water. We were almost running out of water. The one inch of bath water was brown that morning. I made coffee from soda water. Not to be recommended.

This is why we were meeting AL KHAN and AL KHALIJ off the coast of Trucial Oman.

AL and AL were a fresh water and a fuel barge. We were tanking up for our return.

Near to the shore, we turned the bend of the peninsular. The dry mountainous land was without bush, tree or blade of grass. Where was the fresh water going to come from among those sandy coloured barren rocks.

The only other colour in the landscape were the dhows with their beautiful lateen sails in orange and chocolate. The dhows skimmed around, fishing on the bright water.

94

The crew passed the time fishing

The AL KHAN was captained by another northern Englishman, his welcome came over the VHF just as the sun was setting. I could see the oil refineries cut into the craggy inlets and buildings in the laps of the hills now, etched with purple shadows. A bleak place but with its own beauty, the fishing boats against the blazing sun and the silvery sea.

It took all night to fill up with the fuel and fresh water for our onward journey. The crew passed the time fishing, no ban it seemed in that place and we were at anchorage, not in port.

The radio operator caught seven huge barracuda and others three or four each. The sea was exceptionally clean and brimming with life and the lights from our ship attracted every creature.

In the early morning, having coffee on the bridge before we sailed, we saw shoals of fish jumping in every direction and more of the sea snakes I had seen in the Arabian Sea. The snakes were poisonous they said, as were the Portuguese Man of War jelly fish. This made the idea of swimming less attractive and it looked so inviting too.

Night sailing in the Arabian Sea brings the wonder of the fascinating phosphorescence on the curling waves at night and fabulous starry skies, but I awoke one night as we approached the Indian Ocean startled by the most incredible sheet lightning. The room was lit up, every second it seemed, flash upon flash upon flash.

I was alone as Tomas was on the bridge and I knelt up on the bed at the window, looking directly out along the full length of the ship.

We were lit as if by a strobe light in a disco, on and off, on and off. The sea in contrast was calm, we barely moved from side to side. It was eerie, but I couldn't take my eyes away, even though the light was painfully bright. Then in a tremendous flash, lightning struck the ship and around the main mast a brilliance flashed forth, yellow and green, dancing around, up and down. It must be. Saint Elmo's Fire. Goose bumps covered my body. I laughed like a cartoon witch with the exhilaration of it all.

Then heavy rain splashed down onto the deck and except for the few ship's lights softly shining out into the night, we were once more in darkness.

There was no question that we were sailing east. Each morning the sun rose directly ahead of the ship's bow, shining across the sea and in at our cabin window.

Once again in the Bay of Bengal and surrounded by patches of blue and huge puffy clouds and the ship swinging in a swell from a distant storm.

Renalto's cabin was across a passageway from the ship's office and through the open door I saw Tony knock, tentatively at first, then returning, the knock becoming more and more robust.

I was writing at the desk. Tony returned after the fourth attempt with Ernesto and the master keys. They went into the darkened cabin.

"Everything alright?" I called across at them. Ernesto did that Philippino silent expression of tilting the head back with raised eyebrows which means OK or I agree but Tony came across to me when Ernesto had left.

"He drunk" he whispered, with relish I thought. "Electrician. Drunk."

He covered his teeth and laughed.

"You should ask him to 'show a leg'," I said, typing away.

"I not understand."

"Show a leg. It means, well, when there are ladies visiting..." Tony feigned an innocent expression but I knew he would enjoy the explanation, especially coming from me.

"No lady. Only Electrician," he said solemnly.

I knew I was on the path to nowhere land but continued for the heck of it.

"Years ago, maybe when sailor's slept in hammocks. You know, a sling, a net, strung up on the wall." I knew I had lost him but I ploughed on. "When the Boson or officer wanted to start up the day, wake the sailors up, he would say that."

"Say what?"

"Show a leg. Then he could see if it was a woman or a man in the bed."

"Why he want to know?"

"So he could make the occupant of the bed wake up and get to

97

work. Presuming they let visiting women stay put for a further forty winks once they knew who it was."

Tony mused on this, then started up the cleaner. After a few moments he switched it off and came back over to me.

"What if leg is like a woman?" he demanded to know.

"What your leg for example?" I guessed, getting into deeper water.

Tony lifted his trouser leg a few delicate inches and showed me his obviously shaved and smooth leg. I had noticed that he plucked his eyebrows.

"Well you just might have to show something else." I said, straight faced and still typing. I felt him looking at me but continued typing.

Before starting the conversation I had not thought it would be delving into Tony's possibly ambiguous sexuality. I had seen him emerging from sailor's cabins from time to time without cleaning equipment and looking very jolly, and with all the months at sea deprived of affection it would not be too surprising. Whatever service he provided along with the vacuum cleaner was his business. Once he had proudly shown me a photograph of his girlfriend back home.

Whoever was gay on board was not discussed among the officers. Perhaps the crew knew and made the odd remark, but tolerance is a necessary part of life at sea when it comes to sex. There was also the friendly helping hand on occasion as well, a small secret that straight men think is not known by women, that some will allow a gay guy to be nice to them if there is no other opportunity around for a long time.

On the other end of the scale, there are those who would run a mile from the thought, and with my macho man, it was a delicate subject. I had made the great mistake of making a comment to him after a ship's barbecue and I had thought for a moment that he was going to make me walk the plank. It was simply that two sailors who were sitting at the party holding hands, disappeared together, then re-emerged both looking very clean and shiny, obviously from the shower, their wet hair slicked back, their faces rosy and smiling from ear to ear.

"Ben and Lopez had a good time tonight," I said to Tomas to be saucy, as we climbed the stairs to our cabin that evening. I did not realise it would turn into a major discussion. I was 'commenting' on things that should not concern me. I was 'interfering in ship's business' and by the time we went to bed I was pretty angry.

"Just what was I implying?" Tomas had said, which I thought was a ridiculous question.

After Tony had finished cleaning the office and gone on his way, a very rumpled and sleepy Renalto emerged from his cabin, dressed in boiler suit but not looking at all ready for work. He stood in the passageway holding his head.

"Fernet Branca," I called across to him. I went to the bar and poured him a shot.

"What is?" he asked suspiciously, looking down at the small amount of thick brown liquid.

"Something the Italians know about," I said. "What we call in England, the hair of the dog, but with other things in it."

He looked suspicious, his normally handsome face was puffy and creased all over.

He took it manfully in one go. I thought he would explode. His face went bright red.

A stream of expletives in Portuguese was followed quickly by his usual charm

"Sorry, sorry, but terrible. I not taste anything like. Ugh. I think you poison me."

"You might find you feel better in just a few minutes," I said encouragingly as he limped away clutching his stomach.

I had just finished my letter when he re-emerged, looking decidedly brighter.

"Well, this is miracle. I must know what this is," he said reaching for the bottle I had left on the side, and preparing to take another. I took it away from him gently and placed it in the cupboard.

"It won't work if you have too much" I warned him, aware of the high alcohol content it had, along with herbs and 'secret ingredients'. "In any case, it belongs to Captain."

This was always a certain way to stop anything being used up.

"I think I can work now," he said, examining his hair in the mirror, a sure sign that he was back on form. "Thank you." He bowed, accidentally making a small fart, which we both ignored.

I took my mug of tea up to the bridge where Tomas was changing course slightly, temporarily he told me, to avoid the enormous dark rain clouds ahead of us.

"Is it a storm?" I asked, looking through a pair of binoculars.

"Just rain showers. It's for the men on deck," he said indicating the group below, painting away.

How convenient. I had often been painting outside in Scotland, peering anxiously up at the dark clouds. It would have been very helpful if I could have moved the house out of the way while the paint dried.

The nine o'clock world news was on. An American oil prospecting ship had overturned in the Gulf of Thailand in the worst typhoon to strike Thailand in thirty five years. There were ninety seven crew on board. They don't expect to find survivors. Other cargo ships and fishing vessels are missing. This news will be little more than a small paragraph in British newspapers unless there was one British person on board. The ninety seven on the American ship were probably Asians. The glaring discrepancy in reporting the loss of ships at sea, compared to aeroplanes, comes under the heading of what is deemed to be of interest to the public, and sells newspapers. You cannot expect headlines and a three page spread every time a cargo ship goes down, but the statistics would surprise people.

I once telephoned the desk on BBC World news. It was very late at night and they had given a short bulletin concerning a cargo ship going down in the sea without naming the ship or the company. There were other items in the headlines, and as I listened avidly, to the full reporting of the news, the cargo ship was not mentioned again. They had mentioned the place where it happened in the headline, it was where Tomas' ship was at that moment, so fear had prompted me to call them. This was not the first time this kind of thing had happened I explained to the sympathetic man on duty on the news desk, and other wives and relatives must go through the same thing. If it is an oil spill, you'll hear all the details. If its a passenger ship, certainly. Otherwise not.

"Better you don't mention it at all, than fail to mention the ship's name" I explained.

Four whales on the starboard side that afternoon. Two large and two smaller, probably mothers and young. They stayed almost stationery in the water, huge and rubbery looking and just below the surface, their curving over dorsal fins just above the waves. Giants. Thrilling to see.

About an hour after this we saw silvery streams of oil on the surface of the water. It went on for miles. This was the first pollution I had seen. I thought of the whales.

As I stood looking out, everything stopped. The lights went out, the radio went off, the ship's engine died and in seconds we could only hear the wind and the sound of the sea.

We were in the Bay of Bengal again, the place where the ship with the steering problem had confronted us before. A spooky coincidence. Were we meant to die here?

Tomas was on the phone to the Chief Engineer in the engine room. I went out onto the bridge wing and watched as the bow of the great ship started to turn south.

Within fifteen minutes of the full 'blackout' we were seriously drifting south, on our way to Antarctica and nothing, no landfall, in between.

Thousands of tons of steel loaded with kerosene and the sea made light of us in no time at all.

When the engine started up again, Tomas showed me how far we had drifted off course in such a short time.

"What happened?" I asked, not thinking before that the relentless thundering of pistons under my feet would be so welcome a sound.

"Someone pressed the emergency button by mistake," was all he replied.

Never knew if he was serious or not.

Back on the Malacca Straits highway, well on our way to Singapore now, where we will be out on the roads, not in port, picking up provisions and spare parts, and all important mail, before taking off to Korea with our cargo.

The day before we arrived at the anchorage, we had an incident. It was lunchtime, we were eating in the officer's mess, quite a distance from the crew mess as there were kitchens in between the two large rooms. Even so, we could hear the noise. It sounded like high spirits, a lot of laughter and whooping. Allonzo the substitute cook explained to Tomas that it was 'Carlo the pumpman's birthday' and they had given him a 'present.'

Later in our cabin sitting room, Tomas was reading and I was attempting to do some ironing as the sea was fairly calm.

We started to hear a lot of shouting and thumping sounds through our open door, and up the stairwell Mario came bounding, looking distressed with blood on his shirt.

"Sir, sir, It's Gedung sir, he try to kill everybody!"

"What do you mean?"

Mario was shaking and pointing at the stairs. "He coming now sir! He really mad sir, help us!"

Tomas went off down the stairs. I leant over the banister, listening to the slamming of doors and the yelling.

Then Tomas appeared, also with blood on his shirt and holding Gedung, the Indonesian Voyage Engineer, firmly by the arm.

Gedung appeared to have a large gash over his eye.

Tomas dressed his wound and he appeared calm for the moment, explaining in great gasps of distress and fractured English what had happened.

The 'present' Carlo had been given was a bottle of whisky. Carlo had poured Gedung half a tumbler full apparently, or in any case a lot, and offered it to him. Gedung had been urged to drink it down.

He was a very sweet natured man normally, I had seen him dancing around at the previous Saturday barbecue, doing a wonderful traditional Indonesian dance. There were three Indonesian Voyage Engineers on board. They were travelling with us on a

102

temporary contract to do welding. The Philippinos, often feeling themselves to be the underdog, were not very nice to them, as is the way of things, they felt they had the opportunity to be over someone for a change. The three Indonesians were therefore isolated and kept their own company.

It must have been a surprise therefore when Carlo invited Gedung to share his whisky and the happy group celebrating his birthday.

Things quickly went very wrong indeed when the next thing Gedung knew was Carlo telling the others to pull Gedung's trousers down.

It may have been a silly joke but Gedung had taken great offence, understandably.

"I not like that sir" he protested, his eyes watering under the swathes of bandages Tomas was wrapping around his forehead. "And now I kill everybody" he continued sounding quite sad about it.

"Well you haven't killed anyone yet," said Tomas.

"I know. But I will," said Gedung, as if he was announcing something quite normal.

Tomas took him firmly by the shoulders and looked him in the eye.

"You go and rest now. Second officer will take you to the hospital," he said, although Ernesto was nowhere to be seen.

The ship was strangely quiet now and there was not a soul in sight.

Tomas took Gedung along the passageway himself and let him in to the hospital.

I was still ironing. I took the clean shirt from the board and handed it to Tomas.

"You should take a shower." I advised, the unspoken spectre of Aids lying between us.

Tomas went to do so. I continued to iron.

Then the noise started up again. Gedung had left the hospital bed and was once again flying around the ship, banging on the locked doors where it seemed most of the crew had gone to hide. "I KILL YOU ALL!" I could hear him screaming.

Tomas emerged from the bedroom, still damp from the shower, pulling on his clean shirt and now, furious.

He ran back down the stairs. Once again I heard them at the bottom of the next deck landing.

Tomas was holding Gedung up against the wall. Gedung had torn off the bandages which hung in bloody strips around his shoulders, the wound bleeding all over Tomas' clean shirt I noticed.

"YOU WANT TO KILL YOUR CAPTAIN!" Tomas roared in his face.

"No sir, no sir," said Gedung, then raised his voice defiantly. "BUT I KILL ALL PHILIPPINOS ON BOARD!"

Tomas frog marched him up the stairs. "CHIEF OFFICER!" Tomas roared and a quaking Mario appeared. "GET ME THE STRAIGHT JACKET!" Tomas yelled and Mario dashed off.

Calm restored and a second clean shirt later I peeped into the hospital where Gedung was lying on a bed in the straight jacket, fast asleep. On either side, like visiting relatives, the other two Indonesian Voyage Engineers sat looking at him. Resentfully I thought and I was right.

"They are all taking their meals in there and will spend the night in the hospital," Tomas told me. "I cannot risk more problems. They will all have to go ashore in Singapore. Something starts like this and you don't know where it can lead. The other two may decide to take revenge."

Ernesto arrived with keys and Tony with food and the trio were locked in for the night.

In the morning we anchored with the now familiar skyline of Singapore some distance away. It seemed months since I joined the ship instead of a few weeks.

Tomas was sitting at the computer writing a letter about the Gedung incident.

"What happens now?" I asked him.

"I am making a report to the company." I looked over his shoulder at the screen. Tomas had not made a big thing of it, but said the voyage engineers were not 'compatible' with the Philippinos. Most of the welding was finished in any case and it was more prudent to repatriate the Indonesians here instead of in Korea. Other crew could complete the work.

Tomas was sorry to have cut their work short for no real fault of their own. He gave them a simple letter of recommendation and twenty five dollars each from his own pocket. He can be a kind old sausage at times. The agent arranged their air tickets to Jakarta.

I watched the barge come to pick them up. Gedung had woken up like a little lamb. He was not used to whisky and was very apologetic about the whole thing. Carlo carefully avoided Tomas for several days after this and Rolando received a ticking off for supplying the whisky, especially in the middle of a working day.

While we waited at anchorage for various supplies and things to arrive, Tomas received a message from the company to say that a sister ship was going to anchor nearby. Would he be prepared to go over and make a visit? The Indian Captain was having some difficulties was all that they said. Tomas thought this would be a good opportunity to have a lifeboat practice, and accomplish the two things together.

We had the old fashioned kind of lifeboats on board, the ones that had to be let down on cables. It looked horribly dangerous and could be, even in calm seas and without the boat listing as it might do in an emergency. One of the many hazards was if the boat failed to stay even it could tip people out. Although cables were greased and the lifeboat checked periodically, it hadn't been used. The ship was old, its general condition was far from perfect.

Once the boat was released, it was not the easiest thing to get it hooked back on again and hauled up, something you have to do for a practice unless you want to lose the lifeboat each time. Looking down at the sea from the deck, it was as if you were standing on the roof of a five-storey building.

Tomas had made a special request to Boson. The crew should be chosen specifically for their seamanship. They lined up, dressed in orange boiler suits and lifejackets.

The lifeboat's engine had been checked by Garcia and at the last minute the Chief Engineer had actually volunteered to accompany

Tomas, in order to visit with the Engineer on board the other ship who was also a Croatian.

On the boat deck I kept out of the way as the heavy little boat was swung out on the davits. Two of the chosen seamen were on board to balance the boat and it was lowered carefully to just a few feet above the surface of the sea. I was terribly glad I wasn't going with them.

The sister ship was quite close to us but there was a strong current flowing and a lot of vast sea beyond that.

It was because of the speed of the current that they held the lifeboat just above the water. The remainder of the crew of twelve slid down the rope and after the Chief Engineer had started the engine one more time, Tomas took the pilot ladder and followed down into the boat. It was released with a splash onto the water, its small size and the actual swell and speed of the current very apparent as soon as it was in the sea. It bobbed about like crazy.

"START THE ENGINE" I heard Tomas command and it chugged into life. The Philippinos looked up at the big ship with all their mates looking down and waved as if they were off on an outing. "RELEASE THE PAINTER!" (The painter is the last rope attaching the lifeboat to the ship.)

So, off they went, for exactly two minutes. Then the engine died. Quick attempts to start it again failed. The current was now in charge and the boat was taking off in the opposite direction to the sister ship and us.

"TAKE OUT THE OARS!" I heard Tomas roar, but no one seemed to know how to hold an oar and even less how to use it properly. The lifeboat was really drifting away now, gaining speed on the current with a will of its own. "START ROWING" I heard Tomas voice, a little bit fainter now. The Philippino crew in the boat were actually laughing at their own antics and lack of expertise. Their laughter echoed back across the fast moving sea.

It made Tomas so mad that he took off his hat and hit the nearest seaman on the head with it.

I didn't know whether to laugh or cry. It was turning into real slapstick but with the horrible realisation of danger. There were many ships around, at anchor, true, but also arriving and taking off.

A small boat with neither engine nor sails in a strong current is a real problem.

The Philippinos were serious now, as Tomas tried to teach them to row and get back to our ship, the 'visit' to the other ship a luxury now forgotten.

Chief Officer would have to up anchor and chase the lifeboat at this rate. More attempts were made to restart the engine but rowing was the only real option.

Now the Chief Engineer came into his own and showed his seamanship. His often gloomy refusal to get excited about anything was what was needed. He and Tomas with cool heads and strong hands managed to scull against the current and between them got the boat back alongside.

When I saw Tomas' gloved hand reach for the painter it was a welcome sight.

It was because of this incident, that visiting chandlers and the agent were surprised to see, in the day or two following, puffing seamen heavily working at mock up rowing boats that had been rigged on deck. Even in their mess room. Apple boxes served as the 'boat' and the oars from both lifeboats balanced and rigged with ropes.

"You would think with seven thousand islands in their country they would have known how to row," said Tomas, furious for days afterwards. It was such a fundamental part of a Scandinavian seaman's training he could not believe that these 'islanders' did not know how to row. They were all actually from Manila or Quezon City and were as urban as someone from the heart of Birmingham. Big motor ships they knew. They had trained for that. But handling a rowing boat or sailing was something you did in the Philippines if you were rich or a fisherman. The Philippino fishermen skim over the coral in a 'Banca' made from bamboo, but they use the engine more than the sail. I had never seen anyone rowing when I was there.

The lifeboat engines were overhauled, again, but the truth was that the engines were old. I had learnt a convincing lesson. In emergencies, it's better that you stay on board until you really have to leave the ship.

Still at anchorage off Singapore, the night before we were to take off for Korea, two small boats without lights skimmed around the ship. In seconds someone had thrown a rope and was on board. The man walked along the deck, bold as brass, and Tomas spoke from the bridge over the loudspeaker. "THAT MAN THERE! JUST STOP! RIGHT WHERE YOU ARE!"

Boson and two burly Able Seamen had already been dispatched and the man dived off into the dark waters. One of the slim boats came around to pick him up. I am astounded at the cheek of it and the speed with which he got on board such a large ship.

"They come up the anchor chain" said the Boson, up on the bridge to report. "This one had a rope and hook." He held up his souvenir.

"What do they hope to do? How could they carry anything and get away? We're out in the ocean for God's sake," I said.

"Anything he find. Maybe our mooring lines. Heavy things he throw to his friends in the boat and be off in seconds. You saw him dive off the ship. He can carry plastic bag in his shirt, fill it up with stereo or radio or money he take from the first cabin he enter. Tie around the waist. Then take off, just like you see him do. You won't see him come or go. You just find your things have been stolen. This can make trouble on board."

"Other people get accused?" I asked

"Can happen. Especially if someone is packed up ready to go ashore on their leave. They are the first to be suspected. I saw someone killed once and when his things were searched, nothing. He was not guilty. Probably someone came like that, on board when at anchorage." He had given me the shivers. I went downstairs to our cabin, and looked around at the many items left about on the shelves, chairs and coffee table. My jewellery too on the chest of drawers in our bedroom. What if I found something missing? I would have suspected one of the crew. It was too horrible to think about. I imagined them all lined up like an identity parade, including Ernesto with his cigarette, Mario with his smile and Tony with his smooth legs.

I started to pack things up. We were taking off soon but I made a resolution not to leave things around for the passing athletic pirate.

CHAPTER 6

SOUTH CHINA SEA   TAIWAN   SOUTH KOREA   OKINAWA
THE YELLOW SEA   INCHON

Before light the engines rumbled and we were off once again, this time for a journey of eight days, through the South China Sea to Ulsan, South Korea, where winter was coming and our kerosene would be in demand.

We sailed into a headwind caused by the North Eastern monsoon. The ship was heavy with cargo and travelled well but its a different ride than what I had experienced before. More like a bucking bronco. The waves were extravagant, several metres high, and the bow of the ship sent the turquoise water shooting up in an arc of white foam spreading along both sides of the deck with a gurgling sound.

We took the eastern passage, past Taiwan, to pick up the Kuro Shio, the Japanese current that would add another two knots to our speed.

The ocean was still a toe tempting twenty six degrees centigrade, even though we were riding over a depth of three thousand metres. I knew this, not because I had put in my toe but because of one of the gauges I had read up on the bridge.

The water was to chill considerably by the time we came to dock. Ice forms in November along the North West Coast of Korea, spreading down from Siberia, and stays until March.

I was about to change my wardrobe, reducing the previous feeling of guilt at having brought so much. Woollens and puffy jackets were going to be required after all.

Bao-Dao, or Treasure Island as Taiwan was once called, made me think of Robert Louis Stevenson and if this inspired the title. Also called Formosa, from the Portuguese meaning beautiful, and named by Portuguese sailors in the sixteenth century. More romantic names than Taiwan, which simply means 'terraced bay'. This last name was the one in a report sent to the Emperor Of China by Cheng Ho, the famous eunuch navigator (one way of being certain that your man would not waste too much time ashore) who apparently kept on going, as the Ming Court prohibited emigration at that time.

In this part of the world you are thinking about the Chu-Feng, the Supreme Winds, or typhoons.

On the weatherfax, one could be seen south of us, heading for the Philippines, only recently hit badly by one a week ago. When I was working there a few years ago, and naive to a degree about the weather, I asked 'how many' occurred during the season and was told about four or five a month. That was one every five or six days! Every week, the fear that your nipa and bamboo house would be in the path of one and be totally destroyed? From the discussions on the bridge, I understood that Taiwan's weather can change dramatically at any time of the year and one of the reasons it was called beautiful is due to the tremendous rainfall. It's very green.

The sea was rough as we passed at night. In the light of the full moon you could see the white topped waves all the way to the horizon.

The next morning, the tell tale jade green in the deep troughs and the finer spray flying as high as the bridge made me feel reckless, like going too fast downhill on your bike when you were six. Exhilaration tinged with fear. Thankfully not tinged with seasickness. Oh lucky me, for luck is all it's about and nothing to do with mind over matter.

I thought about those marvellous busty figureheads that used to dip in and out of the waves. What a pity modern ships don't have them. The talisman (generally a taliswoman) that led the ship home and gave it its character. Bring back the 'Saucy Nancy'!

Perhaps when I die I could apply to come back as one and dip my laced buxom bodice in and out of the waves, my thick swirling wooden skirts tucked beneath ship and sea, my calm painted eyes always staring ahead to the next port.

I had an ambition to be a mermaid when I was a little girl. Then I read Hans Christian Anderson's story and how the mermaid had seemed to have been punished for wanting legs, for when she walked it was as if she was walking on swords. Is that a moral lesson for

110

being content with what you've got!

A modern cargo ship is a kind of a robot with no heart, compared to the creaking sailing ships of old. Fish may disappear deep into the calm beneath the storm and a sailing ship would hove to, but our ship knows only to churn ahead along the charted path, a belly full of kerosene and no mind of its own.

On the outskirts of the harbour we were met by a grey haired Korean Pilot and two tugboats, SUN JIN NOG and the CHO KWANG. It took a bit of nautical jiggery pokery to get our heavily laden ship alongside the refinery, due to the wind. Its 'half astern, then 'slow astern' then 'dead slow ahead' and back again, and there we were, lined up inches from the jetty by what seemed to me nothing short of a miracle. The weighty ship could cut through the concrete dock like a sharp knife through cheese but we had moved crab like, sideways on, and the lines cast ashore provided the finishing touches to the manoeuvre. Giant squares of rubber fixed to the dockside squeezed us into a snug fit.

Ulsan Gang (Ulsan Harbour) had about twenty-five other ships docked around. I went to my usual bird's eye view on the bridge wing to see how far we were from the town.

The harbour was surrounded by dusty hills, reminding me of California, and checking the latitude I could see why. South Korea has more of a contrasting climate and the winter is bitterly cold.

Above the hills I saw what I thought was an escaped kite, changing shape with the wind, but through the binoculars discovered it was seven ducks who came flying over the ships and then out to sea.

The Korean Pilot who was just leaving told me that these were the 'Blue Ducks' who leave Korea in November to WINTER in Siberia. No wonder they are called blue.

After the unloading had begun, which would take hours and hours, and all paper work had been completed, I raised the idea of Tomas and me going ashore for an hour or two. Then came the news that Boson had badly injured his foot.

This meant telephone calls to the agent and it was arranged that he should go to a local hospital for an x-ray.

No one could actually walk off the ship at the dockside refinery due to the highly inflammable cargo (knowing that almost all the crew smoked came to my mind as a factor) and a boat would take anyone ashore from the accommodation ladder on the sea side of the ship.

Only loading masters and those directly involved with the cargo were allowed on the jetty side.

As the Boson could not walk, Ernesto and others had strapped him onto a stretcher.

I watched from above. As the anxious group of almost half the crew came to see him off, one of them passed him the cigarette he was smoking and Boson took a drag, just like a wounded soldier in a war movie, before angrily telling him to put his cigarette out. ('No smoking on deck'.)

The people at either end of the stretcher had a debate as to who would descend first, while the spluttering barge waited below, tipping about in the wind.

After much turning this way and that, the smallest of the stretcher bearers for some inexplicable reason started down the steep metal steps first, a poor decision, immediately apparent, as Boson, like one of those cartoons in an osteopath's waiting room, slid right down the stretcher, leaving his legs and feet strapped to the other end.

The little Able Seaman, finding the Boson's head and heavy shoulders buried into his lap, took rapid backwards steps. Boson was about to end up in the sea, strapped, helpless, and drowning before our eyes. Everyone rushed to save the day.

This changed Tomas' mind about going ashore. We would visit Boson in the hospital to see if he was alright.

The young energetic shipping agent, a Mr U.S. Lee, was waiting on the dock to take us into town. His initials prompted the obvious question but he told me that the 'U' pronounced 'oo' and the 'S' pronounced 'sun' meant 'foolish honest'. I was fascinated by Korean letters which looked like Chinese designed by computer. Chinese is all wispy artistic strokes of trees and houses and people. Korean is bold and geometric and looks as if you should know what it says. It was King Sejong, in the fifteenth century, that introduced the lettering, the Hankul Alphabet, as he was concerned that as the people could not read or write they could not present their petitions to him.

We drove speedily into town, passing many rickety shops built of concrete and open-ended stores with tin roofs.

Padded jackets and woollen hats hung everywhere, and the other noticeable items, strings of segments of metal stove piping and new oil heaters lined up on the pavement.

Our kerosene was certainly going to be used here.

Other signs of winter were the people filling huge barrels with Chinese Cabbage, garlic, ginger and red pepper. The famous Kimchi, the Korean staple, eaten all year round, but traditionally supplying necessary minerals and vitamins during a cruel winter. To those who haven't eaten it, a warning. It ferments, which is deliberate, and produces what some may say (like me) is a truly offensive smell. It does no favours for your breath. If you have the slightest problem with your stomach it can attack your duodenum with a ferocity that can make you devour an entire box of Rennies at one go. No fridge required (that's the idea) so if purchased by your loved one, can sit like a Gorgon on a plate filling your nostrils morning, noon and night, even in the bedroom. These descriptions are from personal experience. Tomas loved Kimchi.

All the Koreans I met had 'bear's breath' and prompted you to lean away as you spoke to them in self-defence. I knew the reason. It was the Kimchi.

We sped on up a side street and stopped at a sign with a red cross on a building wedged between shops.

The hospital was rather grim. Dark, bare and cheerless. Poor Boson had one of the 'better' rooms. A narrow cell, with a bed, two wooden chairs, a shaky table, and one astonishing feature, a simply gigantic clock, two feet in diameter, on the wall above his bed. It ticked loudly and the hands made a clunk every time they moved another minute on. It made me think of Edgar Allan Poe.

It would have driven anyone mad. Better not to mention it. Instead I examined the opposite wall, while Tomas spoke to Boson. I went outside in the corridor. Lots of partitions and more narrow rooms. Boson's room was the end portion of what was once a huge main room, probably a central hall or reception. But why on earth leave the clock for the unfortunate patient in Room 12? If it had been me, they would have been carrying me out, strapped to that stretcher he had arrived on and carting me off to the mental hospital after one night. Tick! Tick! Tick!

'Oh God! What *could* I do? I foamed – I raved – I swore! I swung the chair upon which I had been sitting, and grated it upon the boards, but the noise arose over all and continually increased. It grew louder – louder - *louder*!' [3]

"We'll see what we can do," Tomas was saying to Boson. "Won't we?" He said turning to me.

This meant I had been allocated a job. "Do what?"

"Bring Boson something to read."

I looked around. The poor man didn't have a book or magazine, only a newspaper in Korean. You would soon get fed up with looking at the photographs and trying to guess the captions.

"We can send some books with the agent."

"Good idea. We'll do that," said Tomas, meaning me. I made a mental note.

We stepped out into the dusty noisy street, the cars zooming by threatening our toes. After five weeks at sea, I needed a few personal items. We started to explore.

The people in Ulsan were on the short side, square and strong looking, with pleasant rosy faces and for the most part, dressed in ridged padded coats and trousers. It was like stumbling across a town of miniature Michelin tyre people.

Most roads were without pavements and the cars sounded their horns all the time. It was cold and it was dusty and did not improve our mood. It was also difficult to find anything we wanted.

I bought three jars of what I believed was honey but found to my

---

[3] The Tell Tale Heart – Edgar Allan Poe

delight later that one was marmalade, something we did not have on board.

Looking for a place to have lunch (pictures of things to eat) or place to have a drink (cocktail glass neon sign) we discovered that these establishments seemed to be below ground. We read a sign in English "COFFEE," so down we went.

Through a heavy wooden door we emerged, like Dorothy, into another world, an American Coffee Shop with booths and all the familiar items.

The Korean lady behind the counter adjusted her Pierre Balmain scarf and asked us if we wanted 'telephone' with coffee. Very puzzling. Just coffee please.

We sat down. I noticed that she stood with her glossy red lips only an inch away from a microphone. The place had soft lighting, flowers, and the latest coffee making equipment.

As we waited for our coffee we noticed that we were the oldest people in the place. This was not so difficult, but simply everyone else was under twenty-five, mainly teenagers.

The telephone rang on the scarf ladies desk. She picked it up, answered then cooed into the microphone. Another telephone rang to the right of us, in a booth where six teenagers were sitting, giggling and talking. One picked the phone up and started to chat.

This was before mobile phones had become the ubiquitous personal accessory of today.

"I get it," said Tomas. "Coffee and you can make and receive telephone calls."

A phone rang somewhere else, the scarf lady spoke softly over her microphone and the market for coffee and conversations continued.

The most interesting thing about this novel coffee shop was the atmosphere. Compared to one passenger using a mobile today on a train or in a restaurant where the entire place would be subjected to loud dialogue, the 'Ulsan Chat Shop' as we called it, was calm, pleasant, and not intrusive. Very Asian in other words. And the coffee was very good.

Outside again and directly across from a man selling hot roasted chestnuts at a makeshift brazier. I had to have some. Memory of childhood. A London street and chestnuts after a visit to the cinema. Watching his gloved fingers turning the chestnuts around on the tin plate over the fire I remembered how my mother would give into my request, but complain that "I would get it all over my coat." How amazed I would have been then to see the mountains of popcorn, bars of chocolate, packets of sweets and twenty varieties of ice cream in the cinema foyer today, but nothing to compare to the taste of those hot sweet roasted chestnuts on a cold night.

Up the street munching, we turned a corner into a great covered market hall selling nothing but fish. It must have covered the area of three football pitches. Row upon row of all varieties hanging on hooks, swimming last swims in tubs, or lying in mountains of salt, expiring.

In the centre, a large group of women were squatting on stools, their copious laps enveloped in plastic aprons, chatting away and gutting fish at a tremendous speed. They looked up at us, the only non-Koreans in the place, and were very amused. Laughing at us and with us, their half moon eyes crinkling and disappearing into their rosy faces, they passed remarks to each other, looking us up and down.

I forgot to mention, that when I had purchased the honey, my eye had fallen onto some flat plastic shoes displayed in a basket. My feet were aching in my leather boots, too many days in a hot climate, my feet had spread like pancakes and the boots felt tight. Not wanting to buy a pair of shoes I didn't need, I thought a temporary pair would do the trick and allow me to continue walking around. I soon discovered like the Ugly Sisters, that my feet would not fit into the dainty sizes and I had to turn to the men's display, where I found a pair to fit. They had a large embossed sign on the front of each: DUCK SUNG and became known when I was looking for them thereafter as my Duck Songs. They were very large, very ugly and very bright. I was wearing smart conventional clothes and if you were looking at me and then got down to my feet, you would have the impression you were looking at a hasty dresser to say the least.

Further into the fish market you came to the cooking section.

Bubbling woks, shrimps dipped into batter, and an oblong shaped omelette made with stringy bright green vegetables.

The stall holders, mostly women, were wrapped up against the cold wind that was blowing through the market place. A wind that carried on its wings, a bouillabaisse of fishy smells that had started to wrinkle my noise.

Tomas was in his fishy element, darting from one gruesome pot or gutting to another, exclaiming at the variety, the quality and the size.

I poodled off on my duck songs to yet another cavernous section, this time piled high with packets of dried fish. Stall upon stall had mounds of cellophane bags filled with dried everything and above the stallholder's heads lines of more fishy things in bags were pegged up for display. It was a Gunter Grass nightmare.

I staggered on, to the opening, towards the harbour wall and the sea beyond. I could actually see our ship's funnel poking up in the distance.

Outside, rows of stalls, no one selling here, but more fish, this time drying in rows and rows, with 'washing lines' of squid that flapped in the wind. I turned around as Tomas came out from the market, laughing at my face. He took a photograph of me, surrounded as I was, by the hundreds of rows of drying fish.

This was also the place where the fish gutters brought the residue of their labours and here and there were barrels of fish guts swimming in seawater and blood.

"HELP! I shall never touch fish again!"

We had needed to pee for some time and started to look around for a hotel or cafe where we could stop, without success. No public conveniences here.

We started to consider an alleyway as our need was so desperate, but I remembered a colleague in Mexico once, with the same idea, who had disappeared into a dark alley, only to come flying out again, his trousers undone and screaming at the top of his lungs. Having directed himself into a corner, he had stirred up a cloud of flying insects and cockroaches, which had of course attacked him, in all parts.

Tomas found a petrol station and we were shown a hole in the floor kind of toilet which was as welcome as the powder room at the Ritz.

Bells were ringing as we strolled down the street on our way back to the ship. The houses in that area were more traditional with deep grey curving tiles on the roofs and carved beams. Some were painted in bright colours and others had tiles etched with patterns or designs of birds and flowers. More bells ringing as we turned the corner, and then a wonderful scene. Groups of Korean women in traditional dress, holding up their skirts away from the dust, looking like large coloured bells in their high waisted gowns. The women rustled by us in their full skirted embroidered silk, broad sashes flying.

The men were super smart in suits and ties holding the hands of their tiny children or arm in arm with their teenagers.

Everyone was walking in the same direction and we then understood that they were all on their way to church. I was even more aware of my awful duck songs.

After we left Ulsan we headed directly south through the East China Sea. Our destination, Okinawa-Jima, the island that lies between the tip of Japan and Taiwan. I awoke one morning to see a shima to the left and a shima to the right. Shima is Japanese for island, I was told by Mario, who was on duty on the bridge. There were 'shimas' and 'jimas' all over the chart.

I had dressed hastily, excited by the tropical blue rings of water and sandy beaches I had seen from the bathroom porthole as I took my shower.

On the larger chart, directly east of us, but hundreds of miles away, are Iwo Jima, Midway, then Hawaii and eventually the United States. The names provoke thoughts of the Second World War and as we dock, I realise that it is actually American Thanksgiving, the last Thursday in November. At that time there were over 12,000 American army, navy and marine corps and their families stationed at Okinawa. This was before relations had turned sour due to several terrible incidents. The agents and chandlers that came on board were relaxed about the huge American presence and only had good things to say then.

Of course the Americans brought business, but to the older generation of Okinanawans there was a profound sense of history and even gratitude.

The Okinawans do look Japanese but many have a more elliptical eye, and certainly darker skin. Some of the people were closer in resemblance to Hawaiians, or Pacific Islanders, not reserved as Japanese generally are at a first meeting, but immediately warm and friendly.

Our shipping agent there, a man in his late fifties, spoke freely of his memories of the war. In 1941, Japanese soldiers came to Okinawa and killed half the population, needing the island produce to feed their soldiers. The shipping agent was a young boy at the time and had run into the mountains with some of his family and survived. His father had been shot.

When the Americans came, they tried to help the people. He had memories of American soldiers carrying the children to safety. Writing this now, makes it all the more terrible that the American servicemen's reputation on the island seems damaged beyond repair.

When we arrived in Ulsan, seven ducks had flown over the ship. In Okinawa, seven, yes truly seven again, not ducks, but giant Huey military helicopters, roared overhead, heading inland to the base.

We were docked in Kin Port, not a conventional port but an oil refinery, which seemed sacrilege among the lapis lazuli waters. At least the tanks were painted pale green and the dockside lined with small trees in pots. Japanese sensibilities, those gardeners, who even there, had decorated the oil refinery with grace, order, and something green and growing.

We were there to load gas oil mixed with kerosene, or LSD, low sulphur diesel. When I had seen LSD on the telex I had wondered.

During the journey from Korea, the crew had been cleaning the tanks ready for the next cargo, flushing them with sea water, a lengthy process that is governed by the number of particles per gallon and all the pollution regulations in mind. Boson had got left behind as his foot turned out to be fractured, so one of the more experienced Able Seamen had been promoted temporarily until a replacement was flown out to the ship. Not so very far from the Philippines, in comparison to most places in the world, the new Boson would be arriving in Okinawa.

The business of transporting fuel revolves around the deadly sounding term, 'flash point', the temperature the cargo can reach before it produces inflammable fumes that can ignite at a spark.

NO SMOKING signs are everywhere but it only takes one unthinking sailor to stroll out of his cabin and onto the deck with a cigarette at the wrong time.

Allonzo was caught doing exactly that. He had not entered the deck area but on his way out of the accommodation main door, when Tomas was coming the other way. Next time we had a fire drill he was chosen as the fictitious person who had caused the fire.

The drill was conducted at sea. Crew dressed in their fire suits, looking a bit like astronauts, advanced towards Allonzo who was told to stand in the middle of the deck. Tomas had told the crew not to actually turn the hoses on at that moment, the blast would have knocked Allonzo overboard, but along with the joking, perhaps something was remembered. We would hate someone's Marlborough to be responsible for blasting us into space.

At Kin Port there was a bus service to take crew into town for a couple of hours. To my delight Tomas agreed to take the bus with me, interested to see the island. He was generally reluctant to leave the ship. "Something always happens," he would say.

We drove along dusty roads, passing fields of sugar cane and long rows of lush looking vegetables, flowering bushes, trees and plants in pots. The houses were simple, mainly cement buildings with flat roofs, the more opulent ones with concrete terraces, but everything was covered or surrounded by greenery.

The oil refinery had brought prosperity and jobs to the island but I wondered at what environmental cost. There are no oil wells on Okinawa. Crude is brought from elsewhere, like the Gulf, then processed into products for sale on the island. The agent said it had prevented a mass exodus of young people from the island and he spoke about his children who all had jobs at the refinery. They were earning a good salary.

This was reflected when the bus stopped in the city of Nahu where there was an over abundance of shops and nightclubs. Every side street seemed to flash signs beckoning the American to spend their dollars. The signs were mainly in English THE WHITE TIE and THE POGO POGO. THE LUCKY LADY and POPEYES.

Just as I had done in Ulsan without success, I searched for typewriter ribbon cassettes and correcting tape but the art of writing by hand was very much alive in Okinawa, as it had been in Korea. I was all for that, but short of visiting the American Airbase, I was going to be out of luck.

Stationery shops had every kind of pen and brush, inks and paper of every texture and colour, but no typewriter supplies. Electrical equipment they had in abundance, this was Japan after all. We met crew from the ship, staggering under gigantic boxes.

The many computer and computer game stores were brimming with images jumping about with overpowering robots and snarling monsters.

We discovered Pachinko, the big Asian obsession, as we entered under a sign that simply said BAR and were confronted only by rows of backs and bottoms. One or two turned to stare then returned to face the machines with great concentration, their arms working furiously.

The clatter and clamour and the ringing of the bells was like being in a factory. It looked like the old fashioned Bagatelle game, silver balls being released inside pathways created by springs and rows of nails.

In 1989 there were 14,500 Pachinko parlours on mainland Japan. Today there must be many more. There on Okinawa, you were not allowed to win money, as gambling was illegal, but you were given a voucher that was discreetly exchanged for goods in a shop around the corner.

We couldn't stand more than a few seconds of the frenzied atmosphere and headed for POPEYES, which turned out to be a cafe/restaurant of modest size, but serving far from modest portions.

No one spoke English. This wasn't Tokyo after all. Okinawans speak Japanese but have their own dialect.

Writing all over the walls, ceiling and counter in Japanese letters, and no picture clues. We took the plunge and pointed at two lines of writing on the menu. When our plates arrived we thought we had a made a mistake. The plates were platters, and the amounts, two Mount Fujis of rice, shrimp and chopped meat, were enough for five people.

Then we looked around us at the diners at other tables, and at the line of people seated eating up at the counter. Some had different kinds of food, but all had the same enormous amounts.

I noted the long row of enviably neat bottoms at the bar. Not one bottom overlapped the tiny seat.

"If I ate like this I would look like a Sumo wrestler in two months."

"We do look like Sumo wrestlers," said Tomas comfortingly, "Compared to these people."

Why wasn't I born with Asian metabolism?

"It's the diet," Tomas continued, munching his way through Mount Fuji.

"But its mainly rice," I countered, "Isn't that carbohydrate?"

Across the room, a tiny Okinawan, aged about three, was ploughing his way through his platter, an elbow confidently propped up on the table. I caught his eye and he waved which I returned with a modest wave of my fingers, not to distract him. He enchanted me by blowing me a kiss in return.

"Happy Thanksgiving" I said to Tomas, suddenly remembering what day it was.

"Makes a change from turkey," was his reply.

When we sailed, in the middle of the afternoon the next day, it was light enough to look out and see the islands and mushroom shaped rocks on narrow necks that jutted up from the sea all around.

The soft volcanic domes of rocky islands, large and small, remembered from Japanese paintings and embroidery, were a wonderful sight, but I read in the Pilot book on board that many had poisonous snakes. On Amami Shima, it said, there was a particularly poisonous snake, with black stripes, only ten inches long and the thickness of a cigarette. These bits of local information are given to sailors in case they get shipwrecked I suppose, or think of tying up in an unscheduled place. If you achieved the impossible and climbed up the rocky stem of the island, scrambled limpet like under the shelf of the overhang, and got to be on the flat part on top you would be a mountaineer as well as a sailor. Having got that far, you should then look out for the devious little snakes who would certainly leap on the only living thing they had seen in decades.

Another rocky islet, Tori Shima, is frequented by vast numbers of seabirds, their cries morning and evening can be heard for miles, says the Pilot book. That would be eerie, especially if you were on a sailing boat and could hear. On board our ship, the noise of the engine thundering away would drown all that out, but on a sailing boat, you might feel you were being seduced by distant sirens.

The new Boson, having arrived in time before we took off, was causing a small stir, trying to prove himself by arm wrestling with everyone.

The news of this reached us when we saw Garcia the First Engineer, with his arm in a sling.

Several others had had their egos bruised and there was a disgruntled air in the crew mess room at lunchtime.

It had the knock on effect of making everyone complain even more than usual about Allonzo's cooking and he had gone into a sulk inside his cabin, declaring that he would do no more. Tony was seen knocking timidly on his door, out of sympathy perhaps, but also fear that he may have to be the one to cook dinner that evening.

It had been weeks since the women had been on board in Singapore, or the crew had been ashore in a place where they could have the odd fling. Since then we had been to the Gulf and at sea. Ulsan had been busy and Okinawa the same. It seemed important parts were feeling deprived, and with no satisfaction for either stomach or manhood, the arm wrestling took on gladiatorial proportions.

"I not wish to break of your arm," sneered the Chief Engineer, as Jerry, the new Boson asked to take him on. He strolled out of the room with a superior air in his greasy boiler suit with its sagging droopy seat. At least Boson had the good sense not to call him back.

"Come on Tony," Ernesto cried, as Tony came back into the mess to clear tables "Lets see what you can do."

Everyone laughed. Tony was tall for a Philippino, and slim. He did not look like a contester, and his fastidious, slightly feminine air did not lend itself to the image of an arm wrestling champion, but to everyone's surprise, he put aside the dishes he was holding, whipped off his apron and sat down opposite the Boson.

This made everyone laugh even more. The place was in uproar.

The new Boson, a burly type of about forty-five years of age, with muscles just turning into fat and a bit of a beer belly, was still very strong. Several members of the crew had been beaten by him, their arms laid down on the table like matchsticks. The Boson had grown louder, looking sweaty and pleased with himself. He was certainly not a diplomat, having been on board only twenty-four hours and previously unknown to any of the crew.

Tony took the Boson's right arm, arching his thin eyebrows and smiling slightly into the Boson's face. The Boson grinned. He had a gold front tooth that gave him a piratical air.

Down. The Bosons knuckles struck the table.

There was a gasp from everyone. A nervous giggle. Could this be? Boson held out his left arm. Down. That too?. Boson looked astonished.

"You're making a joke." Ernesto accused him. I was thinking the same, until I noticed the Boson's expression. He was very puzzled. He looked sideways at Tony, then held out a middle finger to him.

Grimly Tony and the Boson hung on. Then the Boson winced and sprang away. Blood spurted from the Boson's finger. Sadly, no one cared, the cheering and shouting took over and everyone wanted to clap Tony on the back.

He stood up, smiling away, bathing in the attention.

Tony. The champion. Who would have thought it.

Even Allonzo had appeared from his cave, unable to resist and wanting to know what all the noise was about. "I will make you a cake tonight!" he promised Tony, which made everyone laugh more than ever. "Oooh, one of Allonzo's cakes! You so lucky!"

When the crowd had dispersed and the Boson had had his finger bandaged and was back out on the deck, I saw Tony sitting on one of the mess room tables, smoking, while Allonzo was whistling in the kitchen and stirring pots.

"That was well done," I told him, as I passed on the way to the laundry room.

"I am younger than him and I not have fat."

"That's true."

"I watch him. He also wear himself out before. I not wrestle six men before like him."

I liked that he shared that bit of honesty with me. It made his success even more of a triumph.

Not just brawn had won the day, but brains as well.

When you look out of the porthole each day, you see many paintings of sea and sky, and some get frozen in the memory.

We were now in the Yellow Sea, but that morning it was pale pink.

We were passing Sho Kokuzan To, one of the hundreds of small islands on the South West Tip of Korea, and there were several traditional fishing boats around us, silhouetted against the rising sun. Huge seabirds flew around the boats and the tiny conical shaped islands we were passing. One moment the birds and the boats were sharply etched dark shapes, and the next they were revealed in detail and coloured pink and gold. It was wonderful. Beautiful. And no photograph could have captured it so well as the mind's eye. I see it still, today.

The islands where the fishermen lived were rocky and infertile, with only the barest covering of scrubby grass and layer of soil. Steps led up to small stone and wooden houses perched on the top or clinging to the side of a shelf overlooking a tiny beach.

Fish had to be their principal food and the only way to earn money to buy anything else.

Later that night, the dark sky was lit up by dazzling rows of lights. The fishing boats were now fishing for squid, which were attracted to the lights. I remembered our ship in the Gulf, surrounded by fish at night. The fishing boats had a conveyor belt device suspended from the sides of their boats, rotating continuously from deck to water, scooping up squid by the ton.

We were bound for Inchon, the gateway port to the capital Seoul. The raggedly west coast of Korea reminded me of the west coast Scotland, but Korea has many more islands and inlets.

Also the waters around Scotland are deep, allowing the biggest ships to pass and dock, a fact that was no small contribution to the boom in shipbuilding there long ago.

The inlets on the west coast of Korea however are very shallow, only the smallest ships can land on most of the shore, until you come to the great Yom Ha River, which leads to Inchon.

The mouth of the river was as wide as the sea and full of islands.

The Inchon Korean Pilot boarded our ship and we took two hours to travel the twenty-four miles of river to our anchorage in the harbour, navigating past islands in a strong current.

Four Korean Naval destroyers sailed by, and I thought about both wars, the Second and the Korean, when Inchon was so strategic. Enemy ships could hide behind any of these islands.

The tugs that came to help us berth did something new to me, they talked to each other by sounding their horns. They have different tones. One goes beep and the other goes honk.

I remember the traffic in Ulsan. A Korean thing? If everyone was honking about in the harbour it would seem to lead to chaos, but we docked alright, although they had ominous names, DIE YOUNG (DAE YUNG) and DIE SOON (DAE SUNG).

The Korean seamen on the dock who were helping to moor the ship, and others waiting, the agent, chandler and immigration, were marching up and down, flapping their arms and stamping their feet. Out on deck your face froze instantly.

The Koreans there were very different to those in Ulsan. In Inchon the Koreans were tall and slim, their faces long and pale compared to their Southern cousins.

Our LSD from Okinawa will take sixty hours to pump ashore. There is not a lot of room between us and the muddy bottom, so when we sank with the tide, the swell gave Tomas some concern. The ship is like a pregnant whale about to give birth. This puts Tomas on alert and although aware that the ship only had this margin, before docking, Tomas wants to stay with her like an expectant father.

It was also necessary to give the officers and crew time ashore, at least in shifts, and so this was a port I would visit on my own. Again we had to take a barge ashore on the seaside, although the distance to the dock was only a few hundred yards. I say 'we' because I was accompanied by almost half the crew for the short trip to the shore.

The immigration and officers in the custom hall were gathered around a pot-bellied stove topped by a gigantic copper kettle. We all trooped in and an official stepped away from the warmth to inspect my passport.

He looked at me and then smirked back at his friends.

"You much younger here. This photo long time ago?"

"No, but I'm rather tired today and I'm wearing glasses." I removed them.

He looked at the long line of crew lining up behind me, amused at this middle aged British woman who seemed to have fifteen sailor boyfriends in tow.

He said something to the other officials in Korean, and they all laughed, but he stamped my passport and waved me though.

The crew did not have such an easy time. The customs gave them body searches, looking for guns I understood as we were close to the Northern Korean border. I hovered around anxiously, looking at the ways guns and drugs had been smuggled before. Wouldn't that give people ideas? Or was it meant to say 'We know what you can get up to?' The punishments, which were severe, were listed in Korean and English.

Everyone eventually emerged unscathed and piled themselves into several taxis.

I took a taxi into the centre and bought a ginger jar in a department store. Then into a restaurant where the menu was translated on one side into English. It didn't help as a plate appeared with a giant squid that I was sure I hadn't ordered.

"Lady. Sloe Gin" the waiter kept saying, trying out his few words of English, so I agreed, not quite sure what I was drinking when it did arrive.

The waiter brought long white radishes and a pickle type sauce.

The squid continued to stare with baleful eye as I nibbled a radish. A bread basket appeared with no bread but two sweet doughnuts inside. An influence from the Americans no doubt, but a stomach churning idea if they were meant to be eaten with squid.

"Lady. Sloe Gin?" said my friend the English speaking waiter and afraid to shake my head from side to side in case it meant 'yes', I waved my hands and put one over the glass.

The gin still arrived. I passed him the plate of squid in exchange. He looked sad.

"Egg?" I ventured. "Omelette?" I pointed in the menu. I had a thought that the English may not match up with the Korean. Opposite the various omelettes described, the Korean could be saying boiled cod's liver. To my relief, an omelette appeared, although very fishy tasting, with shrimps sticking out at angles from a very soft interior, like pink caterpillars from custard. I swigged down the rest of the gin and took a few mouthfuls of the omelette, longing to get out of there before something else inedible arrived.

The bill was fifty American dollars. Knowing you're being cheated does not help when you have a language problem and you want to go to the bathroom.

More doughnuts for sale on the street. Rows of stalls with oil sizzling in woks and balls of white dough waiting to be sizzled. Hot dogs on another stall encased in what looked like doughnut mixture. These were observed at speed as I was not going to risk being offered any of them and I was on my way to look for a taxi.

"Have a good time?" asked my beloved as I wrapped my ginger jar and swaddled it inside a drawer full of sweaters. "Why don't you leave that on display? Its very nice."

"It was very expensive and I don't want to risk breaking it."

"How much?"

"Ten dollars. Ten dollars plus fifty for lunch and twenty each way for the taxi, so as far as I'm concerned it's a hundred dollar ginger jar."

As we left Inchon it was bright and sunny and sailing back down the river I had no desire to go ashore again. Too much like hard work. Sitting up on the bridge wing with a glass of cold wine in my hand, I felt I had become a real sailor, happier on the ship than ashore. That was then.

Within an hour of this summery scene, we entered into a band of heavy sleet, snow and icy rain, which lashed across the ship reducing visibility to a few yards.

There was yet another typhoon forming on the weatherfax report, still out in the Pacific but heading west at about the same speed as our ship. Permission to increase speed was requested by telex, as it obviously consumes more fuel and costs money. To be preferred to being in a typhoon however, even by the company.

We tore along in a race for a couple of days then Irma flicked her tail and headed north-east, away from us and away from the Philippines just as a military coup began.

The radio officer picked up Morse code messages, passing along the political news to the anxious crew.

Out on deck that night, the isolated beauty of being out on the dark sea under a perfect crescent moon, gave a deceptive feeling of serenity. Not so very far away, guns were being fired in the streets of Manila. How the crew must wish they were home with their families.

Back in the South China Sea and again on the way to Singapore, we pitch and roll every day. We are riding high in the water, as although we have ballast, seawater taken to balance the ship, we are empty of cargo and toss around like an empty tin can.

I woke up every hour and got up every morning with backache. Looking out on the terrible waves ten and fifteen metres high, I wondered if anything else was at sea, I hadn't seen another ship for days. You would think that, then suddenly just in a wink of an eye, you would see a tiny fishing vessel, battling along in the trough of huge waves, miles from shore.

I still was not seasick, could not believe my luck, but what was not so good, when eating three meals a day with little exercise. Everyone knows about friends returning from sea cruises with moon faces and wide hips, and that's after three weeks. What I would be like after four months I could not bear to think. And what about exercise you might say. Well just try to exercise in a Force six or seven, let alone a Force nine. Just staggering up the stairs to the bridge or down to the mess room, clinging onto the stair rail, you risked a twisted ankle.

Anyway, that was my excuse. I could have eaten like a bird and gone into hibernation or something but I was told having a full stomach staved off seasickness. Even on Allonzo's cooking I managed to eat everything.

The Chief Engineer appeared in the middle of this weather carrying ear protection and boots for me to wear. "You want to see engine room," he said, more a statement than a question. He had remembered our earlier conversation and his promise.

When the door was opened the noise and blast of hot air took my breath away, as did the open iron steps that lead down into the chasm below. He was attentive and strict. "Not for you put foot there, walk this, like this. No touch that. Mind thing on floor."

There was an office and control room in the middle of this din of thundering pistons and hissing valves, a few decibels quieter, not much. He yelled at me what each one was for and I nodded like an animated grinning puppet, not understanding a thing but not wishing to offend.

"Marvellous!" I screamed over the racket. "Fantastic!"

Out from the control room, the tour had only just begun. We passed endless pieces of machinery, each one was explained to me in loving detail. The ship was still bouncing about and there was nothing to grip onto that wasn't hot or covered in grease. In the bowels at the back, men were actually working, cleaning odd-looking pieces of machinery.

"These are the oilers," he explained at full volume. Then the piece de resistance, the propeller shaft. Really scary. A spinning shining huge tube of steel, gleaming with oil, thundering along for yards and yards, leading out to the final thing, the propeller. All of this vast hall of what-have-you was really only geared for this final thing, to drive the propeller through those huge waves that I knew were all around us.

As I staggered out into the comparative peace of the ship's corridor and removed my ear protection I only had one heart felt thing to say. "How can you work down there?"

"I used to it. I like to know everything working properly. Now you see who really running the ship," he added proudly. This I would not repeat to Tomas.

Tomas had been looking for me. "We are passing Anambas Island" he said as I joined him on the bridge. "This is where that Chief Engineer went overboard. I thought you had gone to join him."

I explained that I had been having a tour of the engine room. "And believe me, if I ever had to spend my days down there, I would be jumping overboard before too long."

After the visit to the engine room, there was a change in the Chief Engineer's attitude to me. It wasn't a huge change, but friendlier. We even shared the odd joke. Before we arrived once more in Singapore, he started to talk to me about his family.

Now I had entered his world and was genuinely admiring of anyone who could work there, a barrier had been broken. Sadly this was a bit late, as he was going on leave when we reached port and we were to have a new Chief Engineer.

However, there we were, the only people in the mess room after lunch, and he produced a bottle of wine and poured us both a glass.

The story was one that became familiar over the future times I spent at sea. First the children mentioned with pride, and dog-eared photographs produced from a wallet. The children's interests and achievements spoken about at length. During the conversation it became clear that they were estranged from their wives, probably divorced, and the snatches of time they spent with their children when they were one family, had become even less. A sad, sad story.

There was little comfort I could give, except by listening. Sometimes I would try to explain how it was for the waiting wife back home, but this was generally brushed aside with "I sent money home, she wanted for nothing." Wanted for nothing. I thought about all the times their children may have been ill or exceptionally difficult, the times she had been worried or lonely, the times she would have been racked by jealousy when the ship was delayed in port. There would be a strong desire to end that anguish and find comfort in someone new, someone who was there all the time. It wasn't the people. It was the job and the long separations.

From the seaman's point of view, his life was also lonely, if he had the occasional fling in a port it meant nothing to him and was quickly forgotten. Most of the time away he was working and out on the sea but the perception of his life from ashore was different. Men envied him and women were suspicious.

Before he left we shook hands at the door to the engine room. "Maybe we will be on the same ship again one day," he said, and I hoped so too. I would even miss his continuous moaning, which had now taken on a new poignancy after hearing his story.

CHAPTER 7

SINGAPORE   TAIWAN   HONG KONG

The new Chief Engineer came on board the moment we docked in Singapore. He was from Manchester, rather fat, and his gloomy disposition was not a good sign.

"He has his wife with him" Tomas told me. "Go and say hello to her." I went along to the cabin. The door was half-open and a pretty woman was hanging up clothes. I guessed her age to be around thirty.

"My name is Anna," she said, extending a small hand with perfectly polished fingernails. She was slim and very elegant, her tiny feet trotting about the cabin on delicate strappy high-heeled shoes. She made me feel like an elephant and I was suddenly conscious that my grooming had gone down hill somewhat since I had been on board.

"Have you been on this ship before?" I asked her

"Not this. But other ship" she said, hanging up something whispy in the closet and tossing a teeny bikini into a drawer. She was certainly going to turn a few heads.

"I come because we go to Hong Kong," she said. "I like very much to go shopping."

It was the first I had heard about our next port.

"Never been to Hong Kong," I said.

She looked me up and down, in my giant sweater and corduroy trousers.

"You will like I think. They have many pretty things to buy."

All three sizes too small was what I was thinking but I smiled and we agreed to see each other later. I guessed her to be French by her accent; she was actually from Mauritius.

I could not imagine her somehow with Wayne, the new Chief Engineer. He must squash her flat, I was thinking, rather indelicately.

"We're going to visit another ship," Tomas announced after lunch.

The ship was moored alongside. It was managed by the same

company. On board I noticed it was a bit shabbier than ours. We found the English captain in his sitting room, a tall man with a diffident, weary air, about forty five years old. Across from him a young Thai woman was seated, savagely filing her nails. They had obviously been in the middle of an argument and our arrival had cut it short.

"Coffee?" the captain asked, getting it himself. The Thai woman filed harder and then spoke angrily, directing her words at us.

"He no want to take me with him!" she said as if she and I were old friends.

"Don't involve other people Sal," said the captain, as he passed our cups to us.

"I understand you're looking for a cook," said Tomas ignoring the outburst.

Ah, now I knew why we were there! I had heard Tomas tell Mario that the company were refusing to replace Allonzo and allow him to become the assistant cook once again. They felt he had managed well so far.

The captain sat down looking tired. "I'm sailing in a couple of hours. They haven't had time to get one and my next port is Lagos."

"I don't envy you," said Tomas sympathetically. Lagos was notorious for corruption and I had recently read of a ship being boarded and robbed while at anchor there.

"I'm going to be in West Africa for the next three years," said the captain.

"Good Lord," Tomas replied. I was starting to feel sorry for Allonzo.

"Yes. The old WAWA. I find myself saying that too often. I've been there many times so nothing will surprise me."

"What's W, A, W, A?" I asked

"West Africa Wins Again," said the captain, "It's not an easy place and I don't want to make it more complicated than I have to."

"You just don't want ME to go," said Sal vehemently.

"About the cook," Tomas broke in loudly. "I have to be here for three days, so I can get a replacement. We can call the company and arrange for the transfer." Poor Allonzo.

"Is he a good cook?" the other captain asked. This was it.

"He's OK," said Tomas without batting an eye.

"There is no way I can expect the crew to put up with poor cooking for another voyage," said Tomas as we went back to the ship to break the news to Allonzo. "In any case, they will find out from another ship as they don't seem to want to listen to me." He had apparently told the company that the cooking was poor, but the fact was, the cost per head for food had remained the same during Allonzo's tour of duty, and this was their main concern. It had stayed the same because Tomas had ordered the stores and dealt with the accounts for him.

When we returned with the news the unexpected happened. Allonzo was sorry to leave a crew he had got to know over the last few months, but was quite interested to go to West Africa as he hadn't been there before, he said. What was unexpected was the arrival of one of the fitters, in tears. He was a rather ugly man with a huge stomach and pock marked skin.

"If he go, I go too," he announced, weeping copiously to Tomas' embarrassment.

"Now we are getting complicated," said Tomas raging about the office.

The fitter was sitting outside in the passageway, refusing to leave.

I wanted to say, "Well he's obviously in love with Allonzo," but knew it would add fuel to the fire.

"Then I go ashore," said the fitter through his tears. It was heartbreaking to hear him.

It was better I left. This really was 'ship's business'. I poured a cup of tea and gave it to the fitter as I passed by, and went down to the kitchens to make myself a sandwich.

One of the Able Seamen who was often the helmsman on the bridge, was talking to Tony. "We talk about Christmas Ma'am," he said politely.

"Will it be in Hong Kong do you think?" I said, as I fixed my sandwich.

They both laughed. "No. Usually it is at sea. Nobody want to work in the ports and they are closed for part of Christmas. Company won't pay for us just to be in port."

"Well what do you do? Do you have a party?"

"We have some nice things to eat you know," said the Able Seaman, whose name was Ricky. I thought about Allonzo trying to cope with Christmas cooking.

"We are going to have a new cook," I said, but they knew already of course and just laughed.

"This is why we speak about Christmas," they said.

"Hmm. The Festival of the Nine Emperor Gods. I am glad I missed that." Ricky and I were sitting in a shopping mall ashore in Singapore having a coffee break and resting our feet. I was looking at tourist guides I had picked up. "Slashing themselves with blades while priests write charms with their blood?" I read aloud.

"And how about this one in January? 'Thaipusam. Gaily decorated kavadis are fastened to devotees' bodies by hooks, skewers and spears, blades pierced through tongues...' Ugh, I can't read anymore. I thought festivals were supposed to be fun."

"They are for religion," said Ricky, dipping into his ice cream, "For keeping faith."

"Like Christmas, of course." Ricky wore a large crucifix, as did many of the Philippinos.

I had come ashore to buy a few goodies, hoping to make Christmas more fun for the crew. I had organised a collection on board. Now the money would be spent for everyone to get a present. The presents would not be the same in value, but that was the idea, to make it more of a gamble. They would have a number on them and there would be a Lucky Dip.

Tomas wanted someone to help me with suggestions of what the crew would like and to help carry the shopping back on board.

After my recent conversation with Ricky, he seemed to be a good choice, someone who would get into the spirit of the thing.

Ricky however, was startled by my humour. I wanted the cheaper gifts to at least raise a smile, but he completely disapproved of my choice of brightly coloured Australian surfer shorts and plastic wind up toys. I decided not to be too influenced by him and bought them anyway. He did approve of the more expensive electronic games. There had to be a jackpot present and this was decided to be a remote controlled toy truck with giant wheels and the full works. This went over the budget but this would be Tomas' and my contribution. The truck was greatly admired by Ricky. He talked of nothing else as we made our way back.

"Someone certainly lucky to have that present" he kept saying. "I would certainly like that for my son" I was a bit weary. Buying twenty-six presents, all for men, was not easy.

I realised that none of them were going to be a surprise as Ricky would tell everyone what we had bought, but it wouldn't matter, even increase the speculation when the time came. "You never know, you may be lucky," I told him.

"I probably get underpants," he said gloomily and I understood that he had mistaken what the surfing shorts were for.

Our voyage north again was on a different route, passing Southern Vietnam. We slid by in eerie moonlight, rustling through the calm water. The shore was some hundred miles away but there was a strong smell of a pig farm on the breeze.

Tomas and I were leaning on the ship's rail, looking out into the night. The air was hot and humid and we had gone out on deck to feel cooler, without much success.

I had an unnecessary feeling of insecurity, thinking of yet another war. There were probably boat people out there in the dark and the predatory pirates ready to pounce on them, the newspapers were full of terrible stories. If they made it through to their intended promised land they would be cursed and unwanted.

Next day was going to be Christmas Eve. What a contrast our ship of plenty was to the fate of boat people, with our stores full of good food and the brightly wrapped presents waiting by the Christmas tree in the officers' mess.

It inevitably was a 'Karaoke Christmas' as this was the crew's favourite way to have fun.

Everyone had a 'turn' before taking a number for the lucky dip of presents, which made for many performances of loud warbling over the super sonic microphone. A lot of the singing was good but some was painfully bad. Then they started up the small percussion band, but it was fun to be with people who knew how to enjoy themselves.

The new cook, a serious man who was known to some of the crew, had surpassed expectations. There was a roast pig complete with apple in mouth, a fabulous turkey, and diplomatically, he had rustled up an English Christmas pudding.

The crew had transformed both crew and officer's mess with an ingenious use of coloured toilet paper in addition to last years decorations, and made a kind of a bower for Tomas and me to sit in, which was not terribly popular with El Capitain. They had made a drawing of the ship with hearts and flowers above it in pink paint and our names Tomas and Jill painted over the top in gold. It must have taken ages to do.

I gave Tomas a look as if to say, "It is Christmas," and we sat on our 'thrones'.

All the doors were open to the deck and the tropical breeze played with the streamers. At one point the Christmas tree fell with a crash and many hands rushed to put it up again and secure it with nautical skill and several ropes.

Ernesto won the truck and nearly cried during his thank you and Happy Christmas speech.

The Philippinos 'big heart', as Tomas always called it, was surely on display for the two days we celebrated together. They must have been thinking of their families and missing them, but they put all the gusto and spirit they could into helping each other have a good time.

Even the fitter, who had decided to remain on board after all, got up and sang a carol in a surprisingly sweet voice. 'Silent night, Holy night' he sang out into the warm night air.

I had given all the crew a padded Chinese Army Hat, as the last time we had been in the cold in Korea, I had noticed that few had hats and the hoods on their jackets were not warm enough.

The padded hats had earflaps and they all put them on, tied the flaps under their chins, sat me down in the middle and a photograph was taken, while perspiration streamed down their faces.

When Tomas and I left, some were still dancing around in the hats in spite of my protest that they were meant for the cold weather. They were keen to enjoy everything, and I think they were also teasing me, just a little.

Rolando had won the surfer shorts and was wearing them over his trousers and boogying away to Percy Sledge singing WHEN A MAN LOVES A WOMAN at full volume as we passed the officer's mess. He had just come off duty, so his Christmas was just beginning.

He had a drumstick in one hand and a beer in the other.

Tomas was on his way up to the bridge to relieve Mario. "You off to bed now?" he asked as we came to our door.

"I don't think so," I said, trying to be noble. "I'll come up with you." It was going to be four hours before Tomas would be able to go to bed. It seemed mean to leave him on his own, it was Christmas after all, I was thinking, but after ten minutes of sitting in one of the swinging high chairs my chin dropped onto my chest and I was sound asleep.

Anna, the Chief Engineer's wife, had not appeared throughout Christmas as she had the flu.

On this voyage, we were to stop in Taiwan, in the port of Kaohsiung, a city of some fifty-nine square miles and second largest city after Taipei. We would see none of it however, as to begin with it was shrouded in thick fog, and we were not at the dock but anchored at the port entrance to receive two new anchor chains.

The procedure, which was obvious to those on board, but a mystery to me, had started several weeks ago in the dry dock where we had renewed the 'tenth shackle' on both starboard and port anchor chains. A ship that size would have anchor chains of ten shackles, the tenth is attached to the ship inside the chain locker. We would now be renewing the other nine that are attached to the anchor, taking the anchors off one at a time, and replacing the anchors once the new chain was in place. The anchors would lay alongside in the barge, while work was in progress, but we would only do one at a time, or we would start to drift away!

139

A shackle is a length that when let down in the water, measures fifteen fathoms, or twenty-seven and a half metres. When we have been anchoring before, I have heard Tomas ask the Boson over the radio "How many shackles in the water" as the crew on the forecastle worked the gypsy wheel and peered over the side of the ship at the anchors progress into the water.

We sat in the fog while giant ships loomed up at us and disappeared, going to and from the port. A day or two went by. It was just as boring and unnerving as sitting in a car at the side of a foggy motorway, and although under the radar control of the Kaohsiung Port Control, there were small fishing craft without radar that could run into us. An unfortunate sailor was dispatched therefore to ring the anchor bell continuously up on the forecastle, to act as a warning. I strolled up the deck to see where the bell was hanging and almost laughed at Ricky's miserable face as he hung onto the bell rope, his hair plastered to his head and his trousers clinging to his legs.

The actual fog signal, the mournful sound of the horn, is used only when a motor vessel is underway. These we could hear out in the sea.

It was now New Year's Eve, and although as of 1912, Taiwan along with China had adopted the Gregorian Calendar, the month long celebrations of the Chinese Lunar New Year seemed to be the real occasion. So that day, and possibly the next, were to be working days when the chains would be delivered and attached. The fog was lifting at last. Any idea of New Year's Eve party on board was out of the question, as all needed to be fully alert for the procedure and if all went well we could be underway early on New Year's Day.

First, port side anchor was detached and winched onto the heavy barge alongside, and the new chain, weighing many tons, was fixed on. We hung on, anchored on the starboard side. I was still unsure I understood how the whole thing was going to work, everything was so horribly heavy. I was out on deck to watch. The sun was starting to shine through. I could see the city shoreline, heavily industrial, with steel works and smokestack factories. There was very little 'formosa' in this part of the island.

As the fog cleared, and I was marvelling at the size of one of our anchors lying in the barge, I saw that everyone had stopped their close attention to what they were doing and gazing up at our ship, but above my head to the radar deck above the bridge.

I squinted upwards, expecting to see that one of the radio masts had broken or similar eye arresting disaster but it was Anna, in her teeny bikini. She was leaning on the railing in a pool of soft sunlight, surrounded by the last wisps of fog, like Venus emerging from a heavenly cloud.

She looked down at the craning necks with no expression of recognition, and when everyone had registered how exquisite she looked from the front, turned and lent her back against the rail, so we could all appreciate her bottom.

There was a loud exclamation from the barge as one of the workers crushed his hand under the anchor chain links, and the first of the 'Anna' disasters began. This one caused a delay of three hours as the injured man was a key worker who now had to be carried away and replaced.

No reaction to this from Anna, who then strolled off to lie down on her lilo in the centre of the radar deck to sunbathe.

At that time, I didn't think a lot about it, but it wasn't long before the 'Anna Effect' was apparent. She was such an eye catching beauty, that she really needed to be encased in a nun's shroud if she was going to be on a ship of twenty six hungry men, and if she was going to be a tease, there would be trouble.

She appeared at lunch in her bikini with an almost transparent sarong loosely wrapped around her slender waist and Rolando burnt his thumb in the soup.

Tomas growled his disapproval. It wasn't as if he was unappreciative of her womanly charms, it was simply that you cannot present a gourmet dish to starving men and not expect them to think of ways of cutting each other's throats in the hope that they may be the one to get it all to themselves.

Her husband Wayne, the new Chief Engineer, came to join her at the table. He beamed around at everyone, obviously proud and enjoying the attention. He was thinking of course how envious everyone must be of him with such a lovely wife.

"You'll have to tell her to dress herself when she comes to the mess," said Tomas crossly to me as he went back to work.

"Me? I can't say anything. She would just think I was being bitchy or jealous or something."

My protest went into empty air. I was certainly not going to say a thing to her. This, I decided, was 'ship's business'.

At dinner, it was the sweater with the plunging neckline and mini skirt that made everyone bump into each other. The crew were all grinning like fools and Tomas was in a bad mood as he had had a long day and I was refusing to co-operate.

"As a woman you can tell her," he insisted.

"As a woman I certainly cannot tell her," I replied firmly. "Maybe if I was her sister or something. But I've never met her before."

The Chief Engineer's cabin and office was on the next deck down to ours, close to the ship's office and therefore the electrician, Gorgeous Renalto's cabin.

I went down to the office to pick up a video for the evening. Anna was there, looking along the video shelves. "I have seen all these I think," she said. She bent over to inspect the lower shelf, displaying the edge of her panty lace

Ernesto was looking for something in the ship's files. He pulled the drawer out too far and the contents crashed to the floor. This was turning into a French farce.

Renalto was passing to his cabin and I noticed that he at least was not going to electrocute himself at the vision of Anna's apple bottom, as he looked in briefly, then went to his cabin without so much as a backward glance.

"I think I go to crew mess to look what they have there" said Anna, which seemed a bad idea, but who was I to tell her.

As I was leaving with my film, Wayne came by and asked me if I had seen her.

"I think she went to the crew mess to look for a video," I said. He looked at the four shelves of three hundred titles behind me. "Said she had seen most of these." I continued feebly.

He frowned, but instead of stomping off to the crew mess, he simply went into their cabin and shut the door. Oh well, I thought.

While we were watching the video, we heard a commotion down on deck. As we were still at anchor, we could hear it above the soundtrack. Disco music and a lot of shouting and singing. Coming from main deck.

"Someone's having a New Year's Eve Party," I said. I looked down, out of our bathroom porthole. About ten of the crew were dancing about outside the open door to their mess room. Anna was rocking and rolling in the middle of them all. Wayne was not in sight.

I went back to the film, saying nothing. Tomas picked up the house phone.

"Second! Whatever is going on down in the mess room has to finish shortly after midnight. We have an early start tomorrow. See to it."

When the film finished, the sound from the party came roaring up from below. "We can go and wish the crew a Happy New Year," Tomas suggested.

We reached the crew mess just as the fight had started.

The new Boson of arm wrestling fame had taken the CO2 cylinder from the kitchen and sprayed one of the able seamen in the crotch as a 'joke'. Later we heard it was because he had been dancing too close to Anna and the erection in his trousers had become obvious to everyone. Boson had had one or two beers and went for the CO2.

What we saw was the able seaman, with a huge white patch on the front of his trousers, swinging away at the Boson, who was jumping around, still holding the cylinder.

Five other crew were trying to intervene between them, and a few pushes and punches were starting to be exchanged among the helpers.

Anna was sitting on a high stool, swinging her legs and laughing.

One roar from Tomas and they calmed down. They were read the riot act and the able seaman and Boson were to see Tomas in the morning in the office.

"I suggest you go to your cabin," Tomas said rather abruptly to

Anna, who raised her eyebrows but slid off the stool and departed.

Not the best New Year's Eve I had experienced. Tomas and I went to bed in silence.

The next few sailing days, on our way to Hong Kong, the sexual tension increased. A sunbathing Anna in her string bikini could be seen at various places around the ship depending on the direction of the sun, and at other times she would jog around main deck in short shorts and sun top. There was evidence of stubbed toes and bruised thumbs as concentration evaporated.

The whole ship was in love with Anna. I was starting to feel like a Mrs Grundy, worrying that I would round a corner one day and find her in *flagrante delicto*. To be honest, I told myself, if you had a lovely body like Anna wouldn't you want to show it off to so many admirers? What puzzled and concerned me was her husband. Would Wayne emerge like a steaming frenzied monster from the engine room one day and take his revenge on them all?

I glanced at his podgy pink face as he chomped his way through a steak at lunchtime. Perhaps he was simply content that he was the one she climbed into bed with every night.

Two black and yellow butterflies escorted us past the beaches at Stanley on the southern tip of Hong Kong Island. They flew in the slipstream of air flowing over the bridge windows and then around the radar mast and back again. Appropriate escorts to 'Fragrant Harbour'. In 1990 it was still in the hands of the British, but before long, it would once again belong to mainland China.

As we picked up the Pilot at Green Island, I was excited by the variety of ships and boats all around. Fishing boats like small galleons. Ferries and cruisers covered in red and gold dragons with pagoda roofs. Pretty yellow canopies with golden silky fringes atop decorated barges. All these, competing with fishing boats trawling nets, and the last, only metres away from ships like ours and the super speedy hydrofoil on its way to Macau.

The harbour was so full of life, I ran from one side of the bridge to the other.

Eight small sailing boats, little more than skips, were being towed by a single tugboat, two by two, off to find calmer waters to sail. Each sailing boat with a skipper and streaming pennants. Toys against a super tanker passing on our starboard side.

Many floating cranes chugging along on huge rafts, rowing boats and windsurfers darting in and out along the shore.

A Jumbo Jet roared over the harbour, the boats and the skyscrapers, coming into land, a stock shot I had seen many times on film.

Honeycombs of buildings in Kowloon with flags of washing from every window, the display of many windows adding credence to the statistic of many thousands of inhabitants per square kilometre, less than nine square feet of space per person.

We took the Star Ferry as we were far away from the main city and docked at a refinery on the island of Tsing Yi.

The first thing that struck me about the centre was the noise. People shout and traffic thunders. Trams rattle and clatter and everything roars around the waterfront. You cross on concrete bridges and hurry to the side streets that are jam packed with chattering people.

Tomas and I went to a restaurant in Jardine Street and sat upstairs on the mezzanine looking down at rows of plucked ducks and chickens that hung from every beam on the ground floor below us. The smell of the raw poultry had a bad effect on our appetite and we left after eating only a salad.

We had been told that if you go to the Excelsior Hotel at sunset you would find sampans and you could take a mini dinner cruise.

When we found the hotel it was across the road, six lanes of whizzing roaring rush hour traffic, separated by yet another concrete flyway. In the litter filled harbour, a hard faced Chinese woman with a shrill voice offered us dinner aboard her sampan. We looked to where she pointed and saw white plastic chairs and tables fixed to the deck facing a television screen. The price for this so-called treat was high, and not the romantic experience we had expected. Tomas marched off angrily. I followed along the noisy road passing the famous Royal Hong Kong Yacht Club. Looking through the iron gates, I saw a covered cannon and thought of 'In Hong Kong they strike the gong and fire a noonday gun'. In this traffic, no one would hear it.

Now we needed to rest our feet. The miles of cameras, binoculars and goods on sale were having an effect on me. I only wanted to go back to the ship. Urgh, get away, stop trying to sell me something, I wanted to shout at the smiling beckoning shopkeepers.

We went to the swanky bar at the Mandarin Hotel and before we could order two large gins and tonic, found ourselves almost sitting next to Renalto. He was alone, but not for long, as a lovely Chinese girl in a red satin dress slid into the seat alongside us and Renalto introduced her to us.

"This May Ling my old friend," he explained and ordered her a drink without having to ask her what she wanted.

May Ling was in banking and was smart and funny.

We had a good time with them, and several drinks later tottered off to a taxi, leaving them still at the bar.

Back on board all was well and for once we were able to enjoy our evening and slip romantically into bed without interruption.

Very early in the morning however, we were woken by loud knocking on our door. Tomas wrenched the door open and confronted another figure in a dressing gown.

It was the Chief Engineer, very distraught.

"What is it?" barked Tomas. "Why don't you use the house phone?"

Wayne stumbled into the sitting room, so Tomas closed the door. It was about five in the morning and unloading had not yet begun out on deck.

"It's Anna," said Wayne, staring at Tomas with a red face. "I can't find her."

"What do you mean? Did she go ashore?" said Tomas, as I reached for my dressing gown in the bedroom.

"We had a row. I said a lot of things..."

"Sit down, sit down," said Tomas and I put the kettle on.

"She has probably gone ashore to a hotel. She will be back in a few

146

hours," Tomas suggested.

Wayne shook his head. He looked close to tears.

"No. The watchman told me no one went ashore after ten last night, and he would have noticed Anna. He saw her come back with her shopping in the afternoon and helped her carry things from the taxi. He knew who I meant."

"Have you looked around the ship?" I asked him. He looked up at me as if he hated all women. "Maybe she's watching a movie in the mess room." I added, passing coffee around.

"I looked. But I think I know..." he broke off, shaking his head.

We waited, both of us suspicious of what may come next. A minute passed.

"I heard her voice. I heard her talking," Wayne blurted out.

"Where? What are you saying?!" Tomas said severely, not really wanting to know.

"Across the..." Wayne's eyes filled with tears.

"Come on! Pull yourself together!" Tomas barked.

I retreated to the bedroom, but of course, was listening.

Now Wayne sounded angry. "That fucking electrician. That Brazilian git. After she slammed out of the cabin, I waited a minute or two to see if she would come back. Then I went to look for her. I passed his door when I came back and I heard her voice. In there!"

"Then why didn't you knock?" Tomas was asking.

"Why should I? If she wants to be with him then let her. Fucking Brazilian."

I couldn't understand this for obvious reasons. I went back into the sitting room.

"Wayne, Renalto was with us ashore last night. What is more, he was in the company of a very lovely lady and when we left them I was under the impression, well, they were together."

"That's right," said Tomas. "I think you should just calm down and go back to bed. There is little point in disturbing other people. It may not have been your wife in there you see. Have you thought of that?"

"What if something has happened to her?" said Wayne, looking a little brighter and taking another tack, but Tomas was already

147

opening the door to let him out.

"We can talk about that in an hour or two. If she is not ashore, she is probably alright" he continued, showing him out.

"What a mess!" Tomas raged, as we got back into bed. "I knew that woman would be a problem. Well I'm not chasing around looking for her in the middle of the night."

"He's been with the company some time hasn't he." I said. "I'm surprised she doesn't, well, has she been on board before?"

"You think I would have let her on board if I had known she was going to stir up things like this? I told you to have a word with her. Now look what's going on!"

"Don't start to blame me! I'm not responsible for her. You seemed rather keen for me to meet her when she first arrived remember."

I thought it was MARGARET. The one I KNEW. I had no idea he had divorced and married this one. He needs his head examined.

"His head had nothing to do with it," I said and I felt Tomas chuckle in the dark.

"I'm going to stop this before it gets any worse," he muttered.

Tomas was pressing buttons on the house phone. He was showered and dressed and I watched him sleepily from the bed. "Who are you calling?

"Renalto? This is Captain. I'm coming over right now. OK?"

Tomas put the phone down and marched out. I was all agog.

I was coming up the stairs from lunch when several crew started down, carrying boxes and suitcases.

"Where are you going with that?" I asked but they ignored the question.

Then I saw Anna follow. I almost said something like Wayne was looking for you or where have you been?

"I bought so many things I don't know how I am to get on the plane" she giggled.

"Are you leaving?" I asked, surprised.

"Of course!" she gushed "I only come to shop."

She leaned towards me, confidentially "I cannot say I like so much to be on the boat"

"You live in Singapore?"

"Yes, we just move there. You know England? My God it is raining, raining."

Wayne appeared with the last of Anna's bags. He gave her a look.

"You better get a move on if you want to catch that plane" He hurried by.

I said goodbye to her and she went out into the blazing sunshine and down the steps.

The crew took her baggage to the taxi but they neither lingered about nor waved.

The mood and the message had gone around the ship.

Wayne briefly raised a hand from the top of the steps, then went into the engine room door.

I felt depressed. Perhaps because we were leaving ourselves the next morning. It was the end of my voyage as well.

The relief captain arrived at lunchtime and Tomas was so busy passing the ship's details over to him that I didn't get a chance to ask what had happened about Anna that morning.

In the evening we had dinner with the captain and Tomas and he told each other stories about ships and companies they had known and the shortcomings of all of them.

I went up to finish the packing and was asleep by the time Tomas came to bed.

In the morning I tried to see everyone on board to say goodbye, they felt like old friends now, family even. I may see some of them again or not I was thinking as we went down the accommodation ladder to the waiting taxi.

"Now you have to tell me what went on yesterday," I said to Tomas as we swept away along the dock. I looked back at the ship. No longer our ship, someone else was in charge now. I could see one or two familiar figures moving about the deck and Rolando waving at the top of the steps.

"So what happened?"

"When I went to Renalto's cabin, he opened the door. He was

dressed and he invited me in.

I asked him right out if he had had a visitor in the night, as 'someone had gone missing' and at first he lied, and said no. I expected to see his friend from the night before, and I asked if he minded if I just took a look for myself, you see. She was there of course, standing behind the shower curtain, looking as if she had dressed herself in a hurry, her hair sticking up and standing in her stocking feet."

"Who? Who was there?"

"Anna."

"No! Poor Wayne. What will happen now?"

"Nothing. I got her out of there very quickly. I told her she was going to be able to save her face because she was to lie to her husband and give some other excuse. That she was to leave on the first plane the agent could arrange and no more would be said. Renalto of course knows full well not to say anything. Otherwise it would have been impossible and I would have had to send him ashore as well."

"Where does Wayne think she was all night?"

"That she got shut into the laundry room. I locked her in myself. Told her to wait for a few minutes and then to start to bang on the door."

"You think her husband believed her?"

"He was given a story he would like to believe. He also had Tony apologising over and over again. Tony let her out and wondered if he had accidentally locked her in with his set of keys."

"We will never know if it works out alright."

"Oh yes we will. It's a small world in the shipping business. Everyone on board knows what really happened, and before we reach the airport, at least five other ships in this port will know the story as well. If Wayne and Renalto kill each other, we'll find out, don't worry."

CHAPTER 8

AT HOME IN THE GLEN   SCOTLAND

Each time we returned to Benbuie after months away, it was always a joy to come over the hill and see the familiar white shapes of the geese grazing on the big field in front of the house.

Most of the time I came back alone. Tomas, with a month or two to go before the end of his contract, would follow on later. That early spring, when we came home from Hong Kong after my first experience at sea, we were together.

The taxi stopped at the first gate and the mossy earthy smell of the glen brought back all the memories. We were home.

Home to work. As we strolled around the house and out to the pond it was clear that there was much to do. In the mild autumn and early winter of South West Scotland grass can continue to grow at a fiercesome pace. Fox gloves, red campions, ox eye daisies, tansy, hogweed, ragged robin, and the many varieties of wild flowers had bloomed, spread their seeds and now stood in vast brown clumps waiting to be cut. The soil around needed weeding to make way for the new seeding, in the herb garden up the steps, and especially in the half acre vegetable field.

Gus the cockerel came around the corner with several of his ladies. Gus was potent year round and was always hopping on and off an unsuspecting hen as she bent to examine a tasty insect in the grass. He was a good provider and would always look around for something for the object of his desire to eat immediately after the act. 'Sowing his seed and making sure it was nourished' was Tomas' description but until I lived so close to chickens I had no idea that they had personalities and could be very different to each other, especially cockerels.

If you brought food, Gus would wait until all the ladies had eaten before he had his share and would call to them in a soft burbling coo, raising and lowering his head to show them where to eat. When Tomas was digging, he would come running, calling to the hens.

From every corner they would come, rushing along as if it was opening day of the sale at their favourite department store. He would select fat worms right from under the thrusting prongs of the fork and Tomas' boots and drop them one by one to the hens without eating one himself. I would try to give him one, but no, he wouldn't take it until all the ladies were satisfied.

This may not be unusual, but I found out just how special Gus was when I allowed one of his sons to grow up. I thought it was the right thing, as one day, Gus would be too old and die and would need a son and heir. It was a mistake as Son of Gus was not a chip off the old block.

He serviced the ladies alright when he came of age but he was nothing like his dad in other ways. Son of Gus would rush ahead to take the food first and would peck his way through to take an especially juicy morsel before any of the hens got a chance.

When I cleaned the hen house Gus would always come to inspect what I was doing. He would jump up among the hen laying boxes and get into one himself. The first time he did it I thought it was because he was enjoying the fresh sweet smelling hay. Then he began the cooing noises that he made when he called the hens to eat. Several came rushing in of course and there was big Gus looking too large for the hen box, and a bit out of place. One of the hens would jump onto the top of the box and would then get in beside him. Then he would get out, having shown her, as if to say "See how clean it is? Now you can lay an egg."

He was so smart, never aggressive with us, but a brave warrior if he thought anything or anyone was going to attack the hens. In comparison, Son of Gus was a playboy.

Our two border terriers, Feisty and Fiona, gave him a wide berth. They had been trained from puppies not to chase sheep or anything with feathers, especially domestic poultry. They could be fierce at the fox, or at a passing dog who dared to cross the line, but teeny baby ducks, chicks and goslings could march passed their noses in perfect safety.

Jock appeared at the window within an hour of us getting home with some heavy wire, rope and a long pole. He had been checking on the pond while we were away as the outlet was constantly damming up with fallen leaves, twigs and weeds, preventing the flow and flooding the lower field. Although it wasn't the moment and we were both a bit jet lagged, we went with him to thread wire and rope through the feed pipe that led from the stream into the pond.

It was amazing to be plunged back immediately into the world up the glen, culture shock of the nicest kind, but Tomas was tired and stressed from his weeks on duty and overwhelmed at the work our overgrown seven acres was presenting.

Tomas would say that he didn't have a short fuse; he had no fuse.

We had finished the house the previous year and now the outside buildings and land needed the attention. The stable roof was leaking and things we were storing had to be draped in plastic sheeting. Wood for the fire, tools and hay for the hens got too damp to be used. The roof would have to be replaced when we could afford it. Tomas worked hard on everything at once, repairing, weeding and planting but he was not always in a good mood about it.

I didn't like to throw things away, especially wood, but Tomas had a Swedish concept of what should be kept or thrown away. Most of the gates on the property were pronounced to be 'rotten' or possibly 'rottening'. 'Rotten' meant they were wrenched from their toppling posts and thrown onto the waiting bonfire. 'Rottening' meant the same fate would be put off for a week or two. All those picturesque, sloping, moss covered gates that I loved? What did it matter if you had to give it a knee up or a kick to close it? We had eight gates on the property, closing off fields, or leading up to the forest or the glen road. Tomas was proud of Swedish seasoned wood and straight growing timber, strong iron gate hinges and hand made hooks and could not understand why I wanted to keep the old gates. My immediate argument was quite truthfully that we couldn't afford to replace them all at once, but the gates offended Tomas' eye.

I came from the house one day to see that Tomas was at the bottom of the pond field about to remove a gate that would actually allow cattle to come in that grazed there in the summer.

"You're not throwing that way!"

"What!?"

"That gate. The cattle will get in."

Tomas was ignoring me and still pushing the holding posts to and fro to pull them out.

He stopped for a moment to yell at me at the top of his voice.

"What is it you want!? You want to keep it!? It's ROTTEN! Look at it!" He grabbed at one of the bars on the gate and smashed it in two. Tomas could have done the same thing with a new gate and his action made me furious.

"Don't break it! You're making it worse!"

"Making it worse!? Are you totally crazy!?"

"I LIKE the old gates. I don't WANT to throw them away!" I screamed.

I marched back to the house.

Two minutes later the kitchen door crashed open and the old gate, half in pieces, was thrown in at the door, followed by the large branch of a tree complete with newly sprouting leaves.

I had never felt more angry in my life.

"BASTARD!" I screamed and struggling by the dirty wood I rushed out in pursuit. Tomas was stripping off his gloves and walking off down the driveway.

"YOU BASTARD!" I screamed following him.

Tomas was passing one of our industrial type wheelbarrows complete with shovel and spade. He picked up the lot, wheelbarrow and all, and threw it in my direction.

"BREAKING SOMETHING ELSE NOW!" I screamed, then took off myself in the other direction to sit by the stream on the other side of the house, muttering 'bastard' every few minutes. The dogs came and sat next to me wondering as they always did when we had a row, if they had been the cause of it all. We gave each other a cuddle. It would be a few hours before normal relations would be restored but love would win in the end.

We had rows about how to do many things, and the geese. The geese had come to live with us for two reasons. Tomas had wanted to "stop all the ridiculous grass cutting" and secondly, Jock told me that there were four geese living on a tennis court at a big house just outside the village. The owners wanted them to have a better life, more out in the countryside.

"There's an old one, his name is George," explained Jock, "They say he's about twenty two years old. Sometimes when they get out, you come across them walking down the middle of the main road into the village with him leading. Old George knows a thing or two. He says to the others, there's got to be a better life than this, and he takes off to look for it."

"Don't they have a pond?"

"That's the trouble. Can't breed without a pond. Geese are too heavy. Old George, he hasn't forgotten how, you can bet. I think the other three must be virgins."

I took off in our one and only car with four large cardboard boxes left over from the move.

Geese. What did I know? People were afraid of them. The Romans used them for guards. There they were, staring out from the wire mesh fence surrounding the tennis courts. I could see that they had a plastic dustbin full of water. One dipped his beak then lifted his head back up to observe me driving up to the house. They were huge. They let out loud cries at the car. I had never handled geese before, I was to learn, but at that time was relying on the previous owner who spent nearly an hour trying to get near them. A gardener came to help and between us we managed to place them into the boxes in the back of the car.

Half way up the glen road they got out of the boxes. First a neck appeared, then a wing, then with struggling and flapping they emerged. You haven't discovered country living until you have driven several miles up a narrow road with four geese trying to fly out of the car.

When I pulled up at the house, Tomas stared in at me in the chaos. Both myself, the windows and the interior of the car were covered in grassy poo droppings. The plan had been to keep them in the stable for awhile until they got used to their surroundings. Tomas had been preparing a space.

"We just let them out and see what they do," said Tomas

"I'll put the dogs inside," I said, whistling them into the kitchen.

155

When we opened the car door they were afraid. Old George peered out, extending his neck. He was immediately identifiable by his lop sided bottom and his beak which he held slightly open at all times as if he was wearing ill fitting false teeth. He saw the pond. GAGAGA! He cried, caution to the wind, and half flew, half jumped out of the car, followed by the rest.

They careened along at such speed I thought they would take off and fly away, but no. Into the deep pond they jumped, swooping down under the water. Then up on the surface with a joyous flapping of wings. The obvious happiness at their new home was infectious.

Tomas and I sat on the old seat by the pond, laughing, delighted.

Three of the geese were big white Embdens usually referred to commercially as 'table birds'.

One of these was George who had managed to escape the table for all those years. The other two were smaller. One had a long thin neck we called Cecil. His girlfriend was a round bottomed female. The fourth was believed to be a Greylag. She had beautiful dark grey markings, black tipped wings and a white front. We called her Griselda. Griselda proved to be our first Mother Goose and I had a guarded but special relationship with her.

Geese are only aggressive when they are in season and protecting their young. The ganders will rush at you with neck extended if you come to close. They can give you a bad bruise on your thigh if they get a hold and you can get to know what they consider to be 'too close'.

Tomas, and I noticed other males, found this a challenge. Tomas thought it was insufferable. A personal attack on him when he was giving them a good home and feeding them bag upon bag of expensive corn in the winter? "Don't go too near the nests," I would say. "I cannot go where I like in my own home?" would be Tomas' reply. You can actually see an attack off if they are just being provoking and not defending their territory. You simply extend your own arm and advance towards the gander as he is coming for you. They will generally back away but if not if you are near a nesting female. It was a privilege to get to know them. Geese are not 'stupid' just different. People would say 'he can't say boo to a goose' when I was a child, maybe they still say it, meaning someone who could not defend themselves. With Tomas this was certainly not the case. I was just concerned about who would win.

It was thrilling when they started to mate and produce eggs. Local people told me that geese could be difficult and temperamental mothers. They told me that others had not had success hatching eggs locally. Geese can sit and then decide to neglect the sitting half way through the time. The undeveloped gosling can die before it has a chance to hatch.

In spite of these gloomy stories I was excited when Griselda started to sit on her ten eggs and fed and nurtured her in a special hutch along the driveway that I could watch from the kitchen and bedroom window. When the sun was warm, she would want to come out for a swim and I had to trust her timing that she would know when she needed to get back to her eggs but I did not feel secure after all the stories. I was often on my hands and knees in my nightdress in the mud worrying about the fox sneaking up on the eggs while she was away from the nest for her daily bath. She would preen for a bit on the bank of the pond and then with a scream suddenly take off at some mysterious instinctive alarm in her head and go rushing back to the nest.

The day I woke up and saw a flash of bright yellow fluff, heard the distinctive call of the first gosling, was a memorable day. Griselda took the full day to hatch seven. They were cocky little things, putting up their heads to see the world, their beaks sticking out like long noses and making the running-up-the-scale sweet little call that sounds so much like a question. When they are alarmed the call turns into a penetrating peep peep peep.

After her efforts, Griselda now wanted her bath and banged ferociously at the wire netting to be let out. I was fearful what to do. Her anger could damage the new babies. I opened the hutch and she rushed out without a backward glance at her new brood. Inexperienced, I was hoping to keep them in the nursery until she returned but they all started the high pitched peep peep peep immediately. Like water they poured over the edge of the nest and rushed up the drive after her, holding out their teeny new wings to help propel them along.

I ran behind, fearful that one of the circling buzzards would drop down from the sky, that a weasel or rat would pop out of the dry stone walls or a fox from the hedge.

When Griselda reached the pond not one of the seven hesitated. To my fear, they all plunged in after her. The other geese in the pond were curious and not at all careful and rushed up to see these new specimens of themselves. They made waves and tossed the goslings about.

I knew from the books that they could easily die of hypothermia as they had no goose fat on their down at that time, not enough for the cold mountain water of the pond.

Griselda continued with her 'me first' ablutions as she always did, while the babies tried to get under her powerful flapping wings right there in the churning water.

Then she made a sound I hadn't heard before, a deep HONK HONK for them to follow her to the floating island in the middle of the pond. This was a tough place for the teeny goslings as although they were out of the water, the island was made of branches and old telephone poles and had huge gaps between the joins. This was fine for the large webbed feet of the big birds and the ducks but one false move for a small gosling and they would be trapped underneath.

What anxiety. It was now dusk and I knew the fox would be coming. I wanted Griselda to go back to her safe nest and take her babies with her. The midges were biting me to pieces and the sun was slipping behind the hills. I called and appealed to her for an hour. The goslings, wet and shivering, were at different stages of trying to climb to her where she was preening herself on the island. They needed to get under her wings. Perhaps if I pulled on the sea anchor I could float the island over to the bank and get her to get off and go home.

Suddenly there appeared a wild naked figure on the other side of the pond, shouting and waving a stick, half dressed in a gaping old raincoat and felt hat. It was Tomas.

"Never mind this! You have done enough now! Come in now! You will get bitten to death!"

We glared across at each other in the gathering dusk, simultaneously swatting at the millions of midges that surrounded us.

A ridiculous shouting match across the pound continued for some minutes, then Tomas, red in the face and fearful perhaps for his tender parts, stomped off back into the house. It was ridiculous I realised after he had gone. I would have to leave it to nature.

At dawn I rushed out to see and came across Griselda sitting on the bank. The way she adjusted her skirts I could tell something was still alive under her.

Later I saw her out in the field and counted the little bright yellow blobs that were already imitating her, nibbling on the tender parts of grass. "One, two three. Wait, four five , six. She lost one, no! Seven!" That would not be the last time I would do the counting game of baby geese, ducks and chicks each morning after nights of storms or hungry foxes on the prowl.

At one point we had thirty three geese at Benbuie. The fox would take his share, numbers would go up and down. There were good mothers and neglectful mothers. One day twenty five huge heavy goose eggs were stolen from a protected nest near to the pond. Not a broken shell, yolk trails or anything to see the route the thief had taken. The mother had been scared off the nest and she was back swimming around the pond. We found the empty shells far up in the forest on a walk with the dogs one day. The clever fox had carried them, one by one in her mouth. It was probably a vixen as she is the more resourceful. She has to be, to feed her babies as well as herself.

One of the lessons I learnt was to avoid the well meaning rescue of young goslings if they were rejected by their mother, as they often grew up weaker than the rest.

You could come across this half dead, wet creature lying in the mud, far away from the main group who were grazing some distance away. At that point too cold to walk it would have no energy to make a tiny sound. The first time I took one into the kitchen and placed it on a soft towel on the warm hob of the Aga was so exciting. I rubbed it and dried it and it lay there panting for awhile. Then a small sound came, a tiny peep. Within minutes the ragged little bundle turned

159

into a fluffy yellow ball and started to preen itself. I fed it soft chick crumbs soaked in warm water and poured a little warm water down its throat with a thin spoon.

"Look at this," I said to Tomas who was home at that time.

"What are you going to do with that?"

"Give it back to it's mother of course."

"Good luck," said Tomas, somewhat sarcastically. Tomas had been brought up on a farm and had a more practical approach to these things.

I went outside and all the geese looked up at me suspiciously as I seemed to be making a recognisable gosling sound. I carried him and put him down near by and watched from a distance. The group moved off and my orphan tried to follow. Two of the females turned around and actually bit him. He fell over with a squeak.

I ran to the rescue. As soon as I put my warm hands around him he made the 'I am happy now' little questioning noise up the scale. Doo doo doo??

Two or three more attempts, but he was wet again from the long grass. It was August and he was very late to be born. Usually goslings are born around April, May and June like the ducks.

This was why they were rejecting him. They knew he could not survive. The others born that year were already fat teenagers and would have more than enough fat on them when the winter came.

Now I had interfered I was responsible. I took him back inside.

"He's back I see," said Tomas.

"We can use the puppy cage from the stable and put it in the downstairs toilet," I suggested enthusiastically. Tomas slooped off to get it. He has a soft heart when it comes down to it.

We called him 'Augustus'. We packed his cage with fresh straw and a hot water bottle and set him inside. "Doo Doo Doo?" he said, seeming to enjoy his new home. Then we closed the door. PEEP PEEP PEEP PEEP PEEP PEEP! We opened the door again. "Doo Doo Doo?" he put his head to the side and looked at us with one blue eye.

I took my rubber boots off and stood them by the cage. It was fine for the duration of dinner and then he worked it out. PEEP PEEP PEEP PEEP PEEP

"For God's sake!" said Tomas. The sound penetrated the whole house.

Someone had given me a wonderful white toy goose some years before. You could move the head by a pole that came out of its lower chest. It had floppy orange legs and webbed feet.

I went to find it and placed it into the cage.

Augustus immediately started thumping on the toy with his tiny beak and head, to get the stuffed goose to lift it's wing. PEEP PEEP PEEP PEEP PEEP PEEP.

I made the pole opening larger and lifted Augustus a little way inside. "Doo Doo Doo?" Augustus said to the stuffed goose.

"He's happy now," I said as I climbed into bed. Tomas gave a grunt. About a couple of minutes later the sound started up from below. PEEP PEEP PEEP PEEP PEEP PEEP PEEP PEEP!!!!!

Tomas shot out of bed.

"What are you going to do? Don't throw him out! Tomas!?"

Tomas was already down the stairs. He was shouting as he crossed the room to the toilet.

"SHUT UP! SHUT UP!" He wrenched open the toilet door.

"Doo Doo Doo?" said Augustus, looking up at us sweetly. "Mum and Dad?" We had to laugh but it was a problem.

"The light," said Tomas, "You left the light on. Maybe that will do it." We switched off the light and went back to bed. Silence. Until the crack of dawn of course.

Our baby grew fast. I was determined he would be fat and fit enough to last the winter. The cage, straw and floor had to be cleaned every day but I could not think of having him in the house for ever.

Jock smiled wisely. "They say you give your enemy a pet lamb."

"A good source of irritation?"

"Aye. Its alright when they're small you ken, but not so easy when you are attached to a wild animal that wants to live with you and has certain unclean habits you might say."

I already had that problem. "What's that strange smell?" I expected people to say when they came for dinner. Our dining room was close to Augustus' nursery.

When Augustus was about six weeks old and we were

experiencing an Indian summer, I decided to try an experiment. I gathered up some slodgy goose droppings from the gang outside and smeared Augustus with it. He was very used to me of course and I could hold him without him protesting at all. He was just very vocal and terribly loud. I always thought it was because Tomas would shout out at him to shut up if he was calling. It didn't make any difference to Augustus but Tomas let off some steam. Augustus must have thought he was supposed to make just as much noise as 'Dad'.

I placed Augustus in his large cage out on the grass. The geese were quite far away. I could see them on the other side of the big field. I had tied the door of the cage so Augustus would not be harmed if they decided to attack him. They were a very bonded group by now. I wanted to see what they would do but I was ready for the rescue at any moment.

It was autumn again and Tomas had gone back to sea. My brother Peter was staying with me. We watched from the kitchen window. Augustus quickly found he was in a place he was not used to. I had fed him turfs of grass in the house as well as chick super food and gravel that they need to grind the food in their gizzard. He liked the grass around the cage and started to nibble on it through the bars but he was very worried, so being Augustus he started up the sound. PEEP PEEP PEEP PEEP PEEP PEEP!! It was louder than ever now he was grown. Most geese stop making that noise and graduate to conversational sounds and calls when they get older but he hadn't been with other geese to learn the language.

Out on the field old George as usual was the first to hear it and respond. He put his head on one side, "GA GAG GA?" he said to the others. Is that a large baby I hear?

Anyway, he was curious. Where was it coming from? He marched off purposefully down the field and of course everyone followed, swaying along in their 'we are off somewhere important' mode.

When they reached the cage Augustus was completely silent. Goodness knows what he was thinking in his little brain. The crowd gathered round.

It was all over in a minute. Geese are smart at opening things. They nibbled and tweaked and bit at the cage and the string until the door opened. I held my breath but it was a Hollywood ending. Augustus stepped out. The geese chattered and remarked to each other, then they strolled away to some juicy grass near by, Augustus followed and started to graze.

If my brother had not been a witness I doubt if people would have believed me. Because the other geese thought Augustus was 'trapped' or 'caught' in some way, it went against their concept of their life at Benbuie which was total freedom. None of the ducks, geese or chickens were 'pinioned' at Benbuie, the method of clipping one wing to prevent them from flying away. The ducks would fly around in circles, sometimes fly down the river half a mile or so, but they always came back after a few hours. The geese wandered everywhere, around the house and fields. We did lock them away from the vegetable garden but they never attempted to fly over the wall to eat Tomas' veggies which was just as well.

When I took corn out to the geese in winter and they were far away, they would all take off and fly towards me, landing in a semi circle around me with triumphant cackles. Visitors not used to such things and wanting to be there to feed the geese would be alarmed and sometimes ran backwards away from them. "They can fly!" they would say in surprise.

One summer Charles and Elna asked to have one or two geese at their smallholding. After a day or two, as Tomas and I were sitting at breakfast, we saw geese, flying about three hundred feet up in the air, circling around the property. We went outside and there was Charles puffing down the road after them.

Our group on the field started up a loud chorus of cries as they saw the three in the air, and who came into land with a great show. What a lot of GA GAG GA that set up, as they all discussed it, lowering their heads and greeting each other

"Sorry Charles," said Tomas. "They seem to want to be with the others."

Benbuie

Spring in the glen

The geese and 'Augustus'

Ashore

Augustus was the exception to future rescued goslings. He grew up straight and strong and until the fox got him three years later, lived happily with the group. When we leant on the kitchen gate that led to the big field where they grazed most of the time, Augustus would give us a puzzled look, turning his head this way and that. He would also be the loudest in the general cackle for the piece of bread you were holding and you could always hear him above the rest. "There's Augustus," we would say, even when we were indoors with the radio on. "Hear him?"

Approaching Mauritania   October 8th 1990

Dear Jilly,

How are you doing my love. We are now close to Nouadhibou, expect to be there about 0700 tomorrow morning. My birthday was okay until I got a telex from the company which destroyed the rest of the day. However your message gave me inspiration. Everything is fine onboard but of course I am very lonely. I do not mind that at all but sometimes you feel for 'discussing' something.

My radio with a brand new copper antenna, works well and I can listen to Britain, Sweden, but news I have enough of just now. Soon we expect to see grey ships moving around in the Gulf. Company has indicated next voyage will be Argentina to Iran.

Just now we are passing a Russian fishing ship. They swarm around here outside the coast which is very 'fish rich' according to the pilot. Have asked agent to find prices for fresh fish.

Iran will by all means try to stop any conflict in the Persian Gulf. Probably something will happen in Jordan or Israel and the USA will attack if there is an open conflict. Everything is very delicate now in the world.

I had hoped to do some fishing while at anchor here but I have been too busy with the telex. There is a lot of bullshit as usual. I will run this ship as I was trained once. Safety first and all safety equipment will be maintained as first priority. In order to justify his existence, a supervisor had to report to the company, something which of course already was known! Now they pretend to be concerned about safety etc which is a joke when you consider how they expected me to take this to sea in the first place. Superintendents usually avoid to get too close to safety equipment as they know it costs money and time to keep it 'tip top' and up to date. However, now working from 'do best you can' instructions to this 'complaint' I will order all things and see if they meet the costs!!

I hope you and Nicola have a good time together and walk in the hills. It must be an experience for her after Los Angeles. I am looking at Nicola's drawing 'Gentle breeze blowing' it is very comforting for the brain.

I am very tired now so will stop writing.

Love and kisses
Your Tomas

Benbuie   October 9th

Dear dear Tomas,

Your birthday was celebrated by the glen revealed in bright sunshine and washed clean from days of rain. It was also marked by Rumer Godden coming to lunch. Nicola and I lit a big fire in the sitting room and we had lunch in there to make it cosy. Rumer was delighted to see how we had restored Benbuie. She admired your mother's embroidery on the dressing table and loved the pond that she pronounced, 'looking natural'. Nicola asked her what the property was like before. Rumer simply said 'a wreck'. We toasted you at lunch, Rumer saying 'dear Tomas' which she always does when mentioning you. She said how much she enjoyed your company when we went to the opera. Well of course you are a dear, most of the time! She called this morning for Nicola and I to go to see a Nicholas Roeg film at the Burns Centre on Saturday. She is off to Canada Sunday week for a festival of forty well known authors. She only has to read from her works for half an hour or so, as will others. Some 'big guns' among them as she described the other writers. An exercise for people to see writers 'in the flesh'. She is taking one of her granddaughters. There is to be a big Rumer Godden

169

retrospective in the spring and a lot of her books are being reissued.

Rumer brought her dog 'Silk', a little one eyed Pekinese. She spoke about her book THE BUTTERFLY LION which I understood she based on a Chinese legend. The story was of a lioness who became disenchanted by the over aggressive advances of the lion and decided to make love to a butterfly ("If you have ever been kissed by a butterfly" said Rumer "you would know how sensitive they are"). I understood that the Pekinese was the result of the relationship. Silk, in evidence, behaved impeccably. "They do not deserve the reputation they have of being bad tempered," said Rumer, "They have the misfortune of having a weak liver. It's in the breed and people overfeed them or give them the wrong things. If you have known anyone with a liver problem the result is the same." Rumer wrote to the Chinese government on the role of the Pekinese in Chinese history and received the reply, 'We do not wish to communicate on the subject of this decadent predator'.

Nicola and I walked up to 'rabbit heaven' and as we were coming back by the old cattle shed Nicola grabbed my arm. A double rainbow in vivid colours, the arc going from the doorway of Benbuie , across the river and ending up at the top gate. A fierce squall of rainy weather and dark clouds were behind us, the rowan trees blazing with orange red berries in front of us, the circle of seven giant beeches in brilliant autumn leaves on the other hill, the emerald grass in between, it was enough to make you faint clean away. "Incredible," Nicola repeated over and over. I like to think they were your birthday rainbows for luck and that you will be safe. Nicola and I hurried home to find the pot of gold but alas only to discover a great deal of duck poo on the doorstep. Ducks sheltering out of the rain!

Missing you as always.
All my love Jilly

CHAPTER 9

PAKISTAN INDIA THE HORN OF AFRICA THE RED SEA
SUEZ AND THE CANAL GIBRALTAR ROTTERDAM

Just after Christmas Tomas and I had reached the limit of the time we could tolerate apart. So it was that I found myself driving through the rain in the centre of Glasgow, lost, looking for the Pakistan Consul half an hour before it was going to close, a ticket to Karachi for the following morning on the seat next to me.

A few days ago the shipping agency in England had told me that I would not need a visa as I was joining the ship immediately and that the shipping agent in Pakistan would meet me.

Late that morning they had phoned to say I would need a visa stamp in my passport after all.

I was hopelessly lost. I jumped out of my car, grabbed my papers and hailed a taxi. Glaswegian taxi drivers are helpful and cheeky. They make you feel all is going to be alright in the world, and if it isn't? "What ken yer doo aboot it hen?"

Living so long in America, I used to think that 'hen' was short for honey, said in a Scottish accent. They can be a bit churlish at times, but they make you feel you are in safe hands. Just like Tomas.

The driver was true to form and found his way through the heavy traffic and bewildering one way system and we reached the consul just before four o'clock. "Good luck hen!"

How would I get the consul to stamp my passport with only a few minutes before he was due to leave? My anxiety must have conveyed itself as they were supremely courteous and helpful and within a few minutes I was back out into the street hailing the next taxi to help me find my car again, clutching the passport with visa.

When I arrived home there was a message from Tomas on the machine, worried that I would not arrive in time before the ship was due to leave port. He would not be able to delay the ship for me, he was saying, as much as he was looking forward to my joining him.

The next morning at the deck at Heathrow airport, the check in clerk pulled a face. "Only one way?"

"It was issued by the travel agency."

"I see that. But you can't have a one way ticket to Pakistan unless you are a repatriating Pakistani citizen."

"I'm joining my husband's ship. I don't need a return ticket. I won't be returning from Pakistan but another port in another country. I'm just being taken to the ship in port, passing through."

I gave him the telex from the agent in Karachi and the permission to join the ship from the company and showed the consul's visa stamp in my passport. He went to consult someone, leaving me with my anxiety. He came back still looking doubtful. "I can let you on the plane. But these papers you have may not mean anything to the officials in Karachi."

"The shipping agent will meet me," I said confidently.

The conversation made me worried. I was restless on the plane and worried about the ship leaving. This was a familiar feeling this time. I remembered my trip to Singapore in 1989.

When I arrived at Karachi airport my heart was beating wildly.

The official in his box looked at the stamp in my passport, my papers and then nodded that I could go through. Home and dry, I thought, too soon. The airport was very crowded, full of jostling people with serious faces.

As I waited at the carousel I felt someone looking at me. There were two soldiers standing at my elbows. As I placed my bags onto a trolley, they stepped forward and took my arms. They were not rough, merely insistent I was to go with them.

"What do you want? Where are you taking me?" My questions remained unanswered.

I looked around at the sea of faces hoping someone would step forward and claim me, but on we went into an office, where I was told, curtly, to sit down at the table.

I insisted that my luggage was left close by and reluctantly they wheeled it where I could see it.

In my mind was the ship's scheduled departure time. This made me brave and when four or five officials were all arguing around me about the reason for my visit, I spoke up loudly.

"I want to see the British Consul!" I said, like someone in a bad play. "I want someone to speak in English to me and tell me what you want!" They all gave me a cursory glance before resuming their discussion in Urdu.

"Speak in English!" I demanded.

One of the officials, a man with a droopy moustache and poached egg eyes, spoke to me. "You do not have right papers," he said.

"Of course I do!" I said. "The visa was issued by your own consul in Glasgow yesterday."

He shrugged and they all resumed talking. It was apparent that there were several opinions on what to do with me, or how much to ask me for, or simply just which law I was breaking.

"You have one way ticket," said droopy moustache. "You are not resident here."

"I am joining my husband on his ship!" I said firmly. I held up the paper with the Karachi Shipping Company address on it. "This company is escorting me to the ship."

This news did not seem to matter to them at all. Minutes were ticking by. I could see myself peering out between bars in a Karachi jail. Now they were shouting at each other. The place was in uproar. The ship would leave without me! I tried to shout above the din that I wanted to see the British Consul again.

My voice bellowed out, "Where is the British Consul?" They all stopped talking at once. Droopy Moustache made a dismissive gesture with his hand and another uniformed official indicated that I was to go with him out into the airport. I trundled behind with my trolley. What now?

"Is that man?" said the official pointing high over the heads of the crowd at a frantic looking figure in white who was signalling like crazy in our direction. "That is agent?" asked the official.

I was hanged if I knew. Perhaps hanged if it wasn't.

The man in white jacket and trousers came perspiring towards us.

"Oh Mrs Jill. You are late. Ship is leaving. We have to hurry, very much." I didn't even notice the official leave as I was whooshed away, my trolley crashed out onto the uneven roadway and I found myself in a sea of begging arms. The man in the white suit pushed a woman roughly aside. She was holding a baby and another small child by the hand. I stopped for a moment thinking to give her something but was taken and pushed into the back of a small white van. "No, no, no Mrs Jill, no, no. We late. Very late."

There were two seats facing each other and a slim young man sat in one of them. "This my assistant. I am agent," said the man in the white suit, as he drove like a madman out into the dusty road. "Hello" was all I could manage to say as we swerved around and knocked knees.

The scene through the windscreen at the front was like fast-forwarding a documentary film on a third world street. Donkeys and carts and camels and old cars. Coughing buses and loaded trucks belching black fumes and crowds of people.

Then the port and shouted exchange at the barrier as we zoomed in, then along the dock where I could see the ship moored. Then out of the van and up the accommodation ladder and onto the familiar deck. The agent was grinning and waving up at the bridge wing where we could see Tomas looking down at us. The agent shook my hand, so happy to have got me there in time. We were both feeling good about that. He called up to Tomas, "See Captain? Here she is!" Then he ran down the ladder back onto the dockside.

My bags arrived and two seamen were immediately raising the steps. The pilot was on board and before I got to the bridge we were moving away from the dock.

"You cut it a bit fine," Tomas said, laughing with relief. "I was just about! Just about!" he said, "I have been looking through the binoculars up at the roadway. I saw the agent's van coming like a rocket, so guessed you might be with him."

I flopped down on the sofa by the chart table. "Where are we going?"

"Cochin! India! Then to Rotterdam. A very nice trip. You will go through the Suez Canal. You haven't done that before have you. We will go up the Red Sea."

"Oh. How exciting," I said.

It was January 2nd 1991.

In the middle of December, Saddam Hussein had refused to meet US officials before January 12th. The Iraqi invasion of Kuwait was almost five months old and the world was steeling itself for war.

Saddam Hussein had been given until January 15th to pull his troops out of Kuwait.

What it meant for Tomas, myself and the crew to be on the ship, out there in the ocean with the prospect of military action in Kuwait, revolved around the price of fuel. We were bound for Cochin and after that Rotterdam, but the Suez Canal was part of that voyage unless we were diverted around South Africa. That diversion would cost money. Extra fuel, wages, and costs for the ship. Also the cargo if the price on the market dropped during the extra days it would take for the journey around the Cape of Good Hope. It may not be safe to go through the Suez Canal. The ship was insured, that would be the company's main concern. Whether we were in the range of missiles would be a technical point on the policy. There are areas that are considered war zones, usually they are a few miles off shore. Modern warfare must change that. Missile ranges are another matter and so are individual terrorist attacks.

Who was to stop anyone throwing a hand grenade onto our deck as we travelled the slow passage through the canal? We were going to load naphtha, a highly volatile fuel that has a 'zero' flash point. In other words very little tolerance to a spark. A spark alone could send the ship sky high.

The BBC World News Service spoke of little else but the possibility of war. I was happy for us to be together again. We were on our way to Cochin, and I had never been to India. I tried to think only of that for the moment. I was really excited and went to the chart table to find the port, remembering passing by the year before when Renalto had told us a story and I had looked at the coastline through the binoculars. Now we were actually going there.

Almost a year had gone by since I left the ship the last time, in Hong Kong. Tomas had stayed home until May, gone out briefly as a summer relief, returned to Benbuie for July and August and left for sea again in mid September. This time we had been apart for three months. I soon discovered that I knew no one on board except Tomas. All the crew were new. I was disappointed not to see one of the old crew but that was how it was for the crew as well, who could make close friendships but may never sail with that friend again. When a contract is signed with a shipping company, you agree that you can be changed to any ship, time or place even in the middle of your tour of duty.

The Chief Officer was a Sikh. He was friendly and had a big smile. I was fascinated by his colour co-ordination of tee shirt and turban. If he wore a peach coloured tee shirt, it would be a peach turban. Black, a black turban and so on. He was rather handsome but not vain. He was always trying to reach his wife on the telephone in their village in the Punjab on the border of Kashmir, where religious conflict was ongoing and there was fighting. He would pray on the bridge each evening as the sun was setting, for his wife, for his children and for the world.

Chief Engineer was from Montenegro and tall and slim with a thin moustache. He had a way of smiling that made you think he had a secret. His name was Drago and he had been brought up only by women he said, as his father had died when he was a baby. Whoever they were, they had been a positive influence, as Drago was kind and considerate and had a courtly attitude to women, and not just to me, as I discovered when I went ashore with him to shop one day. He liked the company of women.

The rest of the crew were Philippino. Alex was the second officer, a serious professional who always wore gleaming white knee length socks, officer's shirt with epaulets and smelt of expensive after shave.

Third officer, Fidel, was shy. He spoke with a thick accent and most of what he said was a mystery to me. Tomas, with his Swedish accent, which was either thought to be Welsh, Dutch or German by those who wanted to make a guess, could understand him perfectly. They would have completely unintelligible conversations about ship's business and I had not a single clue as to Fidel's half of the conversation. I expected Tomas to say, "What? Say that again" but he didn't, and neither did Fidel.

I missed Tony, but the new Steward was a lovely man. Bernard was fifty five years old. The steward had so much to do, relentless housework, and was also at the cook's beck and call. He had arthritis in his knees he told me. When I was on board I washed and ironed Tomas' clothes as well as my own but the bed linen laundry had its own ship's rotation that I had to leave alone.

There was also only one vacuum cleaner which was always in a different part of the ship, and caused a bit of an uproar if I asked for it, resulting in a full search. It was difficult to help. The men had their routines and their pride. It didn't take much to be seen to be in the way.

I read about Kerala, the state where we were going, in a book about India that I found on board.

Our journey from Karachi took four days and I was full of anticipation every day. Kerala was not only considered one of the most beautiful states in India, it also had religious harmony, it was said. Hindu, Buddhists, Jains, Roman Catholics and Protestants are well represented and churches and temples respected. Could this be true?

As we sailed into the inlet to the port of Cochin, I was thrilled by how lovely it was. Backwaters and lagoons and streams flowed through rice fields, coconut groves and land of the richest green.

Around a bend in the inlet were rows of the famous fishing nets at Cochin, the nets like ship's sails, leaning out from the beach above the water. Strong men were hauling on the timber supports that let the nets up and down. Each time the nets were heaved up out of the water many fish tumbled out in a silvery stream to be sold at the stalls that lined the beach just yards away. No one could say the fish was not fresh as it could come from the sea, direct to the stallholder and into a shopping bag within minutes.

The Portuguese colonised Cochin, then came the Dutch and then the British, the last for almost two hundred years.

I could see all three influences in the buildings we passed, but India it certainly was, and its character mesmerised me. There was an exotic perfume of spice and flower blossom in the air, mixed with smoke from fires where coconut, mango and cashew wood were burning.

We passed trees with branches spread like umbrellas, fronds trailing to the ground. Underneath, old men sat, and goats were tethered in the shade. To sail into the harbour, with town opening up on either side, from a viewpoint as high as the tops of the trees, was like arriving on the wings of a bird.

We were to load 35,000 tons of naphtha.

The fumes from the naphtha had caused a terrible accident, in Cochin, a few years prior to this. A fisherman was out in the harbour at night, casting his nets, and several hundred metres away, a ship like ours was loading naphtha at the dock. Unknown to the fisherman, the fumes from the naphtha had crept over the water, and had reached his small boat. He had a naked flame, perhaps to cook his supper, perhaps to light a cigarette, in any case the result was that the naphtha ignited, spreading in seconds across the water and up to the ship and shore. The pilot told us that about one thousand five hundred people had been killed. This story is passed around the ship as a further reminder of how careful everyone was to be.

Tomas was too busy to go ashore and when Drago heard I was going, he asked Tomas if he could accompany me. "I want to order two suits," he said.

"Two suits?" I looked at Tomas. "How long will we be here?"

"About four days. They are very quick to make something."

"They would have to be. You expect them to be ready before we sail?" I asked.

"Of course!" said Drago. "I have done this before. You may like something yourself."

"Oh heavens no. I have too many things already. But I would enjoy coming with you." So off we went to the tailors.

We walked into the town, which was called Ernakulam. All the way, the hairs on the back of my neck were prickling. India. Here I was. I was in India. The local people were good looking folk and I saw many really beautiful women, slim and graceful in their saris. The community looked prosperous and I was impressed by the many strong looking cars and sturdy bicycles. The cars, a Morris Minor style from the sixties, seemed like the original Ford, to be available only in black. There was a general feeling of bustle and purpose in the streets and few distressed people begging.

Into the more narrow streets of the market place lined with tiny shops selling rolls of fabulous silks and cottons, fruit and vegetables and every spice you could imagine.

I bought a length of dazzling silk. Who knew when I would be there again? In a novelty shop I bought stick on paste jewels for the forehead and arms. Then we were off on Drago's quest, along a wide roaring road of bigger shops, scaffolding and half-finished buildings. He remembered a tailor's shop on this road he said, but the changes that were going on had confused him. Back and forth on both sides we went, Drago carrying my parcels, me perspiring behind him, trying to keep up with his long legs leaping ahead. He was still gracious and charming but I was exhausted with the heat.

When we found the shop, I sagged down onto the nearest chair.

Two extremely long hours later, we were leaving, at last. I had watched with interest at first, from a short distance, as Drago had examined roll upon roll, bale upon bale, of different cloth.

Then it was the style. Pages and pages of suit styles. Then it was the measuring, this behind a screen. Then further discussions concerning delivery, price, and method of payment. My eyes were half closed and I was so thirsty I was contemplating drinking from the overflow from the plant pot at my elbow. Drago was chatting to the lady assistant, complimenting the shop.

Trying not to look like the disgruntled wife, I smiled as the tailor showed us out.

"Maybe we get back to ship now," said Drago as soon as we were on the street. I was looking around for a coffee shop but he leapt ahead again. "But first I make the phone call."

I staggered behind. "Where are you going?"

"Is here somewhere," said Drago, moving quickly.

He saw what he was looking for. The Post Office. In we went. Then standing in lines at the counter to pay for the telephone call in advance. No chairs there. I leant against the wall.

At last he was served. Then to the phone booths on the other side where he shouted on the phone for half an hour, above several Indian languages all shouting into their telephones. Afterwards I insisted on a taxi, which took a few minutes to find, but find one we did.

"I talk to my wife. My wife say you are good person to come shopping with me," said Drago cheerfully as we rode back to the ship. "She never come shopping with me. She no like shopping. I not know why."

I could have spoken volumes. If Drago's wife had spoken to me we could have laughed about it. She knew.

The boatman who ferried us to and from the ship was an outgoing character and he and Tomas had fun, talking about fishing and boats. Tomas loved the casting nets. He enjoyed the skill, and the design of them, and had several from around the world. Problem was they were edged with weights, usually lead, and would either be ALL you could carry in your suitcase on your way home, or would cost a small fortune to send by parcel. The two large nets Tomas had bought this time, that he showed me with pride, were no exception. They would have exceeded our combined baggage allowance ten times over.

"Don't start worrying about that!" Tomas said rather crossly. "Aren't they beautiful? I'm going to try them out on the pond at home." I could not lift either one. If I tried to hurl one around I would have ended up in the pond along with the net.

I filed the problem under the Tomas department. What was exciting was that the boatman had invited us for a trip. It would cost only twelve dollars. We would take the assistant agent with us as well. It was a unique opportunity to go around the harbour and perhaps into the lagoons without being part of a tourist group.

The continuation of the loading had been delayed a little, it was a Sunday and there was little going on, so Tomas left the Chief Officer and Drago in charge and off we went.

The boat was a small motorboat with a tiny cabin. We sped along the brilliant water and turned into the waterways where floating blue water lilies tossed around against the lush green river banks. Exotic birds flew around the trees and the small wooden houses. Canoes slid back and forth between the banks, sometimes loaded with a line of people, sometimes just a small boy on his own rowed by, pausing to stop and stare and letting his boat glide along on the current.

The wider parts of the rivers were lined with houses on stilts, a few businesses and restaurants among them, and children playing, women hanging their washing, animals drinking at the water's edge or lying down in the shade.

We came out again into a wider stretch of water where we could see churches and temples among the trees. People dressed in Sunday best, carrying parasols, were being taken across to the church in narrow canoes from one side to the other, a kind of water taxi, and so charming, with the women holding their parasols over their heads as they sat in the boat.

Faintly, above the sound of our engine, we heard the church bells ringing.

I was sitting up on the front of the motorboat feeling wonderful. It was breezy and cool.

I looked back at Tomas but he was not looking so happy. When the boatman went further and further away, deeper into the lagoons, where the trees were thicker and most of the stilt houses had been left behind, he started to look very serious and spoke to the assistant agent.

I understood we had gone out of radio range. Tomas did not want to be cut off from communicating with the ship in case he was needed, but the boatman wanted to show us his village and his home and family, so we continued.

When we pulled up, we were really in the jungle. Walking ashore, it opened out into a pretty square with a highly decorated church and a shrine in the centre. We followed the boatman down twisting paths through the trees until we came to a small wooden house with bright jade green pillars. The boatman's wife and children came out, and we were shown into the almost bare house and seated on a bench in the main room. A large picture of Jesus was hung over the top of the door surrounded by flowers and tinsel.

The wife was extremely shy of us, and half hid her smile as she brought us a drink in a tall beaker. It was a kind of Lahti, a thin yoghurt and was so welcome. She would not stay with us but hid around the door of the next room, sometimes peeping in, while her husband strutted about and looked out at the neighbours, dozens of whom were now gathered at the foot of his wooden steps, staring in at the open door.

It was marvellous to be able to see his home and the village. The children and dogs followed us as we left, skipping around, the dogs sniffing and barking in alarm at these strange smells.

After covering several hundred metres of water again, Tomas was able to speak to the ship, where all was well and nothing was happening.

"You should go to the Dalghetty Palace," said the assistant agent. "We will pass there."

The Dalghetty Palace was a large wooden hotel and restaurant set by itself on a small island and surrounded by landscaped gardens, probably built in the middle of the last century.

High ceilings and giant whizzing fans, muslin covered beds, mosquito nets and highly decorated wooden balconies and balustrades. Tropical, and so romantic.

We had an early dinner sitting on the garden terrace and as romantic as it sounds and should have been, warning signs came when those green curly insect burners that smell strange and look a bit like a large fire cracker were placed around the tables. Attracted by the smell, a signal that people were trying to defend themselves, giant mosquitoes arrived.

The next day, Tomas asked Mr Singh, the Chief Officer, if he would like to go ashore for the evening, but he said he would not and even looked alarmed at the very idea.

We had heard there was to be a traditional performance in a folk theatre near the park and decided as Mr Singh wished to remain on duty we could afford to go.

We had heard loud speeches over a microphone system during the day and when we went ashore, we saw a group of people in white running along the road with small red flags and surrounding a decorated lorry covered with signs in red paint.

"Communist party," said Tomas and then around the next bend, in the park, crowds were seated, some on chairs, some on the ground and sitting along the park walls.

A stage had been set up, and a kind of a play was going on. Three men on the stage were bellowing over a microphone, and encouraging the crowd to respond, which they did.

One of the men was saying the same thing over and over, in a kind of mantra but it was not religious, more indoctrination. This was apparently an opposing party as they carried different signs.

The crowd was huge. I was thinking what a local politician in a village park in Britain would give to have such an audience for his pre election speech.

The folk theatre on the other hand only seated about fifty people, and when we arrived, there were few other people in the audience. It filled up a little more as we waited for the performance to begin which it did with a bang, a riot of colour and a sound system designed for the very deaf. "HARRAHABALADABAR RA RA!" roared the first character, an extravagantly dressed figure in crimson and gold with a head dress two metres high. Then the most famous character, the one with the lurid green face that is seen on postcards for the area, leapt onto the stage. It seemed to be a story about abduction and sorrow, reconciliation and all the other elements of a ballet, but with loud singing, poetry, moments of symbolic pointing, eye rolling and gesturing and it seemed to go on for hours.

The costumes and performances were very professional but I looked around at the mainly western tourist mix of the audience and saw several glassy eyes and heads nodding onto chests. If the audience isn't familiar with the plot, and in spite of the dialogue being shouted at them full blast, if its another culture and in another language, you'll lose them every time if the performance exceeds twenty minutes.

If it had been Little Red Riding Hood, we would all have been waiting for the moment when granny is revealed as the wolf. As it was, we hadn't a clue when good would eventually triumph over evil.

"Memorable" I said as we walked back to the ship.

"Certainly," said Tomas. "I thought it was never going to end."

There was a moment in the theatre when I quite expected Tomas to stand up and loudly address the actors on the stage. "ALRIGHT! I THINK WE HAVE SEEN ENOUGH! WE LIKE TO GO HOME NOW, THANK YOU!" and to march me out but when I thought of Cochin in the future, it was this performance that was one of the memorable things that stuck in my mind.

We had been listening to the World News and Tomas ordered extra rice and fresh water. He spoke about a situation in 1967, when the six-day war between Israel and the Arab states had resulted in a blockage by wrecked ships in the Suez Canal and other ships in transit had been stuck for months without supplies.

Everyone thought war was inevitable and we were waiting to hear if the company wished us to take the longer passage around the Cape of Good Hope. This would take many more days, cost more, but might result in the cargo getting to Rotterdam, which if war broke out, was not so certain.

It was clear that the company were not going to respond to Tomas' telex. They were thought to be waiting until we reached the point of deviation, or point of no return, closer to the Horn of Africa. Entering the Gulf of Aden for example, may make it difficult to bunker (fill up with fuel) if war broke out.

We were to leave the next day, the 10th of January, the day that James Baker, the US Secretary of State, and the Iraqi Minister, Tariq Aziz, were to meet in Geneva, in last ditch talks to prevent a war.

There was a sense of gratitude, as we left that morning, that we had been in such a heavenly place before taking off on our uncertain journey. The crew had rested and the loading of our dangerous cargo had been unhurried and without incident. There was a red light on now up in the signal mast, day and night, to warn ships that we were carrying an inflammable cargo. Extra notices and warnings about smoking were given out. Tug boats arrived and the pilot was on board, the ship was moving very slowly away from the dock when there was a commotion on the port side, up on the forecastle.

We discovered later that there had been a lack of co-ordination between the Boson and the Chief Officer. Mr Singh had observed that the tug boat was being attached (made fast) to the bollard on the ship incorrectly, and as he went forward to correct it, the line to the tug boat suddenly tightened and whipped across the back of his ankles. He fell to the ground from the pain, and also, as he told me later, because he thought his feet had been cut off, an accident he had seen happen once on another ship when a man's legs had been cut off from below the knee.

It was a strategic moment for our heavily laden ship that had to be kept steady in the current. A launch from the port arrived, to take Mr Singh ashore, but when Tomas and I went down to the cabin to see him, he insisted that all was well and that he could stand on his legs.

"You will need to see if something is broken," said Tomas, but Mr. Singh was afraid to go ashore and to have to travel the length of India back to his village. He would have been twice as vulnerable to attack if he was injured and in the political situation at that time in India, he felt he would not reach his home.

His face was grey with the pain and his eyes full of tears. He was shocked he said, but would recover quickly. He could co-ordinate over the radio to the crew and still do his job. Tomas told him that if he agreed, Mr Singh would have to stay rested. It was a difficult decision. We didn't know what lay ahead of us either.

I stayed with Mr Singh and asked the Second mate, Fidel, to bring him strong sweet tea. Fidel had arrived with a gigantic bottle of iodine to pour into the wounds and I was concerned more with the shock than injury at that moment, I asked him to hold off on any 'treatments' for the time being.

We were well under way now, and when Mr Singh's trousers had been cut off, you could see the bone. The rope had cauterised the backs of his ankles, there was very little bleeding, but the injuries were deep. It was then that he told me he was allergic to penicillin. It would be three weeks before we would be in Rotterdam, if we were not delayed.

I was very concerned about infection. Just what would we do if the wounds became infected and gangrene set in? I wrapped him up in blankets and raised his legs on a stool. The hot tea helped him to stop shivering and as he said he had no problem with his stomach, gave him two aspirins. We keep morphine on board, locked in the safe in the Captain's office, but at that moment, he seemed able to bear the pain. I wanted him to start taking erythromycin and suggested this to Fidel.

I am not a nurse. My experience was like any other middle aged person, based on incidents that had happened to my children or other people over the years. I was concerned not to do something to make him worse, but it seemed making him comfortable and giving reassurance was the most important for the moment. I bathed his feet in warm Dettol water. Fidel seemed to have gone back to work but had brought fresh clean bandages and dressings.

Looking after Mr Singh was mainly what I did for the next few days and as we approached the Gulf of Aden I had not thought so much about the war, but how my 'patient' was doing each day. When I went to his cabin in the morning, I feared to find him in a fever, but except for a slight elevation of temperature for a day or two, this did not happen. He was not, of course, able to stand, especially when the feeling returned. The pain was considerable and Tomas was constantly telling him not to walk about at all.

I gave him a crutch so he could help himself to the toilet and he trusted me enough to allow me to see him without his turban. His hair was very long, down to his waist, and we wound it up in a kind of plait. It would have been impossible for me to try to put his turban on for him, and it was also difficult for him, so he left it off. He pinned a photograph of his wife and child above his bed to keep him cheerful, but he was worried for his job and it was getting difficult to keep him off his feet.

The company still did not respond to the ship's telex messages.

As we passed Socotra, Tomas came up on the bridge and found Mr Singh on duty, saying he was 'better'. We felt differently, but events were to place our concentration elsewhere.

Socotra, according to Tomas, is famous for having giant rats and for being a pirates nest, but I read that the name is from the Sanskrit, 'dvipa-sakhadara', meaning 'island abode of bliss' and among the flora on the island are myrrh and frankincense. Could stories of rats and pirates have been told to keep sailors away? Socotra was in a strategic position for pirates who robbed ships trading between the Red Sea and the West Coast of India. Marco Polo recorded over a hundred such pirate ships in the area in the thirteenth century and the danger continued for hundreds of years, as it did in other parts of the world, like the Caribbean.

A certain Captain Thomas Tew (I read to Tomas) offered his men 'a gold chain or a wooden leg' if they would sail with him to the Red Sea and capture the Moghul's ships. They all ended up with over a thousand pounds each, a fortune in the seventeenth century, enough to buy several wooden legs at least.

No skull and crossbones on the horizon as we entered Bab el-Mandeb, the narrow strip of water leading into the Red Sea, but a heavy propeller plane from the French Airforce. It flew around the ship several times before heading back to shore. We were off the coast of French owned Djibouti.

It was now January 16th. That night, at three in the morning local time, the Gulf War began.

We continued north, holding our breath. Still no reply from the shipping company, and no change to instructions. We were apparently meant to continue as planned. Thinking especially of the cargo we were carrying, we wondered if they took any notice of the news.

The days were sunny. The sea a deceptive tranquil blue.

We suspected the war from the sea could not be fought alone from the cul-de-sac that was the Persian Gulf. The supply ships for the war would use the Suez Canal and travel down the Red Sea. We were in the Red Sea. It wasn't long before the huge shape of an American Aircraft carrier appeared on the radar and then loomed ahead, a fearful sight.

An American voice with a chilling message boomed out over the VHF on our bridge. "AMERICAN WAR SHIP ON YOUR STARBOARD BOW. AMERICAN WAR SHIP ON YOUR STARBOARD BOW."

There were other military support ships around and we felt there had to be submarines. Everyone's heart was in their mouth. Before long, another huge Aircraft Carrier appeared on the port side.

It was now January 18th and through the binoculars we saw the planes lining up on the decks and taking off. They flew around in formation then headed east. It didn't seem real. It gave me a massive headache that was to last for days, knowing that at the end of the planes' journeys many were going to be killed.

I could not believe that we would be allowed to continue on our journey into the Gulf of Suez, between Aircraft Carriers engaged in war. Our ship, with its particular cargo, was after all, a potential bomb. The communication between the Port of Suez and our ship, and what we were carrying, must have been monitored by them, but on we went, unchallenged, our red light shining out with the message, "Here we come with dangerous cargo!"

I could only guess that it was something to do with International Shipping Laws and freedom of passage. They couldn't stop ships from trading and passing through the Canal, or could they? It wasn't everybody's war, but we could still get in the way. Surely they knew we could blow other ships to pieces and block the canal.

We travelled on in great tension. The crew were understandably in strange moods that changed all the time. Fear, excitement, concern, all mixed together. Sometimes behaving like schoolboys, jumping around. Then at others, stiff and professional as realisation crept in. It was difficult to believe it was real, that the planes we saw in the air were actually taking off to drop bombs on Baghdad.

None of us could sleep. We knew Scud Missiles were falling on Tel Aviv and Haifa from the news. Where were we? Would we be out of range? It would only take a spark. Mr Singh rushed around as best as he could on his crutches, his bandages trailing, while I ran behind with clean ones, imploring him to rest. At one point Drago appeared modelling one of his new suits from Cochin. Our little world on our ship. The big world just outside.

When we arrived in Suez, things became more surreal. I was to experience what seasoned sailors call the "Marlborough Canal."

Tomas instructed the crew to lock all doors in the accommodation to the outside, except one, which was to be manned by an officer who would need to be very firm and only allow those on board who were really officials.

This required a lot of judgement as all who tried to come on board swore that they were official. The accommodation ladder was to be lowered and raised for each necessary person and between the creak and crank of this going up and down, there was a great deal of shouting and arguing. Swarms of people were trying to get on the ship. At one point I was amazed at the sight of men appearing over the side of the rails on the main deck. They must have climbed up on ropes from boats below, just as the 'business man' did in Singapore, but these wore smart trousers, shirts and ties and carried briefcases as if they were getting on the eight twenty train to the city.

There was no use in being angry, Tomas told me, as they were experts at getting to you and around things. You can lock all the doors, but in five minutes a nose appears around the side of the bridge door. "Oh Captain. Everyone has something but not me." A good excuse will follow as to why he should receive a 'present' from the ship. There were men professing to be the 'real' agents who knew all about the ship's cargo and destination and wanted the ship's stamp, of course, on the papers they presented. They would be very serious, firm and professional looking, then when that wasn't working they would lean forward in a conspiratorial way and say "Captain. I will tell you something. No one else knows this but you. I have just got married. I don't want any cigarettes...but perhaps a little money?" They would lean across the table for the ship's stamp saying, "I help you Captain. I can do this for myself."

What was this all about? Cigarettes. It could cost as much as fifty cartons of Marlborough cigarettes to transverse the canal from Suez to Port Said, or about five hundred packets. The crew can end up smoking tea leaves. Sometimes its Whisky as well or something from the cook's stores, like coffee. A group handles perhaps ten ships a day.

Salesmen that get on board carry letters of 'recommendation' from other ships saying they are honest men. The souvenirs they sell are not expensive and one or two were well made. I am tempted along with others. Tomas knew one, 'old Moses' he called him, and his sons.

"They are all actors," said Tomas, as the real agent appeared, angry at being prevented from coming on board immediately. He was dressed in a striped shirt and natty bow tie.

"But Captain. I bring Inspector of the Canal. I am most important to you. Why they not let me on board? He give permission for transit the canal. Very important." The Inspector frowned. Tomas patted the top of his own arms. "Perhaps if you wore a uniform," he told him. "Some epaulets. Then we would know." The Inspector looked the same as everyone else, dressed in a pastel shirt and casual trousers.

The agent proved who he was by producing a message from my daughter Claire in Paris. "Don't you think it's about time you got off that ship?" she wanted to know, having just found out where we were. This would require a taxi across hundreds of miles of desert to Cairo. The agent said he could arrange it with someone he trusted, but Tomas would have none of it. I was not so keen either.

I heard a story once about a couple who took a taxi along the coast from Western Sahara. They were on their way to Marrakech but never arrived. The woman's head was taken as well as she had a few gold teeth. This was no reflection on the agent or his taxi driving friend, but who were they against a possible band coming out of the Al-Bahr-Al-Ahmar desert? I was also British. Not the most popular nationality in the area. No. Better to sit on high explosive cargo in the middle of the war with Tomas. At least if we blew up, it would be over in seconds, and that other thing. We would be together.

They were going to let us through the canal. We had our place allotted to us in the convoy, and we went into position, along with our first pilot. He would travel with us as far as the Great Bitter Lake, and Al Ismaliyah, where the main part of the canal then continued straight on to Port Said and the Mediterranean Sea.

The pilot was extremely cordial and attentive to me. A little flirtatious you could say. He was rather short and bald and he wanted Tomas to take our photograph together. As I stood with him

191

out on the bridge wing, he comically placed his pilot's cap on my head. In the background, the grey ships of war sailed by, carrying tanks, large guns and weapons, and heading south.

We took almost two days to travel through the Suez Canal in total, as progress was slow. I could see the ship ahead of us and the one following, perhaps some six hundred metres away. The slow progress was agonising as we were all tense because of the war and the need to get our cargo away from the area.

Without discussing it, we thought of that one person throwing a hand grenade. The fire from our cargo would spread rapidly over the shallow calm water between the banks.

What a weapon we presented to Saddam Hussein. In one simple action, he could stop the allied ships from coming or leaving. With the canal blocked, the only way out from the Persian Gulf would be the very long route around South Africa.

To this day I still cannot understand why they let us through.

Along the banks of the canal, soldiers and trucks were moving to and fro and aircraft guns were pointing up at the sky and there we were, chugging along, a few sparks away from blowing them all up.

The pilot said when he left, he would like me to go ashore with him. He could 'show me Cairo'.

He explained this several times to Tomas. Saying I would be safe with him and his wife would welcome me. Had I seen the pyramids? Then I must go with him so he could show me!

This we both declined, although seeing Cairo with an Egyptian would have been more than interesting I was thinking. I had confided, naively, about the many people asking for 'presents' in Suez, saying it was a bit outrageous I thought. He 'tut tutted' a lot and said we should make a 'formal complaint'. "At such a time of crisis too," he added.

Just as he was leaving he called me over with a beckoning finger. "I wonder. My wife very much likes English tea. As you are English, perhaps you have some packets of tea on board?"

On the morning of January 22nd, we turned west from Port Said into the Mediterranean.

There was a profound feeling of relief although we had nine more days to go before we reached Rotterdam.

The crew were allowed to smoke in special designated areas on board but they had run out of cigarettes due to the "Marlborough Canal effect." The ship's cigarette stores were empty. I was mourning the loss of my precious boxes of Twinings as well but these were small prices to pay for the safe Pilotage through the war zone when you came to think about it.

The BBC World News continued to give the daily bulletins. My country was actually at war. It helped to go back into normal ship routine and before long, Gibraltar appeared on the starboard quarter.

I put a warm scarf around my head and went out on the bridge wing in the brisk wind and the sunshine until the rock disappeared into the distance and we had sailed out into the Atlantic.

We were passing the 'island of terror', Ile d'Ouessant off the Breton coast. This place, with it's striped lighthouse, the most powerful in the world, is at the turning point into the Channel and guiding point for the thousands of ships that pass to and from the Atlantic every year. When I was not on the ship, Tomas always called over the radio from this point, as it was possible to get a connection. He may have been coming up from Africa, or from South or North America, but reaching the Ile d'Ouessant was always a good sign, it meant the ship was close to home.

The Gulf War was continuing, and the mood on the ship was sombre. Light conversations and the telling of tales had been set aside and wherever there was a radio on board, it would be tuned in to hear the latest news. Mr Singh was still trying to reach his wife in the Punjab and was to go ashore in Rotterdam to a hospital. He had no infection, but he was in pain.

Kuwait oil wells were on fire and Iran was appealing for help to clear up the tons of oil spilt into the Gulf. A Kuwait pumping station and five Iraqi tankers had spilt vast amounts of oil into the sea it was reported, and a ten mile slick was heading south down the Gulf. I thought about the previous year when we were in Al Jubayl and how clear and unpolluted the water had been. How concerned we had been about the tea cup of oil that had been on deck.

The Philippino crew were hoping for mail and were also trying to reach their families without success. At that time, we still had a Radio Operator, but within a year or two these officers were replaced by the Global Maritime Distress and Safety System, the GMDSS. The updating of communication systems on board, which technically were an improvement, removed yet another human factor from life at sea. The array of machinery on the bridge for all communication became the responsibility of the officers on duty on the bridge, giving them essentially, another job to do in addition to navigation and the other tasks they did before.

When I joined other ships later on, there was always the sad little room with the old sign over the door, now used for the copy machine and storage. Radio rooms began to look like a feature in a museum, but it was the man who worked there who was missed the most.

The Radio Officer was a position apart. He spoke English well, essential for the job, and was able to help members of the crew who did not. He was a liaison between crew and Captain, someone who could be asked to intervene or suggest something on their behalf. He was usually knowledgeable about the Port of Call and would give advice on going ashore. He held the passports and documents for vaccinations and noted irregularities.

Without putting too fine a point on it, and depending on the man, he was a kind of social worker, an officer who might have the time to put that call through to find out if your sick child had recovered, or a new baby had arrived safely. He picked up essential information from other ships, from speaking to other Radio Operators. He was the human ear of the ship replaced by equipment that only knew how to signal an alarm, and that, I was to discover, was often false.

Standing on the stern deck as we entered the Channel, I noticed a ship, not too far in the distance, who seemed to be following us, move for move. It would be immediately behind us, then when our ship changed course, it would appear to feign disinterest, continuing on the previous route, then change and follow us again. I watched this happen two or three times and went to speak to Tomas on the bridge.

"He probably doesn't have any charts for the area," Tomas explained. "He's just following us, doing what we're doing."

That seemed a bit dangerous to me. "Hope he doesn't get too close," I said, now observing the ship through binoculars out of the rear windows on the bridge. I was thinking how an oil tanker driver on a motorway would feel if another tanker driver was following his every move. "It's a Greek ship," said Tomas, reading the name through his binoculars. "THE GLIDER."

The Channel is a busy place. Ferries and hydrofoils and pleasure boats criss-cross from France to the English coast while merchant ships with cars, produce and equipment plough along from east to west and back again. When you come to points like the Dover Straight where the narrow strip of water condenses the action and the radar is thick with blimps and blobs, your judgement of speed and position of your own ship as well as what the other one is going to do, better be good.

In the middle of all of this, a tiny sailing boat (motor has to give way to sail) can cause a hiccup. The sailor may be entertaining friends or himself and have a CD blasting away in the galley but if the cargo vessel runs him down, it would be considered the cargo vessel's fault. The majority of pleasure sailors that use the Channel are very aware and alert in the traffic separation zones, but you don't have to go to navigation school to drive a motorcruiser. Ignorance may be bliss for them, but for the officers on the bridge of a ship that takes twenty minutes to stop, bliss is not the word when they try to dodge the unwary.

Rotterdam is linked to the North Sea by the New Waterway canal. The Waal Harbour is the largest dredged harbour in the world and life in Rotterdam revolves around shipping. The tall, blonde Dutch Pilot, who came on board to guide us into port, neither asked for a carton of Marlborough cigarettes or a packet of tea. It felt very good to be arriving there.

On the news Israel was threatening retaliation for the twenty-six Scud Missiles that had fallen on their cities and the Gulf War looked set to escalate and spread.

Coming into port

Tomas felt it was better if I went home. He had no control over where the next port of call would be and could find the ship travelling back into the war zone. He asked the Dutch agent to arrange my ticket. I wished he was coming home as well, and probably he did too.

When you leave a ship as a 'supernumerary', the title given to you on the crew list, you have to be repatriated the same as any other sailor leaving a ship. You cannot just drift ashore and make your own way to the airport, even in Europe. The shipping agent arranges that you either see Immigration on board, or you are taken to the office to sign off officially. The dictionary defines the word supernumerary as one that is in excess of the regular or necessary number, or a performer without a speaking part.

Before I left, I heard the news that Mr Singh would be staying in the hospital for a couple of days as he had cracks in his ankle bones. He would feel safe and be well looked after in the Netherlands.

He had promised to send me a pair of special slippers that were made in his village, when eventually, he arrived home. I thought of the Duck Songs and hoped he realised he would have to send the men's version. My European size feet again.

As I went to get into the taxi, Tomas came down the accommodation steps and gave me a long hug and a kiss, prompting a whistle from someone up on the deck, someone who hid behind the funnel as we looked up.

CHAPTER 10

SPAIN AND THE WEDDING IN THE GLEN

Benbuie! February 13th 1991

Dear Tomas,

Today I have been home two days but I still feel in a dream. I cannot believe I am here, looking around at all our efforts, and Gus and the girls pecking around, the drakes starting to lay in ambush for the females. Well it is Valentines Day tomorrow. There are three eggs in the goose house as well. No, your taste buds have not become old. It must be the water, no wonder the whisky has a reputation here. My first cup of tea was heaven and the bread! Your stored potatoes in the sacking were still perfect. I boiled a big pot up for the hens as we have snow on the ground and it is frosty. Yesterday I went to lunch at the Bleazards at Glenjaan.

The roads were not too bad but I decided to walk which was a great decision as I enjoyed it so much and had a good appetite for Gladys' roast pheasant, the tastiest I have ever had and truly a 'local' one I 'm sure. Also spotted dick which was Gladys' special recipe. It' s a steam pudding boiled in a cloth with raisins in it which can be a bit solid, but Gladys' one was like a feather.

We had a lot of laughs about this and that. I am taking Gladys and Jim to the Castle Douglas auction tomorrow where Dick is to sell two heifers. He will leave early in the morning.

As it will be Valentines Day it's a great way to spend it as my love is not here. "We'll have lunch with farmers in pub," says Jim. "We shall have to watch you, being the day and all," said Gladys. "Oh yes. I'm a dangerous woman on Valentine's Day," I replied which produced loud infectious laughter. Someone should pay Gladys to sit in the audience of failing comedians she has such a wonderful humour and that laugh!

Jim was in a better mood since the doctor discovered he had 'polupses' up his nose. "'e removed them thar and then," said Jim, continuing with his graphic description even though we were at the pudding and custard stage.

"'e used a thing like a snare yersee. 'Ooks it around inside like. It dern't bleed mooch. I feels a lot better now."

The day before I went for dinner at Dalwhat. At the dinner was Sam's mother, ninety year old Cathy and her seventy year old brand new husband. Cathy wore rose coloured lace tights and he wore a large hearing aid. They were very entertaining. She is a strong personality if you know what I mean. He kept falling asleep which was a bit noticeable as he was at the head of the table.

She would get up and go to his side to hiss loudly in his ear. "IAN! You're asleep again!"

He would wake like the dormouse in Alice in Wonderland. "Oh, so I am," he would say each time and beam around the table at everyone. "So terribly sorry. What were you saying?"

Delicious food. Mary is a great cook. I think she has her hands full with Sam's mother.

You should be docking in Nova Scotia soon. I think of you and hope there are not too many icebergs around.

Hope to be able to talk to you before this reaches you.

All my love Jill

Halifax   February 12th 1991

Dearest Jill,

I arrived here yesterday after a rather choppy trip over the North Atlantic. Deck crew have been working like slaves and they still are, as we have been ordered or perhaps I should say recommended to clean the tanks again after we had 'inerted' the ship as charterers had ordered us, which brought down soot into the cargo holds. This is normal but already prior inspection on arrival the surveyor remarked that they are not used to inert here in Canada.

It's sunshine outside but the thermometer shows minus 10C and I can see the crew' s frozen features out on deck. Everywhere you can see clouds of steam from the deck winches and cargo tanks where the cleaning is underway. The crew are exhausted and I must say I feel for them but there is nothing to do but press on.

After you left in Rotterdam, the family mail arrived from Charles and Elna and I will give to the agent to send back to you. Even though we did not go back to the Gulf, I am pleased you are at home. The weather has been rough, and it's no picnic here, freezing wind and bad weather forecast for the next few days.

Kisses from your Tomas

Tomas letter from Halifax arrived with the forwarded mail towards the end of February. I had no idea where the ship was at that moment. The company said 'delayed' and that the port was Europe but not fixed. World News weather reports of severe storms coming across the Atlantic were worrying me a great deal. The few weeks we had spent travelling close to the Gulf War had brought new feelings of insecurity. I went out walking with the dogs several times a day.

Now the snow had started to melt the Dalwhat Water was flooding across the road at the river run. Benbuie Burn was a roaring peaty brown torrent and I worried that the dogs would become too adventurous and get swept away but they were sure footed and smart. Places where they used to hop over the river were given a wide berth.

The wind roared around the house at night and I was often awake trying not to worry.

"Hello, it's me."

What a relief to hear Tomas' voice. On the satellite phone? Must be urgent.

"Where are you?"

"Well you would never guess."

Tomas was off the west coast of France. He had left Halifax in a snow storm and when far out at sea the deck began to crack open. The ship was old and they were loaded with marine diesel oil. The weather could have broken the ship in two, just like the DERBYSHIRE which had vanished off the Canadian coast in a storm in 1980. "The crack is almost the width of the ship," said Tomas.

"You can see the deck plates moving. I managed to keep her turned so we have not polluted anything as yet but it is touch and go I can tell you. We are on our way now to Spain, hoping to get there in one piece. Taking it as easy as we can."

Tears welled up in my eyes but I wanted to sound brave. I knew the weather in the Bay of Biscay was terrible at that time of year. "Where in Spain?"

"We are hoping to get into a shipyard," said Tomas with an ironic laugh. Fear clutched at my heart. "I will call you again. Would you like to come down to Spain if I make it?" (If I make it?)

"Of course. What do you think?" We couldn't afford it, but what the hell. The company did not pay for wives to join the ship and we had spent too much money on tickets to Karachi and return from Rotterdam, but oh I wanted so much to be with him, especially at that moment.

"I have been thinking that you and I should make things more official. Well we can talk about it when you come to Spain. Have to go now. Don't worry. We'll make it."

The phone call had not reassured me but made me worry more. The ship was breaking up for God' sake! I paced around the house. 'Make it more official?' What did he mean ? Marriage? Marriage. We had lived together now for nearly four years. Of course I wanted to marry him, why not? I telephoned Elna and told her about the ship and the dangerous journey Tomas was making limping into port. Elna and Charles had wanted us to get married and made the odd hint in the past. They were regular churchgoers and thought it was time. Tomas and I had other marriages behind us. I had been married twice before, to an Englishman and an American. Now a Swede? I thought of all the rows Tomas and I had, but we had just as much love in equal measure.

"I think Tomas and I are going to get married," I told Elna. "Would you and Charles like to be our witnesses if we do? It won't be in church."

Tomas still had to bring his crew and the ship into port in one piece. I studied the Spanish map. Where would it be? Probably on the north coast.

At Bilbao airport, the lady in the foreign exchange booth studied my Scottish banknotes with disdain. "No." she said sharply.

"These are legal tender," I protested. "I need pesetas for the taxi."

"Nope," she said again and slid the window shut. She placed a sign. CERRADO. What was this? I turned and crossed to the British Airways office. Also closed. This time in English. Closed from one to three. It was five to one. I tapped on the glass and a young Spanish man came politely to the door. "You 'ave to come back at three o'clock," he said through the glass. "Ye Gods." I sat down on a nearby seat. It must be the siesta.

Then I had a bright idea. Perhaps someone was at the airport from the agency. I walked around looking for someone with a sign. I had had this problem before with Scottish bank notes. They were often looked at as if they were Monopoly money. I should have asked the bank for English notes or bought some pesetas before leaving.

After several circles around I gave up and resumed my vigil outside the British Airways door.

Since that time, which was 1991, the Guggenheim has been built and tourism to Bilbao has increased. They probably keep the offices open all day and ladies at the foreign exchange are now familiar with Scottish currency, but then it was different.

You feel frustrated and out of rhythm if you are hurrying to your destination and then find yourself forced to wait along the way. This was getting to be a pattern every time I tried to join the ship.

I watched the uniformed British Airways clerk unlock the door and sped inside to be first in line. I told her about my problem with the money. She was charming and thinking to help me when a very short square looking man wearing a Basque beret came running into the room. His sign said "Grittit" and I thought of the sign in Singapore.

"I'm Jill Griffith," I told him.

"I look for you. Come," he said and so I followed. He must have taken his siesta as well.

We drove along the industrial looking harbour and shipyards and then started to drive up a hill, almost a mountain.

"Where are we going?" The driver spoke very little English and I spoke no Spanish.

He waved impatiently at me in his driving mirror. "We go. We go," was all he said.

"No Bilbao?" I asked

"Santander. Santander," he replied with wonderful rolling 'r's.

We drove into Santander and down to the harbour wall where the driver parked, got out and hurried across the street to a bar. Men were standing outside with glasses in hand. The driver approached one, began an earnest conversation, pointing at me. The man stared moodily over as I looked from the car window. He did not look happy. He said very little to the driver in the Basque beret but at last he put his glass down and strolled over to the car, passing my window and taking the steps down the side of the sea wall that led to a group of barges that were jostling about on the water.

The driver opened my door, then the boot and took out my suitcases.

"What's happening?" I said.

"You go. You go," said the driver, tossing my suitcases down to the other man who waited on one of the barges below.

There was nothing for it. I stepped gingerly down the stone steps. The chosen barge was in the middle of the others and both men indicated to me that I was to jump from one barge to another to get to the right one. I clambered more than jumped, banging and scratching my legs before ending up in the barge with my suitcases. It had been raining on and off and I was wearing a large green rainhat tied under my chin which I held in place with one hand.

There was a small wheelhouse built for one. I stayed outside in the rain as we set off, knocking the other boats aside and put-putting out into the harbour. I saw by the direction we were going we were headed out to sea. We passed the lighthouse and the breakwater and then out among white flecked waves. It was like sailing along on a ship's biscuit. It was mad. It was reckless abandon.

I began to understand that whenever I turned up there were no real arrangements for me, this one person who was not a sailor, joining a ship that was rarely alongside a suitable place to board a passenger, why should there be? I was a 'super numerary' after all.

I could see the ship was not too far away but could we make even that distance? I held grimly onto my hat, watching for the moment when I would be tipped out into the sea. Now I understood why the boatman had been so reluctant.

Tomas said later that he saw this object approaching, and focusing through his binoculars saw me, standing up, with one hand on my hat, appearing and disappearing between the waves as if I was arriving on the Kon Tiki without the sails up.

The ship was off shore because they were afraid of the possibility of pollution from the cracked deck. Santander is a well known resort with sandy beaches. We were to be going into a small shipyard close by. Tomas was waiting for orders. He had hoped to have been in port by then. I went out on deck with him to see the damage. It was like an earthquake crack, right across the steel plates from one side of the ship almost to the other side. It looked terrifying.

After the ship docked in the yard, droves of people arrived for days on end. Representatives from the company, inspectors, surveyors, insurance agents, but not one said a word to the crew or Tomas to congratulate them or thank them for managing to bring the ship safely to port without polluting the seas. The repairs were going to be very costly, the ship was old and there were many arguments among the conflicting interests as to the thickness of the steel that was to be used for the repair, or had been used in some of the supports when the ship was built.

Tomas was moody and angry and I could not blame him. It was far from a romantic Spanish holiday. We were close to the resort but we never got there. The discussion about marriage did not come up. It was not the time. We stayed with the ship for a further three weeks, then Tomas felt he had done all that he could and gave his notice to the company. "I can find a better ship than this one," he said. As we left, the crew were leaning over the rail, smiling and waving at us. I looked up at their faces and wanted to call out. "Don't stay on that ship. Go home."

The registration office in Dumfries is in the old Midsteeple building in the centre of town. We had passed it many times when shopping but it took on a new significance as we approached and went up the steps to arrange our marriage. Hand in hand and feeling sunny we walked in with a skip in our step and smiles on our faces.

Ten minutes later we walked out again, grim faced and arguing. Tomas had presented his Swedish birth certificate which was the original official paper but, unlike a British birth certificate was brief, the size of a postcard and stamped by the Swedish church. This was before Sweden became a member of the European Community. The certificate was considered an oddity by the large lady registrar who was short in her opinion. "This will not do" she said to Tomas.

"What do you mean?" he said, immediately rattled by her voice and attitude.

"This is not good enough."

"It is good enough to satisfy the Swedish authorities" replied Tomas getting loud.

"But you have to satisfy me!" said the lady, glaring at him.

"I certainly hope not" said Tomas.

Both of their faces were scarlet.

"This is a proper certificate! They are ALL registered with the church in Sweden." They all look like this.

"I cannot marry you with that certificate," said the registrar, turning away to her desk.

"Then we will not get married at all!" said Tomas stomping out.

"What are you doing?" I asked Tomas as I followed him down the steps.

"There is no way that woman is going to marry us. So that's it."

"So you don't want to get married now is that it?"

"Probably not."

"Alright then!"

Later when we had calmed down I had a better idea.

"What about getting married here, at Benbuie? They do that sort of thing in the States."

"Well you can look into it," said Tomas gruffly, then, "That would be nice. Of course."

Easier said than done. The Swedish Embassy had to be involved and approve and by the time we got around to calling a minister (registrars did not marry people anywhere other than the registry office) the minister in Moniaive was away in New Zealand. I had to find a 'stand in'.

This proved to be the Reverend Fergus Macpherson, minister of the Church of Scotland but someone who had spent a great many years in Africa and had only recently returned.

The Reverend Macpherson was uneasy about marrying two people who might have previously sinned and in fact were living in sin. He told me his misgivings at length on the telephone, with Tomas across the room watching my face and interjecting, "What is he saying?"

I groaned inwardly at another hurdle but kept smiling.

The Reverend Macpherson at that moment was saying that he would have to come to 'interview' us first to see if we were suitable.

The idea of telling Tomas that, was not a prospect I cherished. I did not use the term 'interview'.

"What do you mean he has to see us first? What for?"

I was on the edge of really giving up on the whole thing. I was now in the role of almost having to persuade Tomas to go through a ceremony. It was not a good feeling.

"We'll forget it then." I said. "I'm fed up with it all as well. You would think if two Europeans want to marry each other it would be simple."

"Well I suppose we can go through with him coming to see us first. But he better not start to be difficult with me," said Tomas. (Groan.)

The Reverend Macpherson was a dapper man with a small grey beard. He sat down at the kitchen table and we sat across from him like two schoolchildren.

He turned out to be a nice person. He had travelled of course, and so Tomas and he had something in common. I was beyond caring what was going to be said, but the Reverend Macpherson was kind. He had his strong beliefs and feelings. We told him our individual histories. Then he simply asked us which date we preferred.

"What about May 1st?" I said. "May Day. The international distress signal for ships at sea."

Bride, bridegroom and bridesmaids

There is a book about the history of Moniaive, that local people treasure. There are few copies about because it was published in 1910. 'The Annals of Glencairn' was written by John Corrie a local historian and naturalist, who recorded the people, places and plants. He would be astonished if he knew how popular his book is today and the keen price it can fetch in local bookshops. He called Glencairn, which is the valley where the three glens meet (one of which is the Dalwhat Glen where we lived), 'truly a land of romance and beauty.' Moniaive is from the Gaelic *mon-adh-abh* meaning Hill of Streams. There is a small hotel, the Craigdarroch Arms and a pub, The George, which was once a coaching inn and is one of the oldest in Scotland. Moniaive has a famous Flower Show each year, Sheepdog Trials, a Horse Show and a Gala, a Bowling Club, a Fishing Club, Arts Association, and many more clubs and events. A friendly place. That is the best thing of all about Moniaive.

Parts of the village are very old. The Dalwhat Bridge, half way up the glen, was built in 1661. There is evidence in The Annals of Glencairn that there was a house at Benbuie from around the same time. Benbuie means yellow or golden mountain. (and Drambuie yellow or golden drink). If you are asked if you would like a drink in the local pub it would be, "Would you care for a wee dram?"

We had a few drams ready for the neighbours on May 1st that year. My dress for the day was made from the length of silk that I had bought in Cochin in January. The guests were the friends from the glen and the village. The wedding feast, two large legs of local lamb, cooked by the bride. The bridegroom made the wedding cake. It was the best cake I have ever tasted. It was a Swedish sugar cake made with hardly any flour, tons of whipped cream and decorated with sliced kiwi fruit. I have a picture of Tomas decorating it with great concentration. It was a divine cake.

My brother Peter came up from London and 'gave me away' and made a fine speech about us being a 'unique couple'. Charles and Elna were the witnesses, Charles feeding his sheep on our field just before the ceremony in true country style. We gathered by the pond in bright sunshine and a stiff chilly breeze. Tomas wore his uniform, a bit reluctantly. The Reverend Fergus Macpherson came with his wife and they were going to stay for the lunch.

When it came to the exchange of rings Tomas held up his right hand instead of the left. The right hand, his dominant hand, is bigger. I could not get the ring onto his finger. I giggled. Tomas closed his fist around it, pretending it was in place.

Tomas repeated his vows into the cold wind with force and sincerity, gripping onto my hand as if we were on the ship's bow. Later he denied that he had held up the 'wrong' hand until he saw the video. Against the backdrop of sweeping hills and bare trees there we were, struggling to jam the ring onto his finger while Gus and his girls pecked around and the wind threatened to blow my skirt over my head.

In the same week, the first swallow arrived, and in the future would remind us of our anniversary as they always arrived around that time. Hearing the chatter up on the telephone wire we went to the window and watched as the tiny bird preened his shiny wings and announced his arrival.

More would follow in the days to come, rebuilding and repairing their old nests in the stable roof, anticipating the constant supply of midges and insects with gusto, talking incessantly. The line up on the wire grew longer and louder and then suddenly empty as the ladies started to sit and the males had to be constantly on the wing to feed the expectant mothers as well as themselves. The first young swallows that I saw made me burst out laughing as they have a thick yellow upper beak that resembles a moustache. As I staggered in at the door with a bag of hen food they all glared down at me from their perch on the rafter like a trio of disgruntled colonels inspecting a very dishevelled soldier.

On a warm evening, if the midges were not in an attacking mood, you could sit by the pond and enjoy watching the swallows swooping down to the surface and back up into the sky, the next best thing to being able to do it yourself. The last line up would come towards the end of August, mums, dads, and all the broods of the summer, a dozen birds would now be three dozen. They would chatter for sometime, fly several victory passes over the house and then they would be gone, every one, and with them went the summer.

CHAPTER 11

LIVERPOOL   HAMBURG   BREST   THE AZORES   FLORIDA
THE GULF OF MEXICO   YUCATAN   HOUSTON

Benbuie   October 9th 1991

Dear Tomas on the High Seas,

You will remember saying that I would have the pleasure of our 'harvest' when you left.   Today was such a beautiful day so I decided to tackle the carrots.   The smell when you pull them from the earth!   Wheeled several barrow loads up to the house.   Some for the geese and many blanched and stored in the other old freezer in the stable.

The pleasure of these vegetables at every stage!   I am such a convert that I promise not to grumble next time you plant so much, well, the POTATOES would have been too much for me for sure and I don't know what I would have done without Jock to help.   We tipped them out on the driveway and turned them in the sun before putting them in the sacks, but I could not dig them up.   I was the wheelbarrow part of the job.

Jock came early yesterday talking about his nephew (you know, nice John, the one with the Elvis hair) as he was supposed to be up 'being as it's his first day to clean the toilets' (the public ones in the village that Jock usually cleans as one of his jobs).   As John is unemployed, I understood that the job had to be given over to him.   Poor Jock had scrubbed them thoroughly at the weekend in a sad kind of farewell.   "Even took down the spider's webs, although I would never kill a spider," I pointed out a little woolly blob in the corner of the kitchen window.   "Aye, A spider's nest alright.   You better watch yourself lass.   Everything seems to PRODUCE at Benbuie!"

So Jock went off to fish yesterday, having got the time as he is no longer in charge of the LADIES and GENTLEMEN.   I like those signs.   I hope they don't replace them with stick figures like everywhere else.

I'm glad the old short wave radio is fixed again.   I can listen to the World News and know you are listening too.

Have to tell you.   I fell into our pond two days ago.   I had a frustrating conversation with the bank manager and stomped outside to take the dogs out to get rid of the mood. As I passed the pond I saw that the wind had blown the island to the side. Having my shepherd's crook in my hand I jabbed at it to adjust it, the crook part caught on and with no time to let go the island spun away and I fell in, wearing wool hat, raincoat, heavy sweater and rubber boots. The water was FREEZING and went right over my head as it was the deep end. It was like an electric shock.

It was not easy to get out as everything, especially the boots, were clinging to me and full of water. The dogs were running up and down the bank barking just as they do if I am playing a game with them. They thought it was fun! At the kitchen door, water pouring from me, I stripped everything off before going in for a hot bath. Luckily the keys had stayed in my pocket.

When I looked out of the window I saw that Colin the ranger's car was parked up on the hill, you know the way he does, to stand and look around the glen with his binoculars to see if there are any deer!

I also mused on the idea that had Charles and Elna passed that Sunday on the way to church, they might have glanced down our track at the pond and seeing my body floating there would have remarked casually to each other. "I see the wind has blown their scarecrow into the pond."

We had a wonderful week before you left didn't we? Write to me soon. LONG letters please.

Much love from the Jillywife

A postcard bearing my new married name arrived in the autumn.

New Orleans   October 20th 1991

Coming back over the Atlantic! To Liverpool. Please come to spend Christmas. I miss you already!
Love Tomas

So in November I was happy to be off again. The days were dark and cold in the glen. We had many good friends who were taking care of Benbuie while we were both away. There was little to do as everything was practically hibernating . It was enough to make sure they had dry beds and plenty of corn and the dogs were cosy with friends. I thought it would be easy to go by bus from South West Scotland to Liverpool. It was so cold in Carlisle where I changed buses for Manchester the next stage of the journey. My feet almost froze to the pavement in spite of my boots.

There were a few football fans on the bus. They sang loud songs and were having quite a party. The beer cans swished about and they walked up and down the aisle, leaning over to shout jokes to each other, ignoring the driver's orders to sit down.

I didn't mind so much. They warmed up the atmosphere a bit. The cold had made me want to pee desperately. Fortunately there was a toilet at the back of the bus. After I closed the door I realised I was standing in an inch of either beer or pee/beer mix. I had left my long coat in the seat so at least that wasn't trailing in it. The seat was up, so I lowered it to sit down.

At least a litre of pee came pouring off the seat, splashing down the front of my trousers. I have never been so miserable on a bus journey in my life after that. Not only did I return looking as if I had not managed to get to the toilet in time, but I had to sit for hours with someone else's pee soaking into my underwear. My bags were in the hold or I would have changed right there and then, even to catcalls.

In Manchester I staggered into the public toilets, cramming myself and my suitcases into the tiny space. I managed to find fresh pants and trousers. Standing on one leg and bumbling about, crashing into the walls, I could hear someone saying outside "What's she doing in there?"

Liverpool docks were surrounded by freezing fog. It was now dark and after passing the dock gates the taxi driver dropped me beneath dripping concrete pillars.

"Insurance don't allow me to coom further," he explained, sounding like Paul McCartney.

"Where is the ship?" I asked as I tugged my suitcases to my side.

"You said Molasses didn't you loov? Well this is the area."

Through fuzzy lights I could see two ships moored at the dockside. The fog swirled around as the taxi drove away.

I could not move far from the spot as the suitcases were too heavy, as usual. I had Christmas presents for Tomas and the crew, my writing materials and books Tomas had requested.

"HELLOW!" I yelled.

A torchlight flashed out from the deck of one of the ships, then moved up, along and down, and travelled towards me.

"Meesees Veedeebrand?"

As I followed the Chief Officer through the ship I was taken by the wooden panelling and the strong furniture. Tomas' new company was Danish and the ship had been built in Sweden, a few years ago at least, but it had a certain style. It was old fashioned and it made you feel at home.

Tomas stuck his head around the door with a grin. It was always a good moment to see each other again. "I absolutely have to take a shower," I announced, still with my coat on.

"Hamburg?" I went to the chart table where Tomas had spread the section of the North Sea that showed the entrance into the Elbe, the river leading to Hamburg.

"May be a little ice," said Tomas. "We shall see."

I was thinking of Hamburg at Christmas time. Germany, the original place for Christmas trees. It should be fun to go ashore.

"We won't be there very long," said Tomas. "We may not go ashore. It will depend on the passage up the Elbe. If the temperature drops, we'll have to make a quick turn around."

There were five Yugoslavians on board. One Croatian, two Serbian and two from Montenegro. They received news when they came into port, and if the reception was right, sometimes from the BBC. They were not hostile to each other and as far as I could tell, preferred not to discuss the war in Yugoslavia that had begun that summer. If someone spoke about the latest event, like Vukovar when it surrendered or Dubrovnik being bombed, they shrugged their shoulders, but they were far from indifferent, their faces told another story. There was little they could do. They were miles away. They all had families and they knew each other's fears. Better to talk about something else. They must have been worried day and night.

On the Elbe, an icebreaker had thrust ahead of the ship in front, clearing the way. The ice was thin and slivers floated by in a jigsaw pattern, moving away with the current and the waves from our bow.

Two white swans were gliding around in a swirl of water, in an opening in the ice close to the bank. Snow was lying in patches in the gardens of the houses but the trees were black and bare. Perhaps it was not so cold, and not enough to freeze the Elbe.

The icebreaker seemed to be there as a precaution, or was simply returning to port. If the temperature remained as it was, we would have time to go ashore.

In Wilhelmsburg, the commercial docks in Hamburg, the German Immigration officer looked carefully through the passports and documents. He was reluctant to give shore passes to the Yugoslavians. They would have to stay on board. The unloading was going to take time and the temperature remained above freezing.

"Can we..?" I said, "Just for an hour or two?"

As all the officers were Yugoslavian and couldn't leave the ship there were plenty of qualified crew to look after things. Tomas was persuaded.

Hamburg is a wonderful city. It was the first time I had been there and I was charmed by the frozen Alster in the centre and the skaters zooming around, the elegant buildings and tall church spires.

Off the Monckebergstrasse there were Christmas stalls in a market square. It looked like a film set. The goods for sale were hand crafted wooden toys, pretty china, soft toys and the loveliest Christmas decorations, each one a little piece of art. We stopped at a stall selling Christmas punch. No plastic beakers here, and really hot punch in a small glass with silver holder. The shoppers were dressed in beautifully tailored, long woollen coats and everyone wore a hat, the men in Hombergs or German Apine hats, the women in soft furry shapes. I had never seen so many well-dressed people in a market place. The air was filled with the aroma of fine cigars and gentle perfume.

There was also sauerkraut and sausage that tasted nothing like it had before and live musicians playing accordion and violin, strolling through the market, making people smile. The fresh Christmas trees on sale were bristling with health, and would require a truck to take one home and a mansion to put it in, or perhaps you could put it up in your front garden. It wasn't until later that I understood that we had come by chance to the 'Mayfair' of Hamburg, and the wealthiest part of the city. Afterwards, we whizzed around the Kunsthalle Art Museum and bought two small prints to put up on the walls at Benbuie.

Stanco, the Chief Officer, was pacing up and down the deck and came towards us as we climbed the accommodation ladder, on our return.

"Sir, there is a problem." They walked away and I heard Tomas exclaiming angrily as I went up the stairs. Tomas came up a moment later. He picked up the radio and called for the Boson to come up to the office.

"What's wrong?" I asked, feeling guilty that we had been ashore. Tomas didn't answer.

The Boson was Philippino. "You wanted to see me sir?"

"Who can you trust to send ashore to carry out my instructions to the letter?"

"Well, probably..." he stroked his greying beard. What was going on?

"They have to do exactly as I tell them. Is that understood? Who is on board with a shore pass?"

"Posadas sir, and Tolentino. I have them working on the derrick right now."

"Send them to me."

It seemed that while we were ashore, the First Engineer and the Third Mate had started to have a few drinks together and had decided to go ashore. They were both from Montenegro and spoke the same dialect. There was a small bar on the ship and they had been singing loud folk songs to a tape one of them had brought from home. They had been making so much noise that others had shut the door on them. When Stanco had looked for the Third Officer the steward said he had seen them go ashore. Stanco had searched the ship but others returning on board confirmed that they had seen them in town.

"In the whole of Hamburg they bumped into them?" I asked. "They are probably still on board, sleeping it off somewhere."

The two Able Seamen arrived at the door. They showed Tomas their shore passes.

"You know First Engineer Vadrich and Third Mate Torenchi? You are to go to the Reeperbahn and when you find them you are to get them into a taxi and bring them back to ship."

They both looked a little alarmed at this prospect.

"If they give you any trouble, you can tell them they will be fired. Otherwise I have to call the authorities. They are not allowed to be ashore. You understand? I give them this chance, or they can get arrested. It's up to them."

"What's the Reeperbahn?" I asked Tomas who ignored my question, so I trotted off to talk to the steward, a young Philippino called Arny who walked around in earphones all day singing to himself. Arny had a certain sophisticated city air about him, but when I asked about the Reeperbahn he went to pieces and giggled and fell about like a ten-year-old.

"No, no," he laughed. "No, No ma'am" and shaking his head, he replaced his earphones and went on wiping tables.

I got the picture. I went back to the office. Tomas was stabbing keys at the computer.

"You sure that the two you sent after them will come back themselves?" It was like sending two more wasps into the honey jar.

Tomas continued at the computer.

An hour later the two Able Seamen returned empty handed saying they had looked everywhere but were unable to find them. "We tried every place, but we need entrance money sir."

Tomas was now very angry. "I will have to go myself then!" he shouted.

I had been reading about the Reeperbahn in a tourist leaflet on

Hamburg I had picked up at the art gallery. 'Taboo or not taboo' it said, 'that's not a question on Hamburg's lively colourful Reeperbahn where anything goes on the stages of the famous sex clubs as well as in more private surroundings. The Colibri and the Salambo offer a sex show you will never forget'

It made our visit to the Christmas Fair and Art Museum look tame.

"I shan't offer to come with you," I laughed as Tomas wrestled with what to do next, but Tomas was not to be amused by anything. My sexy husband could be a funny old prude at times. He would not find looking for Vadrich and Torenchi a welcome experience, going in and out of the different shows, looking around at the audience of gawping people while naked perspiring bodies leapt about on the stage. He was saved from the 'ordeal', as through the window came the sound of singing.

We went out onto the deck and looked down on their heads as Vadrich and Torenchi climbed aboard. When they reached the deck, they paused on a long note, in perfect barber's shop harmony. Then something made one of them look up.

When Tomas had been in Brownsville, Texas, recently, he had bought two Transylvanian Naked Neck chickens, two Mallards and an Aylesbury. Alive I should add. There was an old swimming pool on the ship and although it was not fit for human consumption as it were, being rather rusty and unable to be filled, it was possible to have a few inches of water at the bottom. Tomas had gone ashore and found a pet shop. He missed our chickens and ducks at home he said.

I went to see the ducks in the swimming pool. The Transylvanian Naked Necks looked like vultures. They would not have been something that would have tempted me to go to all the trouble that they were to keep on board a ship. They were perched on rickety apple boxes. The ducks in the pool looked happy enough.

"The crew will eat them one day when you're not looking," I said, remembering the dog.

The ducks were well fed. Everyone came to see them and admire their progress.

As we took off into the North Sea again, where it was rather choppy, I went to see how they were doing as their water slopped violently from side to side. They were crouched in their make shift hutch on the poolside, looking remarkably resentful.

"I have to have a hobby or I go mad" Tomas said, fending off criticism with his usual exaggeration. He also tried to grow herbs in trays on the bridge wings, and depending on where the ship was in the world, was mildly successful, to the point sometimes that a small bowl of chopped dill or parsley may arrive on the dinner table, proudly presented as 'the ship's own'.

We were heading back along the Channel, on our way to West Palm Beach, Florida, but first we were to stop in Brest, the most westerly city in France as something was being delivered for the engine department.

"You can get a chic French haircut," I suggested to Tomas whose curly hair was starting to look a bit wild. We would be there for a whole day and no loading or unloading to do.

The something being delivered was going to be installed before we crossed the Atlantic.

Brest is one of France's most important naval ports. The town was full of roving sailors wearing starched white uniforms and very French sailor hats. I rattled around in my head for ancient schoolgirl French and Tomas got his hair done without being given a crew cut.

We strolled around the town. It was breezy and sunny and not raining for once. Brest has a reputation for rain, as it is so exposed to the North Atlantic. There were marvellous pastry shops where your gateau or madeleines would be lovingly wrapped in tissue and presented to you in a beribboned box. Red and blue Breton china was the other attraction, illustrated with eighteenth century Breton figures, the man with fishing rod, the woman with bonnet, holding flowers. Egg cups are always a good thing to buy, as they are small and don't break easily.

We sat in a cafe and ate too many pastries and had, of course, wonderful coffee.

I felt ashamed of my poor French. What is it about the English?

Tomas learnt English as all Swedes do, then Spanish, so he is no help in the shops. The proprietors and I stared across the counters at each other, trying to guess what was in each other's heads. "Oui? Je vous l'emballe? Il n'y a que celui-ci. Madam?"

"Er..."

Brest was almost destroyed in the Second World War, as it became a German naval base when France was occupied. The allies attacked it without mercy, even though it was French. They felt they had no choice. The German U boats sat in wait for merchant ships or struck out directly across the Atlantic at the convoys trying to cross from the States. There is a large monument to the people of Brest close to the harbour.

Back on board, Chief Engineer reported that the repair was almost finished. Within minutes there was a commotion. I heard Tomas shouting, angry. He came rushing in holding one of the Transylvanian Naked Necks. It was dead and covered with oil.

I went with him to the 'swimming pool' which was now almost full with black oily water.

"What on earth has happened?" I asked as we tried to reach the other ducks. They were all dead or dying except for the large white Aylesbury now brown and looking very unwell.

I took him into our cabin, threw off my clothes and put a cotton nightdress on. Then I sat with him in the shower, washing him first with warm, soapy water and then letting cool water run over both of us. I had become used to handling ducks and I could catch geese and put them under my arm. It had really been a case of getting on with it at Benbuie and learning by doing as we lived so far from anyone else.

I decided to call the Aylesbury 'Angus' in honour of Scotland. When I had picked him up, he had put his head under my armpit to hide. The water had not only been full of old oil but salty from the sea. "Come on Angus," I cooed. Tomas put his head around the shower curtain. I was sitting down in a corner of the shower tray, covered in oil myself, but Angus was starting to wriggle.

"The bloody engineers backed up some water into the swimming pool when they were doing the repair," he said angrily, "If it was that bloody Vadrich I will kill him." Vadrich of course, of the Reeperbahn fame.

"Everyone must feel terrible. I'm sure they're sorry about it." I held Angus up to show that he now had his eyes open and was craning his head forward trying to make out what was going on. "We can keep him in the bathroom." I volunteered, not feeling so sure about it but trying to cheer Tomas up. Tomas jumped on to it immediately.

"That's right! You can look after him from now and on. You're very good with birds," he added, giving me a rare compliment just to be encouraging.

Crossing the Atlantic with Angus was not so easy. Ducks make large splotchy toilets everywhere, and when bored with paddling about, will suddenly fly up onto something, not always successfully, flapping and falling about on shelves and things, especially if they have a pinioned wing, as Angus did. The shop had made sure he couldn't fly very far. Poor Angus.

It was company to have Angus trotting about behind me, putting his head on one side and looking up at me as I made the coffee, hoping for a biscuit. It was just a pity that I had to walk about all day with a small bucket of water and a cloth. And when the weather was rough, I leave it to the imagination. A ship is not the place for a live duck.

We knew it was Christmas Eve, but we hadn't a hope of celebrating Christmas. Now we were off the Azores and hoped to get a little lee from the islands, as the weather had not improved for days.

If the cook managed to make sandwiches it would be a miracle, I was thinking, but turkey did appear, cut up and piled on plates and manfully brought up to the bridge by Arny who wasn't wearing his earphones and looked rather pale and panting as if he had climbed Everest.

The next day after a fitful night, rolling around with the movement of the ship, I was tired at the very idea of making an effort for Christmas Day. Tomas was again up on the bridge. "We will postpone for another time," Tomas announced, "I cannot get out of this weather for another day or two. It's a lot worse to go north or south of this."

"Hope there are no hurricanes in Florida."

"This is not a hurricane!" said Tomas indignantly. "It's just a squall compared to what it could be. I've already changed course twice."

"Merry Christmas sir," said Stanco, appearing at the door and walking crab like across to the chart table.

I staggered back down stairs to check on Angus who I had put into a shallow bath, feeling he would be better slopping about in water than injuring his legs trying to stand up on the floor.

The floor was soaking wet, but he was rocking back and forth, making small quacks of slight indignation, but at least OK.

I found the whisky bottle wedged in the corner of a chair in the sitting room, poured a large one without spilling it all, drank it down in one go, and got back into bed.

The gigantic woman Customs Officer was looking sceptical. "We don't allow the import of livestock unless you have a permit for it" she drawled looking from me to Angus who was tucked under my arm, having a bored nibble at the buttons on my shirt.

"But I'm not importing him," I insisted. "He's a pet, he lives on board."

She looked most displeased at this, shifting her large bottom around on the seat, trying to think of a regulation to floor me. We were in West Palm Beach, Florida.

"He could bring disease," she said, turning over papers on the table with long red nails.

Tomas was saying nothing. He was rattling around in his desk drawer and he produced something at last, with an air of triumph.

"There you are," he said. "It's an American duck. It's returning home for a visit."

Giant woman stared down at the receipt.

"You bought these in Brownsville?" she asked, as if it were Bangladesh, not Texas.

"Where are the others?" she asked accusingly. Don't say it, I thought, but he did.

"They all died."

"Oh they DIED. What did they die of?"

"They drowned," said Tomas getting red in the face. I had a horrible feeling that if war was declared between Tomas and Giant Woman, Angus would be taken away. I jumped in.

"They were in the swimming pool and it was rough weather," I said quickly, knowing that to say they had OIL on them was to open another can of peas with American officials.

"Are we going to discuss this all day?" Tomas said peevishly.

Twenty minutes after the port officials had left, Giant Woman lumbered back on board.

I was just about to let Angus have a little walk about the deck and she saw me. "I came back to tell you," she said puffing into my face. "Other ducks in the area may be attracted to come visit your duck. This could spread disease."

"Oh, right," I said, trying hard not to smile and to look concerned.

"You should keep him locked up while you are in port," she said emphatically as I retrieved him and put him back under my arm.

"Oh I will," I said, marching Angus off as he squirted all the way down my skirt. "That's what I get for saving you from being locked up in a Florida jail," I told him as I let him back into the bathroom.

It was starting to smell a bit ducky in there, in spite of the clean floor. I bundled up the shredded paper that served as Angus' bed and went off to search for the cook. He was in touch with the chandler and could ask him for a bag of straw.

There was no one in the kitchen but a lot of noise coming from the stores. Boxes and boxes were being delivered via the crane on deck and Arny, wearing a padded jacket with a hood, was stacking things into the giant cold store. He was still wearing his earphones, as I could hear the faint blast of reggae and a cloud of vapour surrounded his head as his lips moved with the music.

Outside the storehouse door, in a thin singlet, our round-bellied Dutch Indonesian cook was perspiring in the sun, shouting orders to Posadas and Tolentino who were guiding in the net of groceries over our heads. Posadas saw me and smiled. As bystander to the Reeperbahn incident, we had a bond. He nudged Tolentino who also looked around and smiled a greeting. This prompted Jan the cook to get a bit excited until he saw me. It's very easy to feel in the way on board a cargo ship.

"I am looking for some straw for Angus," I said as another assortment of orders landed onto the deck.

"Angus? Who is this?" said Jan.

"The ship's duck," I said, trying not to be proprietorial about it.

Jan was checking the stores. "I no order any duck," he said, his mind understandably on food. The empty net sailed out again, across the ship's side and down to the truck on the dock.

I walked over to where I could be out of range of the crane and called down to the men unloading on the dockside. One was inside the back of the truck, the other with a clipboard.

They looked so very American. Base ball caps of course, tee shirts emblazoned with something strange, shorts and what Americans call sneakers, giant trainers. Sneakers or trainers look to me as if they have been carved out of a piece of car tyre, stuck together and painted white. They are the ugliest of footwear, even on the feet of a nubile young lass.

One of the chandler's men looked up. "Hi. Can I help you Ma'am?" The accent made me feel fond. I had lived and worked in the States for nearly twenty years in several locations and there were many things I missed. The terrific work ethic was one, backed up by a deceptively easy going style, and the polite way of handling things.

"How are you doing?" I said, "I'm looking for some straw. You know, like pet straw? I've got a pet duck on board. Could you get such a thing for me? We'll be in port a couple of days. Oh, and if you happen to pass a pet store, you could pick up some duck food if you see any. I'm not allowed to come ashore you see."

One of them disappeared inside the truck and came out with a bunch of shredded packing paper. "This do in the meantime Ma'am? He said cheerfully. "I'll send it up in the next load."

"Don't know about the duck food," said the one with the clipboard, "But I'll sure give it a try."

"He's getting a little tired of smoked salmon and fillet mignon" I laughed, not knowing if they understood my joke. Angus was of course living on the wonderful leftovers from the crew's lunches and was getting rather fat. I only wanted the duck food for a change for him. He was so spoilt he probably wouldn't touch it.

"Why not you go ashore?" It was Torenchi the third officer, who was unable to go ashore for several ports, and not just because of his indiscretion in Hamburg. The war in Yugoslavia was getting worse by the day.

"Oh I can go ashore. I even have a green card. I have to stay with Angus for one thing. But also because Florida is not my most favourite place in the world."

"Dangerous," said Torenchi, perhaps comforted at the thought. "Many sailor get robbed."

"Not everywhere. But perhaps in the places you like to go," I said cheekily.

He laughed, his mouth wide. "You no tell my girlfriend," he said.

A few hours later, the Chandler himself came on board to the ship's office to settle the invoices. Jan the cook was there and the lists were checked before Tomas handed over the money. Most purchases are made in cash on the ship, always in American dollars and this is why people are tempted to get on board. The ship has to carry cash.

I was making the usual coffee all round, when one of the men from the truck came in, weighed down with two enormous sacks.

"What is this?" said Tomas annoyed, thinking groceries were being delivered to his office.

"It must be for Angus. Is it"? One sack of fine sweet smelling straw, the other a huge bag of best dog food.

They waved off any payment for them. I took them to see Angus in the bathroom, who had been getting rather lonely and feeling restricted and was attacking anything he could with his remarkably tough beak. Most of the doors and fittings on a ship are steel but Angus had managed to find the plastic toilet brush. He loved the straw and made great fusses with it, spreading it around and piling it up in a corner, a piece at a time.

It was that, plus the warm weather, that probably accounted for it. The next morning I went down to the mess room where Tomas was at breakfast and opened my hands to him to show him the very large egg.

"Where did you get that? No!" he said, realising immediately.

"Angus is an Angela," I said. "Its the colouring. I've never had a domestic duck before. You know our half wild bunch at home, you can always tell who is what. I'm taking it back now."

"Don't do that! I'll have it for breakfast."

"You will do no such thing!" I said indignantly

"But it isn't fertilised. She'll just sit on it and make it hard boiled or something or it will go bad, you know how it is."

I turned on my heels and went back upstairs. The egg had made me sad. I popped the egg back under the straw. Angus/Angela took no notice of it and was now ready for her breakfast.

I was making a cardboard box ready when Tomas came back up.

"What are you doing?" A tear fell into the box.

"We can't keep her like this. It isn't fair. She should be with other ducks and free to roam."

"You're right of course. But what can we do?" Tomas was already preoccupied.

"I already phoned the chandler. I got the number from his card on your desk. He happens to know someone who has ducks. He's going to take me over there."

"But we're sailing by noon. You can't go ashore now!"

"I'll be back. I can't just hand her over. I want to see she's OK."

The chandler was late coming for me than expected and I left under a cloud. It was ten forty five and Tomas hated tight margins. I couldn't reassure him as I didn't know where we were going and the chandler simply said it wasn't far. I made large holes in the box and strapped it down. Angela was making her protests but settled down once we were in the car, probably petrified. Her egg of course had been included.

We swung out onto a freeway and drove for what seemed miles. The chandler chatted away but I was too fraught to be company. The radio played sad country songs and I certainly felt blue. As usual they were all about someone going away.

I was disconcerted when we turned into what was a very poor part of the country. We drove down dirt track streets passing tumble down houses where broken cars decorated the front yards. At the end of the road, we bumped across a field. I looked at my watch. It was now eleven twenty. I was going to miss the ship. We stopped outside an old wooden farmhouse that had seen better days. I could see the ducks, they were all around, chickens as well. I waited in the car.

The chandler went around the side of the house and re appeared with an elderly black lady in a flowery print dress that she wore over large wellington boots. I got out of the car.

"My name is Esmeralda," she said, "Understand you brought me a new resident."

I took the box out of the car and Esmeralda took me to the back of the house and showed me the pond. It had been paddled a bit around the edges but the surrounding mature shrubs and trees provided shade from the glaring sun. I couldn't rush things. I resigned myself to missing the ship, a plan forming in my head that I would take a flight to the next port.

"How long have you lived here?" I asked her.

"All my life," she answered. "Had twelve children in this house. Now I got babies again." The ducks and chickens ran around her feet and pecked about under the trees. They looked in the best of condition. Esmeralda and I looked into each other's eyes. You can always tell someone who really likes animals. There was peace in the garden.

"I just love them all," she said, telling me their names. "You say the duck was on your ship?"

It was a bit hard to believe. I couldn't begin to explain. I told her how we had thought it was a boy until the egg incident.

"Hard to sex when they is young. But I can do it. They bring me there'n from around the neighbourhood. I'm usually right."

I took Angela out of the box and set her down in the garden. "Oh, she been clipped, I see that," Esmeralda observed immediately.

226

"That'll grow in. Don't like to clip myself." Obviously we had a lot in common. I could have stayed there all day.

"Sure you don't want something cold to drink?" she asked as I went back to the car.

I explained why I had to get back. Angela had already found the pond and was having a grand wash with a lot of splashing about. We unloaded the dog food and straw into a shed.

As we drove back I wasn't feeling sad at all but now we were on our way, I had my heart in my mouth to see if the ship's funnel was sticking up between the cranes in the dock.

"If the ship has left, I can drop you off at the agent's office," said the kind chandler. It was twenty minutes past twelve, but oh joy, the ship was still there. I expected the accommodation ladder to be up, but it was still down. I ran up at speed, then on to the bridge office, my heart crashing in my chest. Tomas was still there typing on the computer. I rushed in breathing heavily.

"Get on alright?" he asked, his eyes on the screen.

"Aren't we leaving? I thought you were leaving at noon?"

"No. Not until thirteen thirty"

"But you said..."

"I knew you'd be late. Put the coffee on will you?"

We were sailing into the Gulf of Mexico and Cuba was on our port side, many miles away, but out there. I leant on the chart table, my legs spread like a giraffe, looking down at the map. I could see by the course marked on the chart that we were through the Straits of Florida now, and as we came out into the Gulf we were swinging to and fro again. I was happy to think of Angus/Angela back in Florida with Esmeralda and not sliding along the bathroom floor. Loaded with molasses once again, we were off to deliver it to the Yucatan, an exciting part of Mexico that I had not visited before. When I lived in the States I had worked and travelled in Mexico but only on the border. The Yucatan is an unexpected part of Mexico, a peninsular as far away from Tijuana on the California border, as Los Angeles is from New York.

Our port of call was Progreso. I looked at the note clipped above the table. It was the list of requirements for the port.

7 copies of crew list, visaed by Mexican Consulate
6 copies of Ship's Stores List
6 copies of Personal Effects Declaration
6 copies of Bills of Lading
Clearance from last Port
Derat Certificate (Rats? I didn't know we had rats!)
Tonnage Certificate
Safety Certificates
Loading Plan
Stability Calculations
Other notes. Safe drinking water available.
Shore leave: No restrictions.
(No restrictions? Torenchi and Vadrich would be pleased.)

We had to wait offshore as it was too windy and other ships were swinging around. A lovely old German Passenger Liner with traditional tubular funnels came steaming by, probably built in the 1960's, looking like a picture in an old storybook

Everything around was a dazzling blue, the sky, the sea, and even the shoreline was a misty blue. From the ship's rails I could make out a line of white sand on the shore.

My first view of Progreso was of a huge reclining figure of Chac-Mool, the Mayan god of rain, seated with head turned towards the sea with knees bent and the sacrificial bowl waiting in his lap. We moored along the dock not far away.

The sculpture of Chac-Mool prompted my immediate enquiry to the Mexican agent. Yes, there were Mayan ruins not so very far away. We would have to go to Merida, the White City, some thirty-two kilometres, and from there a journey of perhaps another hour.

"Forget it," said Tomas. "It will take too long."

We consoled ourselves with removing our hot leather boots and walked along the glorious white sands close to the ship, wriggling our toes in the warmth. We walked for about three miles, right along the beach, passing families at play, the palm trees rustling overhead. One or two white sunburnt men ran by, but there were few tourists and the place had a lovely natural feeling. We stopped at a stall, attracted by the rows of stuffed cloth Toucans swinging in the breeze. Tomas bought the largest. A compensation for the loss of Angus. It still hangs in our kitchen. We call him 'Mr Progreso'.

When we returned to the ship, we felt relaxed and cheerful. The agent was waiting and smiled as we came on board still holding our boots, then quickly looked concerned as I brushed sand from my dress.

"You have not walked along the beach?" he said, his brown eyes bulging. "Without the shoes?"

"Why?" Come to think of it I had noticed that even the children on the beach wore shoes and the joggers were wearing trainers even though the sand was fine and soft. He then explained in detail about a creature, a kind of urchin that was in the sand, or was it a crab, he had difficulty translating what it was.

"If this bite your foot, you die in fifteen minutes."

Well, ignorance can be bliss.

'As slow as molasses?' I was thinking of this with pleasure waiting for the mini bus to pick us up. Our cargo was being delivered into individual trucks which to begin with was a very slow way to unload, plus the trucks were not arriving on time and the waiting in between made it look as if the whole thing was going to take at least five days. There was a question of the molasses being the right temperature to flow, and all this meant that I was able to ask Tomas to hire a mini bus to take us into the jungle.

It was possibly a once in a lifetime opportunity, I argued, and the crew had now had two days of being able to be ashore for the odd hour or two and were smiling more, so could we?

Many of the crew waved from the ship. I was wondering how many senoritas were going to be climbing aboard as soon as our van was around the first corner.

Tomas was chatting away to the driver in Spanish as we sped along. You miss green when you are at sea for days. It was lovely to be whizzing by tropical trees and flowering bushes, even though the journey was long. We stopped in Merida and walked about for awhile to look at the lovely buildings, the fine Yucatan University and the marvellous Cathedral. It lived up to its name as The White City. Purple bougainvillaea and bright yellow flowers fell over the white walls. The streets were swept and the palm trees cared for.

We talked about wanting to go back and stay there one day.

On we went into thicker jungle. We were visiting the nearest archaeological site, Uxmal, city of the plumed serpent. It was still early in the morning, we had set off at six, and the site was just opening when we arrived. This we found out later was a very good idea, although we had chosen to go early because of getting back to the ship, we almost had the place to ourselves, which increased the sense of wonder.

Ci-u-than means 'we don't understand each other', words that were probably said to the first conquistadors. The name stuck, becoming Yucatan. It's well known that the Mayan culture was absorbed, you could say destroyed, by the Spanish conquest. Friars and priests were petitioned by Philip the Second, and a Spanish historian wrote 'Report on Idolatrous Cultures' in 1688. Much can be understood from walking through the ruined cities. The guidebooks were helpful but they gave the facts and could not prepare you for the atmosphere. I wanted to put the books away and simply think about it all and get back to the books later when I had left. Photographs cannot give you the magic of actually seeing. How marvellous it was to be there, among the carved jaguars, snakes and eagles.

We walked silently around the buildings, really in awe, thinking of the population of some twenty thousand who lived in Uxmal and of their struggle to grow their maize in that dry place.

There are, and were, no rivers or streams, the only water supply was rain. They built water cisterns and dug deeper and deeper wells but in this area of limestone much was lost. The people looked to the priests who studied the stars and a calendar was made. The divine, the magical, had to be the answer, and there was nothing more terrifying and powerful to offer than a living human sacrifice. The still beating heart was placed in the bowl in the lap of the rain god. Surely this would make it rain so our chillies and avocados can grow, they prayed.

We walked up the staircase of the Soothsayer's Building to the top, well over a hundred feet high, looking out over the many other ruins and the jungle beyond. The opening to the temple at the top of the steps, surrounded by the geometrical artwork that decorates all the buildings, was where the priests emerged to speak to the crowds waiting below. The priests were called 'Chilam', meaning interpreter. They were the ones who were able to tell the people the messages that came from Chac-Mool the rain god, and the stars over their heads.

As we were leaving, several coaches pulled up outside and people poured out and through the doors of the reception area. We felt very lucky to have been so early.

On the way home, the driver understood from Tomas that we didn't want to visit a fancy restaurant and he took us to his friend's cafe off the main jungle road. The chicken was very tough, I think it had been running about in their yard for years, but the company, tequila and beer were local. What did we care about tough chicken. It was wonderful to be there and we had had a very special day.

Houston is about fifty-one miles from Galveston Bay and the sea. Before I went to sea, I had no idea that Houston was a port, it's so far inland, and that's what it's called, an Inland Port, made possible by man made channels and waterways. Before, I had associated it with land based 'Houston Control' of space fame, the command post for astronauts in flight, and for oil and all those other Texas things, like cattle. The port is huge and very busy.

We were crossing from Progreso to Houston to load our empty ship with soybean oil. There was a great deal of washing off of the residue of molasses to make way for the new cargo and the weather was still rough in the Gulf of Mexico as it was when we crossed from Florida.

There was also a lot of paper work and checking of things, especially safety features and the garbage and stores. I understood why Jan, the cook, had been preoccupied in Florida. The US is very strict. 'Residue of food stuffs purchased outside the continental limits of the United States must be picked up by a transporter that has been authorised by the Ministry of Agriculture" You have to be careful about the garbage, pollution, regulations and immigration, and that everything that is supposed to work, works. On an old ship that's not so easy.

In the swerving swaying ship everyone was busy preparing for arrival, running to and fro from the copy machine, which Tomas said was the most important crew member on board as without it, you couldn't go into port, as everyone wanted so many copies.

In the rough weather, I was trying to pack and kept bruising my arms and legs. I was leaving in Houston, a convenient port for me to fly back to the UK.

Tomas kept hearing stuff rattling about on the ship and sent crew to look into the cupboards to check if anything was loose. He was getting a bit irrational about it in my opinion.

Between the papers flying about and my half open suitcases falling off the bed we were in a terrible frame of mind with each other by the time we started up the channel to Houston.

Then began the miles of smells. Oil, Natural Gas, Sulphur, Lime, Ammonia, Petrochemicals and every other kind of chemical.

Through the gloom and the stench I watched America's wealth go by the window.

"How can they be so fussy about everything," I protested. "Look down into this water!"

It was a memorable journey. Since then, I got to know ships that did this run on a regular basis, Chemical Tankers for example, and all I can say is, the crew earn every penny they get.

When we arrived, Tomas was so harassed by one thing or another, that we hardly had time to say goodbye before the All-American taxi whooshed me away to the airport.

On the plane I looked down to see if we would fly over the ship, but now it was a world away, as we plunged upwards into the clouds.

When I got home, there was a long message on the end of all the other calls. It was Tomas going on and on for about half an hour about the Customs and Excise and everything else that had happened since I had left. He didn't say anything about missing me but I think that was what the phone call was about.

Autumn in the glen

CHAPTER 12

CUBA   THE CARIBBEAN   URUGUAY   RIO DE LA PLATA
ARGENTINA

"It's walking distance from the station," said Peter on the telephone from London. "I'll meet you under the clock." I had been talking to my brother about joining the ship in Cuba. This was before it was usual to see it listed as a resort or was advertised by travel agents to any great degree. It was still a land behind the iron curtain, although the curtain was coming down. I had read recently that 'Old Havana' was being restored and there was a new policy to encourage tourism, and as Tomas was going to be in port, I had been thinking about trying to get a visa at the Cuban Consul in London, something you had to do in person at that time.

"It will be OK" said Tomas simply, speaking over the ship's phone from off the Azores in the middle of the Atlantic. He always made things sound so easy. "Then we are going to Argentina, a long trip." And expensive flight, I was thinking. The company didn't pay for me to join ship, and my travel expenses were higher every year. I would try to fly to Cuba.

I enquired about flights. There was a flight that was direct and inexpensive, a charter, which left from somewhere in South East England. It took Cuban nationals and business people, but the flights were scheduled when they had a full plane. This was too unreliable although sounding very exciting and interesting, conjuring up propellers whirling in the fog and someone saying "Here's looking at you kid." I would save money but could miss the ship.

So, it would be Heathrow to Madrid, then the Dominican Republic, where another connection would take me to Havana. However, first I would take a day trip to London to see about a visa.

It was always jolly to see Peter. He showed me Grape Street in the A to Z and we went off to have our mini adventure. Cuba seemed very exotic and out of reach. We didn't know anyone who had been there, and because of all my years in the States, it seemed more out of bounds than it might.

We walked up and down Grape Street without seeing anything that looked like a Consul or an Embassy. Dustbins and litter were piled around and the street had a Dickensian air about it, as if someone would come around the corner rubbing their hands in fingerless gloves wearing a top hat.

"Number nineteen," I said, looking up at the plastic numbers. It had to be it. It looked like a secret office building, featureless and rather soiled by London dirt.

I spoke into the grill at the door. "Is this...?" The door clicked open, which made Peter and me giggle.

A passageway, no one about. Peter pointed at the large white rectangles along the walls, where previously pictures had hung.

"They've taken down Khrushchev and Gorbachev and are waiting for Yeltsin's portrait to come in," he whispered.

"No Fidel?" I pondered. Perhaps they were decorating or didn't want to frighten the tourists. A small waiting room, reception desk and an unseen office beyond a barrier.

I explained to the clerk about joining my husband's ship and gave them every paper I had been able to muster, including my passport and birth certificate.

We sat at the small coffee table. There were three small brochures about Cuba and simple advertising for tourists, with the usual palm tree on a beach but not a lot of information.

At the end of an hour, I was called to the reception and without ceremony, given a visa.

"Well that was painless," I said as we went off to lunch.

"If you have any problem when you arrive," said the nice English businessman seated next to me on the plane, "You can let me know. I travel here quite a bit. They can be a bit difficult."

I thanked him and explained that the shipping agents were going to be at the barrier and it would probably be alright. I had purchased a one way ticket again. It was a risk, but why pay double when I was joining the ship? The difference in the cost was enormous, but my experience in Karachi should have warned me. He said he would wait and just see that I had got through Immigration alright. Very chivalrous. He could speak Spanish. "They rarely speak English," he added.

The Dominican Republic had looked dark and tropical and appeared a bit sinister. We landed there to change planes for Havana. The high winds and heavy rain had caused an almost complete blackout on the island. We had a bumpy landing. The airport lights were flickering and dim.

Havana airport at that time, was if anything more dark, sinister and tropical. The humidity and heat hit you and stayed with you inside the terminal, which had no air conditioning. It was ten o'clock in the evening and the place was packed. I got in line, wondering if I would see my luggage again, imagining it back in Madrid or on its way to the Falkland Islands.

The desk in front of me was high, like a pulpit. The man in the beige uniform was looking at me but one of his eyes wasn't, which was disconcerting. He did speak some English.

"No," he said sharply. "No. No good."

I explained. Ship. Husband Captain. Cuban agent to meet me etcetera.

"No!" he said. Then something in rapid Spanish to the person behind me who stepped forward. He must have said next please. Was that it? Was I supposed to get back on a plane and return from whence I came? I looked around for the Englishman and saw him at the back of another long line. What about my luggage, perhaps now being removed by curious hands and spirited away?

Perhaps Tomas had been delayed and wasn't even in port yet. I thought of the high winds as we landed in the Dominican Republic.

Another official passed by and I caught his arm and tried to explain what I was doing there. He simply said "Hmmm" and moved on. At least they weren't arresting me. I stood waiting while the rest of the passengers went through the barrier ahead of me.

I looked up as someone was shouting. A Cuban woman, small and slight, was running along the back behind the officials, carrying a black and white photocopy of a photograph of me that I had given Tomas years ago when we lived in California. Having got fatter and older since then, I didn't like him to have it as I felt when he saw me again it would be a bit of a shock that I didn't look like that anymore. Apparently he had put it back in his case. It was strange to see it suddenly like that, flying around above everyone's heads as she waved it in the air. I was also thinking she wouldn't recognise me but her eye caught mine and she called out. "Hill! Hill!"

She was very bossy with the man with a wall eye, presenting my photo and other papers and soon I was through the barrier. "You have good journey Hill?" she said cheerily. She was the shipping agent. Her assistant found my bags and out we went to a large and very ancient limousine which sagged as we climbed inside and smelt heavily of cigarettes.

"Have to go places," she explained as she bounced along the pot holed roads in the semi darkness.

"Is the ship here?"

"Oh yes ship here. Captain gave me photo," she laughed. Of course, how stupid of me.

Along dark streets with the occasional light streaming out from one of the flat roofed cement houses. Skinny dogs crossing in the car lights.

We pulled up at a large building. A soldier was silhouetted leaning in the doorway, a rifle slung over his shoulder, a naked light bulb over his head.

We went in at speed. The agent did everything at the double, perhaps they were closing, or? "Is the ship leaving tonight?" I asked, as it occurred to me.

"Oh no, not until tomorrow afternoon," she laughed as we ran up wide stairs and into an office.

There were more men in brown uniforms. They looked at me suspiciously while the agent spoke in rapid Spanish to them. Then one pulled out a state of the art ancient typewriter, the sort with high metal keys that you have to stab at. I remembered my aunt having one, and how I had broken all my nails trying to type on it one day as a teenager.

The typing began, a two finger operation that went on for ever. Then the paper was given to the agent and off we went again.

I thought we were going to the ship, but no. Another administration building, more papers and talk. I suppose they didn't get too many wives joining ships at that time but I was almost falling down with tiredness. It was already three hours since I had landed.

In just two or three years from this time everything changed and the tourist boom began in Cuba, but then they were just getting used to the idea, after decades of sanctions by the United States.

It was one thirty in the morning when I arrived at last, at the ship. The same ship I had left in Houston, many months ago. I was exhausted, but once on board, the adrenaline started up again, as news from home was required, requested items and presents were fished out of the suitcases. My brother had gone to the Yugoslavian Embassy and bought newspapers in Serbo-Croat for the Chief Engineer and officers on board. It brought grim news, but they were grateful to get them, as they could read about football in the sports pages, and it was news from home.

"I have a surprise for you," Tomas said, and took me up to the bridge. There was a make shift bird stand about two metres tall and sitting on the top was a large Buzzard, the size of a young eagle.

"He came on board from a storm. Blew onto the deck and was so waterlogged he couldn't fly. I think his wing is a bit injured as well, but not broken. He needs to recover, so we're putting him up for awhile."

He was simply beautiful. But of course I looked a bit scathing. Another problem, like Angus. Tomas had attached a strong piece of line to his leg with a long length so he could still fly around, like a falcon from a perch. "He's eating well, bits of raw meat, but I can't get him to drink any water yet."

"He must wonder where on earth he is," I said, thinking, here we go again.

"I've got a parrot as well," said Tomas removing the cloth from a cage that was hanging over head. A small green parrot woke up and squawked at us.

"The Russians gave him to me, so I call him Nikolai, but he's very bad tempered. He bites people."

"So would you if I put you in a cage. Oh Tomas you know I can't bear birds in cages and he might be an endangered species."

"This is my fault? I met these Russians from another ship. He wasn't in such good shape as he is now. I've looked after him. I bought him a cuttle fish even, but he still bites me, don't you, you little bastard? The Russians were signing off, they couldn't take him on the plane."

"Oh, I see," I said, sarcastically.

"We will worry about that when the time comes," said Tomas, "Now we need to have a drink."

It was now four in the morning. Tomas produced something lethal, syrupy and South American, made from cane sugar and I was instantly in another world, mellow and smiley and feeling very pleased that I had made the journey.

"It's all arranged," said Tomas enthusiastically. "I even did a scout myself with the agent today to see if it was alright. We are going to have a small tour and go to a good restaurant for lunch tomorrow."

"Oh lovely," I said peeling off my shoes at last. "What time is he coming?"

"About eight in the morning, before it gets too hot." (Groan.)

I had decided to be very Havana when I had packed my suitcase in Scotland and was now wearing the pastel striped linen skirt, the cream linen blazer and one of the real Panama's that Tomas had brought back from Ecuador one day.

I could hear the agent talking to Tomas in the sitting room and I was late getting ready, having had almost no sleep at all.

"We are waiting," said Tomas in a pseudo cheery voice for the benefit of the agent but I knew he was getting crabby at having to hang around. I grabbed my bag and appeared.

"You look very nice," said Tomas, beaming with pride.

I think I was still a little high from the sugar cane liquor. Everywhere we went, I was floating around, smiling like the Mona Lisa, in and out of pillared buildings, between potted palms, as if I was on my honeymoon. I walked around the Palacio de los Capitaines Generales in a trance. The old colonial terraces and walkways were breezy and cool, sunshine slanting in.

There was a tiny stall in the corner of a church. They were selling small decorated mirrors, the frames were highly coloured curvy shapes and I chose two of different colours as presents for the daughters. There were several small Che Guevara badges with the famous photograph and I also bought one of those, popping everything into my handbag.

"This very famous restaurant," said the agent, pulling up in a side street.

"Hemingway used to come here," Tomas explained.

The people on the street were not used to so many visitors then. They stopped and stared at us as we went into the restaurant. The agent came to look after us, and to have lunch.

The restaurant was charming, not very large, with a bar as you came into the door and small tables arranged under arched white walls. It was very Man in Havana but everyone in the place seemed to be Cuban at that time.

"We like to have real Cuban food," said Tomas to the waiter in Spanish and along came fried plantains, black beans and rice. Delicious.

Cold beer all round and the musicians turned up in no time.

"Yo soy el punto Cubano," they sang around the table. The guitarists were excellent.

This was it, I decided. If I go through hell and high water, it's worth it for moments like this.

Now the musicians were singing something romantic and dreamy. It was so wonderful it was almost embarrassing to feel that good.

We paid the bill and I felt for my handbag.

I was seated against a wall and an open archway into the next room. There was a table quite close to ours. An exotic woman wearing a fitted dress and turban in vibrant colour had been sitting there. She was unusual to look at. Her eyebrows were drawn with a thick black pencil. The man who accompanied her turned to look at us several times during our lunch. I suppose we looked a bit soppy, we were enjoying ourselves so much but I had caught her eye once or twice and then had not looked back as she gave me such an intense look.

"My bag is missing," I said. We all looked under the table. I had placed the bag next to my ankle, against the wall.

Tomas summoned the manager. "There were two people sitting there," he said. A lot of heated Spanish was exchanged between them.

"I saw that woman looking for something under her table," said Tomas to me, "As a matter of fact I was going to mention it to you to help her, but you were so busy enjoying the music. They must have stolen it. What did you have in it?"

Oh what a question. Whenever I get on board ship after travelling, my passport goes with the others on board in a box inside the safe. I also transfer any valuables, especially money.

Having arrived so late, and rushing out that morning, I had simply picked up my travel handbag with everything in it. I wanted to burst into tears.

"Passport, about three hundred dollars in cash, all my credit cards, the gifts I just bought…"

"Good God," said Tomas, turning on the agent and demanding he send for the police.

"We'll never get it back," I said to Tomas. "They got a real bonus when they stole my bag."

"What do you mean?"

"My American green card. It must be worth a lot of money here."

A police car pulled up outside and Tomas went out to speak to them.

The whole street was hanging from the balconies and lolling in the doorways.

The manager told the police that he knew the man who had been seated at the table. He told the police where to find him. They roared off. At another time they may not have cared so much, but this was the new Cuba and they wanted to encourage tourists to come and spend their money without being afraid of being robbed.

The agent's eyes were rolling in his head. "Give me a gun and I will go after him," Tomas was saying to him. I was devastated to lose my green card, almost impossible to replace as I was no longer living in the States.

The police screeched back. They had gone to the man's house, they said, (Tomas translating to me) but the man's WIFE had said he was at work. They went to his work and were told that he had taken a couple of days off. He was running around.

"We will return your bag, madam," they said and saluted. But I had little hope of it.

Back on the ship, we realised what this meant. I would have no legal papers when we came to the next ports. "Never mind," said Tomas. "You stay on board anyway." But I knew this would create a huge problem for Tomas. We were not in Europe. We were going to Argentina and from there through the Straits of Magellan, Terra Del Fuego at the tip of South America and from there to Chile and more of a problem, Colombia. Tomas would be bribed all the way and I could get asked to go ashore. It would, at the very least, cost us a lot of money and be an extra worry for Tomas that he could do without. He would be vulnerable to the future authorities, I had nothing to prove I was his wife, or who I was even.

I telephoned Peter and his mild "Oh dear" was at least comforting after the trouble I had put him through to get the visa just a week ago. He said he would phone everyone and cancel the cards. "I'll let the American Embassy know about your green card," he added helpfully. I was glad for that.

I didn't want anyone to be able to use my stolen card. It would probably sell in Cuba for a few hundred dollars at least.

What a sudden and sad end to a romantic day. Officials and police came on board to discuss it, and to make a lengthy report, but no handbag or contents were found.

I went up stairs to the bridge to visit the birds and make coffee. When I was standing at the machine, the buzzard took off and flew onto my shoulder. I was too tired and miserable to be phased by this.

His wing span was over three feet and he was about two feet high. He balanced around on my shoulder and I moved along the counter making coffee, ignoring him, to see what he would do. He was a bit wobbly, but he stayed there.

I could see his thin fine black talons curved over my shoulder out of the corner of my eye. What had made him take off like that? Of course, the water. I poured some water into a glass and held it out to him without looking at him and he started to drink immediately.

"You managed to get him to drink?" Tomas said, coming in. "He wouldn't drink before."

"It's the glass. Did you try with a china cup? He needs to see the water reflecting, like in a stream. He's wild after all."

"Is he hurting you?" Tomas was looking at the talons on my shoulder.

"No. He just flew over when I started to make some espresso, but I'll have to borrow some workmen's gloves to handle him if he's going to do this."

"You must stay on board. You have to look after Espresso here."

So Espresso got his name.

When he had finished drinking, he flew back to his perch and had a little preen.

Tomas closed the doors to the bridge wings and let Nikolai out of his cage for a fly around. The little parrot went immediately over to Espresso and started to attack him.

The giant buzzard just looked at him in alarm, side stepping away from him along his perch.

Espresso could have killed Nikolai in an instant, but the parrot was outside his experience. He couldn't make out what this little biting creature was at all.

"He's the one you need gloves for," cried Tomas as he went to put Nikolai back in the cage and the biting was transferred to Tomas's bare hand.

In the late afternoon we took off for the other side of Cuba, for the port of Santiago de Cuba on the south east side of the island.

We had made a kind of plan, that I would travel with the ship until Argentina, and go to the British Embassy in Buenos Aires to try to get a temporary passport. How long it would take, we had no idea, but in the meantime we would have almost two weeks together.

When we arrived in Santiago de Cuba I had asked one of the Able Seamen to transfer the perch and I brought Espresso down into the sitting room, leaving Nikolai to lord it over the bridge.

The big bird had become used to me and would let me give him food and water. I thought it was better if Espresso and Nikolai were apart. Nikolai had a tendency to keep attacking Espresso when he was let out of his cage for his exercise.

Tomas had filled the sitting room with many tropical plants, even a small banana plant in a large pot, and I thought the greenery would make Espresso feel more at home.

This decision gave me one of those memorable images. On that ship, the office was off our sitting room, both rooms were large, as it was an old ship, and comfortably furnished so there was no feeling of being cramped, but it did mean that when we were in port, our sitting room ended up as part of the overflow and was filled with heavy cigarette smoke. In Cuba, that was cigar smoke of course.

I was not up on the bridge wing when we came into port, as when the ship turned around to dock, the stench that came up from the mud in the bay was indescribable.

About twelve officials came on board, the Cubans were very polite and friendly but what with the cigar smoke and the smell from the mud, I pushed our door between the office and sitting room shut.

I was busying about and Espresso decided to do one of his swoops around the room just as the door swung open again. Twelve heads shot up from the big table as the huge bird flew into the office and then back to the sitting room, landing, as became usual, on my shoulder.

I glanced back at the door to see a doorway full of faces, all with their mouths and eyes wide open. If they had seen him to begin with when they came into the room, they might have been less astonished, but it was as if Dracula had just flown by. They continued to stare in at the door. Espresso flapped his wings trying to keep on my shoulder, his wing had lost some crucial feathers, and his balance was a bit off. I felt like a sorceress, it was quite an effect.

'Espresso'

I had brought Tomas a new cassette player and radio on board when I came, with fairly decent speakers for its size, and as we sailed through the Caribbean, passing St Lucia's lush green mountains, we played The Planet Suite and Sibelius' Finlandia and other extravagant music, out on the bridge wing at full blast. The weather was perfect and I could understand why the Caribbean was considered to be a dream place for a holiday.

The barbecue out on deck at sunset was memorable against the backdrop of an orange and golden sky. What a difference good weather makes to everything. Everyone was in good mood and full of suggestions of how and what to cook. There was no karaoke on that ship so either we played people's favourite music or someone played the guitar.

Torenchi and Vadrich were still on board, they were not in a hurry to go home to the war. They brought a couple of sticky cassettes to insert into the machine and burst forth into unintelligible song. We had no idea what they were singing about of course, it could have been anarchy, the engineer's daughter or Scarborough Fair type ballads, but they sang well and with rehearsed harmony. The Philippino crew enjoyed it, and responded, when they got a chance, with a song of their own in Tagalog.

Its a long way down the eastern coast of South America. Each morning I went up to the bridge to look at the lines drawn on the chart as we inched down past Brazil.

What a massive piece of the world it is. I was interested to see Argentina, but as this would be a getting off point for me, feeling sad and also angry with the people who stole my handbag.

Argentina has nostalgic memories for Tomas. It was the first place he sailed to when he was fifteen and went to sea. A local shipowner had called him and another friend and they had said why not? Tomas had lived in a small farm on the shores of Lake Vanern, on a small peninsular called Kallandso and had rarely been to the city. Life at sea and Argentina had been a revelation to him. He fell in love with the music, the guitar and the tango and I am sure the ladies, although he isn't too talkative about that part, not to me in any case.

How exciting it must have been for him at that age.

He enjoyed the Argentinean musician's skill and their unabashed straight out way of singing the most heart touching ballads. Romantic, but not sentimental. Genuine music, he would say.

It was a great adventure for a boy and the traditional way to learn about handling ships and the sea. You were just there having to get on with it, mixing with sometimes rough characters and learning as you went along. Then ashore with years at Navigational school and back to sea as a Third Mate to start the climb up the ladder.

I had started whale watching for a couple of days and ran up the steps at a shout from the Boson who had been repairing one of the cranes.

What a thrill to see that giant tail lifting up in the water and then the massive body, curving away, then around and up and then the dive, the tail up and then slipping straight down into the sea. We were out of the dazzling blue and into the fiercer seas of the South Atlantic now, the twirling grey green and dashing waves of something deeper, wider, where whales had the freedom to dive deep, and roam for miles away from ships and men.

As we saw the lights of Montevideo at the entrance to the Rio de la Plata, Tomas told me he had received a telex. There was to be a change of plan. We were not going to Buenos Aires any longer, but up the river to Rosario. And that was not all. First we would be going across to the north bank, to Uruguay. All very exciting, but what about my passport?

"We will manage," was all Tomas would say. "South Americans are negotiable."

It was enough for the Uruguayan official to read the Havana police report. He rapidly skimmed the two pages of Spanish and nodded. "Aqui esta la confirmacio Capitain."

He was tall, with dark, slicked back hair and pale, almost white skin. He had old fashioned manners, and bowed to me slightly before presenting me with a shore pass.

A shore pass! I understood he had explained to Tomas that I must be in his company if I went ashore. I was grateful to him for having common sense on the matter and went away to decide what I was going to wear to go to lunch. The wind whipping around the ship was quite chilly. It was their autumn. I hadn't thought about it. We had sailed so far south and were now in the Southern Hemisphere, and like Australia, the climate was the direct opposite to Europe.

I had thought when Tomas said, that South Americans were negotiable, that he meant we would have to pay money, but what he had actually meant was that they had their own interpretation of the rules and used their judgement instead of always sticking to the law. This was one of the things Tomas liked about South America. He had told me a story about a friend who had decided to hire a car to drive through the Pampas for a few days holiday when he left the ship.

Not too surprisingly, he was held up on the road and robbed. The banditos were curious about him, and sat down at the side of the road to talk to him, although they didn't speak any Swedish or English. The Swede spoke a little Spanish and soon the bottle of Absolut and the six beers that he had in the car boot, were passed around. The banditos pointed out the land around and talked rapidly, most of which the Swede did not understand at all, but there was a lot of laughter about it, and after an hour they were all a bit drunk. One of the banditos produced a small bandoñon from his saddle bag and sang a wistful song. Then they divided the 'spoils'. He got back a fifth of what he had actually brought with him.

They allowed him to keep the car as they had their horses, but they did strip it of it's mirrors and anything else that they found removable.

La Republica Oriental Del Uruguay has low flat pastureland and mostly sheep and cattle. It reminded me of certain parts of Texas and was dry and dusty. We were docked up river where the Rio de la Plata meets the Rio Uruguay, at a small town called Nueva Palmira. The streets were wind swept and the trees bare. Perhaps as it was Autumn I was seeing it at the least attractive time. The houses were flat roofed, square cement boxes with scrappy grass in the front gardens. Behind the wire fencing that separated the properties chickens scratched and dogs barked. There were few shops, mostly small stores, selling a great variety of items. The head and torso of a mannequin smiled out from the narrow window of a clothing shop, a plaster South American man with painted hair and dashing teeth, a sweater knotted around the neck of his winged collar.

The Uruguayan people are almost all descendants of Spain, Italy and other European countries, there are no black people, or 'mestizos', mixed race, I was told.

We walked around a corner, looking for the restaurant, and were confronted by a perfectly preserved 1930's Ford car, polished to a mirror shine. The Mayor? Or the local General?

Across the street the modest restaurant produced two perfect steaks and a bottle of Spanish wine. We asked about music in the town. Did they play guitar? Was there live music?

Tomas was fearful that canned disco music that was already in most major cities of the world, would have crept into South America.

Tomas was so passionate in his questions that the manager took a moment to understand.

"Yes," he said, "As a matter of fact, there is live music in the club around the corner, this very night."

We were suspicious of this, as we walked back to the ship after lunch. We weren't leaving until the morning, and the cargo was small and straight forward, but Tomas felt it would be disco lights and screaming. "Even here, I am sure," he said gloomily. "Or an electronic keyboard."

The work was finished by evening and the Second Officer volunteered to be on duty. The port and the town were one and the same and we could have made the centre in five minutes at a run, so Tomas, the other officers and I went to visit the club to see what it was like. We clomped along the dusty main street like a family going on an outing. It was unusual for us all to be ashore together. Stanco, the Chief Officer was wearing a dazzling blue satin shirt, like a band leader, Vadrich and Torenchi, the First Engineer and Third Officer were wearing similar pastel collarless shirts to each other (in case they might be asked to sing?) and Kadovich, the Chief Engineer, was wearing a blazer which even sported a buttonhole. I was concerned they were all going to feel let down.

We descended on the restaurant and had a quick dinner before setting off. Neither the woman behind the counter or the waitress seemed to understand what we were talking about when we enquired again. "It will be nothing," said Tomas grumpily, "And we will have to pay just to go in."

He was visualising a kind of semi brothel I think, the word 'club' being key.

We decided to go and look for the place. We had not gone very far when we found ourselves walking along with what appeared to be the rest of the town, so we followed.

Around another corner to a large municipal building, with steps, and lights on at all the windows. A coach bringing more people from a neighbouring town pulled up outside.

In the enormous central hall, the place was lined with chairs and packed with people.

Whatever was going on, we were now part of it. We sat down. The people around us smiled in welcome and told us where to find the beer, as if we had joined a family party.

After a few minutes, trumpet music, and in came the children in national costume. The boys were wearing loose black gaucho trousers tucked into high black leather boots.

Over their spotlessly white full sleeved shirts, a small black cape flowed. Their costume was finished by a black Spanish hat. They each held strings with a kind of Yoyo or ball on the end and as they lined up to face us, I heard them click together.

The girls wore red, green and white and held kerchiefs, their dress flowed with ribbon and their hair was tucked under a triangle of cotton scarf.

They began to dance. It was magical and mesmerising. The boys stamped and swung their bolas that made sharp clicking cracking sounds in rhythm with their clicking heels.

Their capes swung, revealing crimson satin linings. The girls pirouetted and offered their bright coloured handkerchiefs. It was

Spanish and it was Latin American. They were all faultless dancers.

Then the teenagers came in, a courtship mime in dance, again with handkerchiefs and this time passing around in a circle in the traditional fashion. They all looked as if they were enjoying themselves; there was laughter from the dancers and the audience. These traditional dances, the Pericon, the Chacarera and the Gato are a perfect illustration of the Gaucho/Cowboy and Spanish culture in combination.

The older folks were next. They lined up the chairs as if they were going to play 'musical chairs' which they did, but not exactly. It was a kind of courtship or marriage game in mime, and was very very funny, with the disapproving characters, the lovers trying to sneak a kiss, the rejected one, the shy one, all acted out with great charm and humour. The audience howled and laughed and so did we. The characters kept changing places on the chairs.

We were the only foreigners in the place and felt really lucky to share their festival. After the show, traditional samba, tango and rhumbas were played and the village took to the floor, and some of us, but not all, joined in. Tomas can only be persuaded to do the fox trot. It was wonderful to move around to hot rhythm after no exercise on board ship. I knew I looked ridiculous, but I had a great time.

In the morning, we crossed between the river islands and into the Rio Parana that would lead us up to Rosario in Argentina.

We had talked about the passport problem again. I did not like the idea of Tomas calling into ports like Buenoventura in Columbia with no official papers for me. They would not be the same as the Uruguayan or Argentinean officials. I had thought the Argentineans would be stiff with me because of the Falkland War, but this was not apparent at all. They were to prove more than courteous, especially to a woman travelling alone.

Tomas spoke to the port officials in Rosario before we arrived and we decided that I would fly to Buenos Aires from the airport there.

'Radio Rosario' blared out from the speakers, a special 'tango only' programme that you can guess, only played tango. Each number was introduced with great relish in rolling Spanish by a very masculine announcer.

Joining in with Radio Rosario

"This goes on all the time," said Tomas rather proudly. "You see, they still like the tango." After two hours of it I had had enough. Doomp doomp doomp doomp, da da da da da, doomp doomp doomp doomp. I liked the tango. But all day long?

Four of our Philippino crew were going ashore at the same time. They were being 'repatriated', going on leave. I watched them go across the gangway first. We were unable to let down the steps as usual, it was rather like it was in the dry dock in Singapore, a segmented iron bridge with very little handhold. The Philippinos were all carrying simply masses of stuff. They had purchased what almost looked like washing machines and armchairs, their boxes and parcels were so huge. "They will never get through all the customs," said Tomas, "But who can tell them?" Two had been on board for ten months and the other two, Posadas and Tolentino, had not been home for nearly two years. They had purchased a lot in that time, much of it they could not even remember where they had bought it.

It was becoming obvious that I would continue home. I had spoken to the British Embassy in Buenos Aires and they had been positive and helpful, but how long it would take, they could not say, I may have to stay in the city for a day or two.

I would have to say goodbye to everyone including Espresso and Nikolai. It had seemed confined for Espresso in our sitting room and his perch had been transferred to the bridge wing where he was out in the open air and could look at trees and down at the silver grey water flowing by. There were no waves and our passage was smooth up the Rio de la Plata. It was fun talking to him as his bright eyes took in everything, his head moving as a small bird flew over, or cranking up on his neck at a sound from a larger bird calling from the river bank. Much stronger now, his wing feathers had grown in enough for him to fly around without crash landing and he was accomplished and poised if he was on my shoulder. I went up to the bridge wing. I saw the broken string and the empty perch immediately and called down to Tomas who was on the deck below. "I think Espresso has flown away. Did anyone see him?"

I looked at the chewed string. It had not been cut. He had released himself.

I was happy he was well and free, but would he survive? I had hoped he could be released at the place where he came on board, but there was no guarantee the ship would be back in Europe. It could be ages. It would have been worse to keep him tied to a perch for months. It was a shock but the decision when and where to release him would have been difficult.

Tomas came up to see for himself. "It's good," he said simply, "It's a varied climate and he can fly into the slopes of the mountains where there will be trees and wildlife he would be familiar with. There are certainly hares and rodents for him to feed on. He saw and smelt it all and made his getaway."

Nikolai looked out of his cage and made a cackle, in triumph I thought.

"And what about him?"

"Oh the boys will take care of him when I leave. They enjoy him to be on the bridge. It's someone to talk to when they're up here alone on watch."

"But Espresso may never mate if there are no species like him in Argentina."

"At least he's alive and free. Better than being drowned don't you think."

I was teary eyed and going on about it. It was the reality of the loss of the handbag and what it had meant to us. Months of separation. We couldn't afford to pay for me to join the ship for awhile, the air ticket to Cuba and now from Buenos Aires was a huge bite out of our budget.

At Rosario airport I expected to see the four crewmen and there they were with their luggage. The plane was small. No room for it all. I saw the airport officials talking to them. They decided to take a taxi all the way to Buenos Aires, sharing the cost between them. Or perhaps a bus, one suggested. I shook my head. "You'll never get everything on a bus." They went to look for a taxi.

A tall, dark and handsome man helped me with my bags onto the plane. There was not the slightest hint from me. He was just the closest in line and he picked them up with a courteous nod. Another dark and handsome man sprang to help on the plane as I tried to put something in the overhead locker, but without that weary 'I suppose I'd better help you' attitude you can get from the British man. Neither man smirked or smiled as if I was to smile back in gratitude. They gave their assistance and then got on with what they were doing. Very appealing.

Flying into Buenos Aires from the country, you can see the big houses, parks and polo fields, lakes and swimming pools of the rich suburbs, the big Rio de la Plata widening out to the sea and the huge man made port. Dozens of ships were at anchor along the five miles of dock. From our little plane from up river, flying low and slow, it was a bird's eye view.

In the city, in a taxi, looking for the British Embassy I admired the majesty and style of the old Spanish architecture and thinking of the Perons and others speaking from the balconies. I was in the capital of a country that not long ago had been at war with Britain.

At the embassy I waited at reception while a man had a long complicated argument in Spanish and my taxi driver outside put his elbow on the window and went to sleep.

When I was finally directed to someone, I was delighted that they had already checked with London. With the photographs I had brought, they could make me a temporary passport. Would I come back in perhaps four hours?

I had a mad thought that I could go back to the ship, but it was still only a temporary passport that would get me home but not through other authorities. I had no yellow fever or vaccination certificates, as they had been in the handbag as well. Still it was good news.

I went to the shipping agency and left my luggage. As my taxi driver looked for the place he suggested for lunch, I saw a car pass by, piled high with suitcases and boxes tied to the roof with rope. More bags hung out of the boot. It looked like a travelling circus. I recognised the four faces inside, buried among other boxes. At least they had made it that far.

After lunch, back to the Embassy, then the shipping agency where I was told the four Philippino crew had been arrested on suspicion of robbery. The four eventually caught up with me in Rio de Janeiro airport where I had a five-hour wait for my next plane. I was slumped in a seat, sleepy and bored stiff after only three hours and twice as relieved to see them as I would have been normally. I had thought I was seeing things at first, as I watched the four familiar figures wandering across the concourse. A lot of flights from Buenos Aires go through Rio. They were on their way to Manila. Me to Glasgow via Paris.

They smiled broadly when they saw me. The shipping agency bailed them out and even managed to retrieve their purchases, some now packed to be sent by sea. The rest they were able to get onto the plane, and checked through to Manila. They looked very happy and were excited to be going home at last. I asked them if they had spoken to Tomas about being arrested.

"Agent speak to Captain. Ship was just leaving." Just leaving.

In Charles de Gaulle airport, I was waiting again, but only for an hour, for my flight to Glasgow. There was a chatty Glaswegian sitting next to me. I told her the story of how my handbag had been stolen in Havana.

"Ach heavens," she said, "The same thing happened to my sister in Peter Jones down in London! They do it with a stick you know. Under the table. Aye. The very same thing."

You don't have to travel the world to have these experiences.

When you are a far flung family, all doing different and demanding things, it is rare to be able to co-ordinate time together. To share an occasion is usually impossible. We were lucky that Christmas. It was in the stars that some good would come of the theft in Cuba after all. Nicola flew in from California. Tomas' youngest son Erik flew in from Gothenburg and Claire flew in from Paris. We met at Glasgow airport in a hail storm and drove home in convoy over the moors and up the glen road to Benbuie.

Christmas in the glen

Almost as soon as we arrived, large flakes of snow could be seen falling passed the windows. That evening the glen was cloaked in thick snow and there we were, lots of wonderful food, Christmas tree, log fires, even Christmas stockings.

Tomas was in another world. The New World.

Buenaventura Colombia   December 29th 1992

Dear Jill,

We are just leaving port. There was more than one incident before I was safely at sea. Nowadays it's more to the point to say that and not 'safe in port'. The temperature has dropped and it is at last comfortable in the cabin. We have had problems with the auxiliary engines and we are low on the electric supply sometimes dangerously close to black out. I am now using electric power only enough to keep Sherlock Holmes going. I need that tape badly at times to return my brain to normal. I took quite a few pictures when we passed through Magellan Straights. It was quite an experience.

The heat has been unbearable. I have had headache for three days.
Do you know that people here in Colombia shoot each other for stealing each other's clothes? We seem to be going back to some kind of an animal stage where human life is worth only what material is hanging on it or what valuables you may have in your pocket. It is not easy to keep the crew safe from themselves. The Philippinos as you know are too friendly for their own good.
The problem here in Colombia is that the bottom has dropped out of the coffee and the banana market. They are cutting down the coffee plantations and what do you think they plant again? Do you think it will be coffee?

It was 32° centigrade in the cabin in port. One thing that is good in this heat. My pen is flowing very well. The windlass has broke down yesterday afternoon after it had done so much work in two months. We anchored four times and moored alongside four times during the loading. During discharge run along the coast we have anchored nine times and gone alongside five times. The old windlass (only one side is working) has had a lot to do. I have been worried too, you can imagine.

Second officer just came after his mission to get charts for the next port, San Jose. He had to take a speed boat to another ship out on the roads that I contacted. He had to pay 40USD there and the same back, but worth it to have charts is it not? He looked as if he had been down at anchor bottom when he returned. He is now very popular with me. Now the agent comes so I say goodbye.

From your Tomas.

Love and Happy Christmas by the way.

CHAPTER 13

SHEERNESS   WEST AFRICA   ANTWERP   BRAZIL
SAN ANTONIO ESTE

"I've got two stowaways."

"What?" I was speaking to Tomas. He was in Sheerness in Kent and so was I.

He was speaking from the ship on the agent's mobile. I was in the shipping office.

"They got on board in Cape Town. I'll tell you about it when you come. I'm waiting for the Immigration this minute."

I had arrived the evening before. Tomas was bringing in a large refrigerated cargo ship, loaded with apples from South Africa. It was almost a year since I had been on board any ship.

Tomas had been home in the meantime and had just left a month before but when we knew the ship was coming into the UK, it seemed a good time to jump on board. I heard it had a swimming pool.

"Can we use it?" I was thinking of the rusty one that filled up with oily water.

"It's newly painted. But you'll have to wait until we're somewhere warm. There's no way to heat it, and it'll just be sea water."

"Where is it?"

"Just about ten steps outside our cabin door, on the same deck."

"Like the sundeck on the QE2."

"Something like that."

The ship was large, white and rather smart looking. This was Tomas' first trip in her and he was very displeased that he had had to report that two men from the Congo had managed to get onto the ship when it was loading in South Africa.

The stowaways had managed to get down into the engine room, and had hidden in a shallow pit under a grating. Oil ran down into this pit and they stayed there until they felt the ship was well and truly out at sea. An engineer saw something move in the oil under the grid beneath his feet as he walked by and the two young men were discovered.

They had been travelling down from the Congo for three years, but when they got to South Africa and tried to work selling things on the street, they were threatened by the local people.

Tomas got to know this because after they had been taken out from the oil pit and allowed to clean themselves up, given fresh clothes and food, they were told they had to write their report on how they came to be on the ship.

They were given a storehouse to live in during the voyage, in the centre of the main deck. They were not allowed to be inside the ship. As sorry as the crew feel for people driven to do these things to try to escape, they know that stowaways may bring disease on board as it would be rare for people so poor to have had vaccinations or immunisations. They may be emotionally disturbed or violent, try to steal or to manipulate the crew to help them. The crew, the ship and cargo must come first. Desperate people on a plane or on a ship can decide everyone else's fate as well as their own, and they may feel they have nothing to lose. It may not be so easy to sink a great ship as it is to grab the controls of an aeroplane, but sabotage is not so difficult, especially in the engine room.

Tomas was angry because security had been broken and everyone was puzzled how it had happened. They must have had the assistance of someone ashore in Cape Town, but it couldn't have been for money. The two young men had nothing, not even clothes now, as the clothes they were wearing were saturated in black oil and had to be thrown away. Perhaps they had given someone all that they had to help them get on board. They may have been helped out of sympathy by those who had permission to be on the ship themselves. There were guards and watchmen at the entrance to the ship. Tomas had sent strong messages back to the port.

Stowaways on board a refrigerated cargo ship have another problem if they try to hide in the hold. If they are well clothed, wrap themselves in plastic sheeting and blankets, they can still be suffocated by the carbon dioxide given off from the tons of fruit that surrounds them.

When I arrived on board, the immigration officer was already seated at the ship's office table, filling in a report. He seemed kindly and I knew that with Tomas having sons of his own, not much older than these two young men, it was not so easy for Tomas to be harsh either. The young stowaways were dressed in ship's issue bright orange brand new boiler suits, the only clothes that could be found on board that didn't belong to someone. The fact that they were such a colour made me think that they probably thought it was to prevent them running away, like convicts. They would have been happy just to be allowed to stay on board. They waved and smiled as they left. Whether they were sent back, or given asylum, we were never to know.

"Did you know that Lord Nelson's body was landed at Sheerness after the Battle of Trafalgar in 1805?" said the pilot who was seeing us out of the estuary and on our way. "And just about here," he said indicating the sea outside, "There is a huge ship still filled with ammunition, unexploded that is, sunk in the Second World War. The RICHARD MONTGOMERY. Can't move it. It would take the whole town with it if it blew up, and a lot else besides. They keep a check on it like."

I mentioned that I had discovered the first Aero Club had been established nearby. I had stayed in a hotel pub at Eastchurch, along the back roads close to Sheerness. The hotel bar had photographs of ancient flying machines and their proud owners on every wall, but the people who worked there couldn't tell me why the photographs were there or their significance. There had to be some connection, perhaps because the pub was called The Aviator. In the morning I discovered what is was directly across the road on the opposite corner. A huge sculpture and monument in honour of the Aero Club established in 1909 in the real pioneering days of flight. The church on the other side had a dedication on the gate.

As I was leaving the hotel, I told the receptionist about the monument. "Sorry love, I had no idea." She turned to a waitress who was passing through, "Did you know?"

"What?"

263

"Anything about these photos on the walls?"

"Haven't a clue."

Rolls and Royce were listed on the monument, along with other famous aviators of the time. Many early flights had taken off from the area across the sea, including Thomas Sopwith who won the £4,000 Baron de Forest prize in 1910, flying in a British built plane. The longest flight from England to the Continent at the time, and he flew from Eastchurch to Beaumont in Belgium, one hundred and seventy seven miles, to win what would be a small fortune in today's money.

As a port, Sheerness is in an important position for the continent, just as it was for those crazy men in those flying machines.

As Tomas is back in his old trade of refrigerated fruit ships and he will return to Sheerness often, it will make it easier to join and leave the ship and less expensive.

We were off to West Africa to load with pineapples. I wondered if the English Captain was still in Lagos and if Allonzo was still cooking for him. We were bound for Abidjan, Cote'D'Ivoire. The Ivory Coast. It would take a week to get there. A week at sea, through the Channel, into the Atlantic, passing Madeira, passing the Canary Islands, then the vast flat deserts of Western Sahara, and Mauritania. Then Senegal, Sierra Leone who were at war, Liberia, and finally the Ivory Coast.

The ship's crew were from Guyana, formerly British Guyana, and because of this they made porridge oats and hard boiled eggs for breakfast each day, and other English influences such as roast meats. They also made their own marvellous food, giant spicy prawns and great fried rice. It would not help the weight problem. Unless you are working physically like the sailors, exercise is not so easy on board ship. Exercise bikes and the like can only be used when the sea is perfectly calm, otherwise you fall off, sprain your ankle, or strangle yourself on the skipping rope. This was one reason I was interested in the swimming pool. You can diet on board, and brave attempts were made.

Other than eating, meals provide social time, when the officers and crew have a chance for conversation. In the evening, the main occupation was watching films on video.

I vowed not to go to lunch or dinner many times, but if you are days at sea, it punctuates the day. "What time is it? Oh it's nearly lunchtime. Perhaps we better skip it for today."

Tomas has a lovely expression. Always fatal. "Well we'll just go and see what it is."

Those with more sedentary positions on the ship, Captain, Chief Engineer, Deck Officers, were all a bit round, especially in the tummy area. The cost per day for food and washing supplies is generally about 5 US dollars per person. With all the variety of the ports of call, this cost would provide a substantial choice and the crew could find themselves eating unimaginable luxuries that would cost a fortune in a European restaurant. Lobster, fillet steak, or fresh exotic fish, purchased from fishermen heading into port with the catch of the day. If the cook was an average cook, the food on board was still plentiful and good.

The Guyanan cook on that voyage was exceptional. He was always smiling, always busy and loved his work. Anything you asked, he would try to exceed your expectations. He knew how to make things tasty.

"Could I have just a few steamed vegetables and a little rice?" I would ask as my zips were getting tighter, and shortly afterwards a variety of colourful, just cooked vegetables would arrive, aromatic with soy, ginger and garlic and decorated with chives, so good you found yourself having three helpings.

There was a small pub on the ship, with dartboard, tiny bar and a music system. On Sunday, the cook would make special lunch in the bar, instead of in the mess. Platters and bowls of steaming, delicious food were spread along a side table. Crispy calamari or roasted peanuts, spicy pickles and chillies were placed along the bar. More downfall. It diminished my resolve, good food was important for the hard working crew, far away from home comforts. I was simply being greedy. I just had to have some exercise.

"Is the water warm enough yet?" I asked Tomas nearly every day. Even off the Canary Islands it was still too cold, but when we were between the Cape Verde Islands and Dakar on the coast of Senegal we were at fifteen degrees longitude and I heard the sound of rushing water coming through the open door.

"You're filling the swimming pool!"

It still felt rather cold as I plunged in, but you could get used to it. I set up the radio cassette on the side, tied it to the rails and swam up and down to Beethoven.

It was a slightly odd, but exhilarating experience, swimming all by myself, in the middle of the ocean, in the middle of the ship, in a completely square tank about the size of the average patch of front garden in a London terrace.

The depth was the same all over, about eight feet, and when the waters outside began to sway, or the ship changed course, the entire swimming pool followed suit. You found yourself being swept to the other side in a huge body of water, rather like the parting of the Red Sea. The only place to cling was the one pair of steps, or the very edge. There was no knowing when this would happen. At times the water in the pool gained such a momentum that it kept on rushing back and forth for ages, almost emptying itself out on the surrounding deck while I clung to the edge, the lower half of my body trying to go with the flow. It was not always relaxing, but I was getting exercise, or at least developing the muscles on my fingers. The water was changed daily and was beautifully clean as we were far away from any coast.

There would be times when conditions were perfect and then it was very special. The crew would not swim during the day time, but in the late evening you could hear them whooping it up out there.

One day I had been swimming and lolling around in the water for hours when I noticed a large seagull flying overhead. His head was on one side, as he looked down wondering just what it was he was looking at. I shaded my eyes to look back up at him, treading the water. It was huge. It wasn't a seagull, it was an Albatross!

I quietly resumed swimming up and down as he continued to keep pace with the speed of the ship, me looking up at his underbelly, him occasionally at me, but mostly ahead.

He was flying about twenty feet above me, sometimes directly overhead, at others, alongside the ship, but always in view. What a moment. He stayed with the ship for about an hour.

Tomas was adamant. We would not go ashore in Abidjan. It was not a good idea, he was saying, which meant, dangerous.

He had had two very irritating experiences there at different times. One had concerned an order for ship's paint that was delivered alongside. The Chief Officer was sent to check if it was the correct type and was what had been ordered. Yes, came the report back, so it was brought on board. Then the agent brought the bill. It was not twice the cost, but TEN times the cost. Hundreds of dollars. "I am not going to pay this price!" Tomas had said, "You can take the paint back. Take it ashore!" They refused. The ship had taken delivery. The ship was of course sitting alongside the dock in the port and therefore still in the country but the officials claimed 'it was now exported'.

Customs Officers came on board and confirmed the situation, this was the law, according to them, what was more this was their price, the price they charged. Sigma, the paint manufacturer who had sent the paint to the port for the ship, had nothing to do with it.

If Tomas was not prepared to pay for goods he had ordered, they would arrest the ship, meaning keep it in port until the bill was paid.

The other incident concerned an 'advance' of CFA francs, the Ivory Coast currency. Tomas had told the crew on that particular ship that, for security reasons, they were not to go ashore. Another reason was that there would be a fast turn around at the port and they would leave as soon as they were ready.

When the time came, he was furious to discover that three crew, including the Chief Engineer had disobeyed his orders. The Second Officer had smiled just for a second until Tomas had had an apoplectic fit. "Chief Engineer fall in love," the Second Officer had been misguided enough to say.

When they came back on board, Tomas was forced to depart under difficult circumstances as the wind was getting strong. The agent came on board and pushed papers in front of him to sign when Tomas was on the bridge about to leave.

After Tomas had been home about a month, the company called saying about three hundred dollars would be deducted from his salary to cover the advance in Abidjan.

One of the papers he had signed was for about 120,000 CFA's which of course he had not received. "What would I do with a currency I can't spend anywhere else?" he said to the accountant at the office. "I was just leaving! Why would I have asked for cash at that stage?" They had his signature and so it was deducted, as the Abidjan officials had put it on the company bill.

So when we docked, I had not expected to go ashore, but one of the assistant engineers had reported a bad toothache sometime after we left England, and it would be several days before we were back in a European port. A car and driver was arranged to take the assistant engineer to a dentist.

When the driver came, the engineer refused to go. The official reason was that his toothache had gone away. He told me that if it came back, he would ask the other engineers to pull it out in the traditional seamen's manner. He was actually worried about Aids. He was concerned that the instruments used at the dentist would not be properly sterilised. It may have been an unreasonable fear, but the result was that we had a driver and car, paid for and waiting on the dock side.

"Come on then," said Tomas suddenly, "But only for an hour."

We would go to a market place.

I dressed in a white cotton long sleeve shirt and white trousers and tied my hair back with a small cotton scarf. I slipped bands soaked in insect repellent around my wrists and ankles. I must have looked and smelt like a nurse.

The driver swung out into the city. There was prosperity there, in patches, Western style hotels and office blocks. We passed a long swampy lagoon of dark green goo that smelt very bad and I thought about mosquitoes. Among the list of diseases given by the health advisory to travellers to the area included malaria, yaws, tuberculosis, dysentery, polio, yellow fever, Aids and many more. I kept checking the car windows to see if any mosquitoes had got in.

For the Ivory Coast, where the mosquito has taken another leap in it's development, travellers are meant to take Larium. This is supposed to work. The problem is the debilitating effect the medicine has on some people, even putting a few into hospital. Our doctor in our Scottish village had been humorous, I thought, but he was deadly serious.

"You can have certain side effects," he had said cautiously, "It can give you a rash, and it can make some people's hair fall out somewhat. Tends to have a negative effect on the nervous system. Puts you on edge you might say" He added that it wasn't as bad as the stuff he had given to a recent patient who was going into the interior of Irian Jaya. "That can have a bad effect on the heart for some," he said, "but better than getting malaria. Malaria is a very serious disease."

"Well if you ask any woman," I said, "If she would like to join her husband abroad, with pimples and her hair falling out and feeling in a bitchy mood, OR take the risk of having a heart attack, I can tell you which medicine she would choose" The Larium cost £40 but I had long decided not to take it and rely on good old missionary type precautions instead like buttoning up to the neck and soaking things in Jungle Formula repellent.

On the ship in port and at sea, the breeze keeps the mosquitoes away, as they can't fly in the wind.

The driver took us to a souvenir shop and we shook our heads. It was the French language again, and Tomas was relying on me. We drove off in the dust. The driver was puzzled about where we wanted to go, then he worked it out, and drove to a huge market place filled with covered stalls. It hadn't been the driver, it was my poor French.

We squeezed ourselves through the crowds, Tomas walking right behind me and saying "Keep on, keep on" and making small nudges in my back. The driver came as well. I did not see one European or

Caucasian in the entire market street and square. The people were very beautiful. The men were tall with perfect gleaming white teeth and burnished, strong, muscular arms. The women and children's faces were lovely, dazzling, and everyone was dressed in brilliant colours. Attracted by the women's vivid dresses, headscarves and turbans, I asked the driver if he could help us buy some lengths of printed cotton.

We went upstairs in a tall rickety building, again full to the brim with people, and among many rolls of patterns I selected two styles and lengths were cut. I was very excited by all the materials in the market, but Tomas was anxious that we returned to the ship as soon as possible.

When we received the mail in Antwerp, days later, there was a letter from my daughter Nicola and son in law Alan. Alan had included a newspaper cutting from the Glasgow Herald and had written on the top, "Hope Tomas didn't shake any hands when you were there."

The article was about Abidjan and dated the same day we had been ashore in the market. Several 'sorcerers' had been going around in the crowd in the market place, it said, shaking hands with men and telling them they had shrunk their penis. As the effect when someone is scared is simply that, when the frightened men looked down into their trousers, they felt it to be true. A crowd had gathered. The sorcerers were accused of causing a distraction while others went through the crowd to pick pockets. Seven people had been set alight and burnt to death.

In the Ivory Coast, as in other countries, a majority of people are animists, believing in complex spirits that can possess people, animals or objects. These beliefs vary among the many tribes, but in a crisis, there can be a common desire to stamp out the devil, the bad spirit that is threatening the majority and punishment can be swift.

On the journey back from the Ivory Coast to Antwerp, where we were to deliver the pineapples, I started to look into a local guide on West Africa and read about the Manatee or Sea Cow. I was trying to read more about the Ivory Coast and it is one of the places in the world where this mammal can be found. The body and habits of the Manatee made sailors believe, in their sexual frustration, that they were women with tails that lived in the sea, or mermaids. 'Stout tapered body. Can weigh up to seven hundred kilos. Makes chirplike squeaking noises when disturbed. Likes to communicate with other manatees by muzzle to muzzle contact. Feeds on seaweed and greenery around shallow coastal waters and estuaries. The Manatee has forelimbs, or flippers, close to the small head, and poor eyesight.'

Not only the Manatee. Sexy mermaid combing her long hair over her naked bosom? Anyone could make that mistake. Especially if they had been at the rum ration.

The pineapple smell is delicious. If the ship is carrying bananas and you can smell them you are in deep trouble because it means they are ripening, but the smell coming from the pineapples is from the green sprout on the top which smells pineapply but does not signify any problem. Better than naphtha any day. Waking up to this perfume is a treat, like walking in fields of fine green shoots with a breeze blowing.

Antwerp was unseasonably cold and drizzly. It is a wonderful sea city and full of history but the entrance into the port and the very harbour itself is so complex and huge it's a marathon to go ashore and find your way back to your ship.

Tomas remembered when he was a young seaman and his ship would tie up right in the heart of the old town. It was so close to the cafes that they would call out from the ship to those seen lingering at the tables on the cobbled square, to let them know the ship was due to leave. Now vast amounts of goods are containerised and the loading is mechanical. The population and demand has grown to such an extent that if we were to revert back to picturesque traditional methods, a lot of people would wait a long time for their bananas, and they would be expensive.

Sadly a lot of the sense of romance and adventure have gone from many big ports in the world. In becoming efficient factories, they have somehow lost their heart.

Out into the choppy busy Channel and then into the Atlantic once again. This time for a voyage of sixteen days to San Antonio Este, a small town far south of Buenos Aires on the coast of Argentina and so small it was difficult to find on the map. Argentina's coast is shallow and super tankers stay away from the shore. Buenos Aires has a constant battle with dredging the silt from the port and the whole coastline is spare of places where ships can load. San Antonio Este has a harbour with a reasonable draft and many fruit ships use the port.

The crew brightened up when they found out where we were going. It seemed that it was a popular destination with everyone.

After a few days out, when the sea temperature had given us the chance to fill up the pool once again, Tomas said he would be stopping the ship mid ocean to allow the engineers to perform a piece of regular maintenance. There was no wind and little drift. We were early for our expected arrival. It was a good opportunity. "You should go for a swim," Tomas suggested.

I was on my way to the pool when Wilson, one of the engineers, walked by and I asked him what they were going to do.

"Pulling a cylinder on the main engine to renew the rings," he told me. He was covered in black oil. I watched him troop away. One of those moments when you feel decadent to be enjoying yourself.

I went to the pool and slipped into the warm sparkling water. Tomas came out.

"I feel bad to be in here when everyone is working," I told him.

"What can you do? I'll give you a spanner and some overalls if you like"

He went over to the rail and looked down. We could hear two men arguing. It seemed to come from the outside of the ship. There was a lot of crashing going on as well.

"Hey! You two down there!" Tomas called. "Get a life buoy in the water on a line."

"What are they doing?"

"Trying to open the banana doors."

I heard a small splash and Tomas looked over again.

"That's better. A bit of calm water and they get cocky. They forget about the current."

"What on earth are 'banana doors'?"

"We don't use them anymore. Everything is unloaded out of the hatches with cranes. They're side doors that open right up, you know, when men carried the bananas off the ship on their backs. Now the fruit is in boxes and palletised and hundreds of boxes are lifted out at one time"

The smashing and hammering down below had increased.

"I asked them to check the mechanism and lubricate. A ship passing us yesterday said that the crane drivers were thinking of going on strike. I'm doing this as a precaution."

"What a racket!"

"They've only got them half open. When things are not used they get neglected,"

He took the steps and I heard him going down to the next deck.

Almost immediately there was a yell and a gigantic splash. I jumped out of the pool and ran to look over the side. One of the assistant engineers was in the sea. I saw him grab at the life buoy. The banana doors were now open. I could see a large square gap in the ship's side about eight metres up above the spluttering man in the water. Tomas and another engineer stood in the gap.

"Get a rope ladder!" I heard Tomas say and the other engineer took off.

"Get your arm hooked inside the ring," Tomas called out. He had been right about the current, the man in the water was being pulled down wind. The line to the buoy was stretched to its full capacity and the engineer was having to work hard to stay close to the ship's side.

A rope ladder was lowered but it took awhile for the rescue. As soon as the one who fell in the water got back on board, he started to shout at the other engineer.

"Never mind all that!" shouted Tomas. "Just get yourself changed."

In the cabin I put the kettle on. Tomas came in to change his shirt.

"I got there just as the doors suddenly flew fully open. Not a bad day for a swim at least."

The incident of the assistant engineer falling out from the banana doors went around the ship like wildfire, as anything unusual that happened did, prompting stories of who had fallen into the sea before and when and where it happened.

Tomas and I took our coffee up onto the bridge wing to look out at the calm blue sea with not a ship in sight. Tomas was talking about his early days at sea which I always enjoyed listening to.

"Accidents happened, people fell overboard, but that didn't stop men from having the urge to jump into the sea on days like this when it was hot," said Tomas. "It was a daredevil thing. Showing off to each other. Naked too if there were no passengers on board. From here, off the bridge wing or from the mast"

"It's such a long way down," I said, my stomach turning at the idea as I looked over the edge.

"They always had a line attached, and a life buoy out, but the real daredevils did it when we were underway"

"When the ship was going along?"

"There was a crazy guy on one ship. We were in the Caribbean and he had planned it of course. He had a line tied onto the stern. Went up into the mast, dived off, set off the alarm but even before the captain had had a chance to turn the ship around, he had climbed up the rope and was back on the deck as if to say, 'Well, here I am' . This kind of a folly was forgiven and not discussed in an official way as it would be today now the lawyers and insurance men have so much to say about everything. People weren't afraid to have fun then. Who was suing who or asking for compensation? Never!"

The Chief Engineer Davich had come up to the bridge to report on the progress of the repair. "This is when we were fit and young and you did a lot of things by hand. Make you strong you can believe. Now the machines they take away our muscles."

"Look at this," said Tomas patting his stomach. "I used to climb up the anchor chain when I was a young seaman and painting outside the ship. When it was time to go for something to eat, up the anchor chain and into the hawse pipe not thinking if the chain would rattle out and kill me. You were so strong you felt you would live forever."

Tomas told us a story about three young apprentices who planned to jump overboard one night when the ship was in the Caribbean. They wanted to find an island and live like Robinson Crusoe. They threw a life raft overboard and jumped immediately. The ship must have been making twenty three knots. All was quiet until it was time for two of them to be on watch at four o'clock. The captain saw one of the life rafts was gone and he called the American Coast Guard. The ship went up and down for awhile then continued on its voyage. The coastguard found the trio on a remote island and sent them back to Sweden. "They were all under twenty years old. The company did not write them off as idiots however and they were allowed to go back to sea. Adventures were not encouraged, but the adventurous man was felt to be an asset. It was what was expected of a sailor. I had one of those apprentices on board some time after that. I used to call him 'Robinson'."

"So you two can't have adventures now, now that you're both so old," I said.

"The ultimate 'jumper' I knew was about your age," said Tomas to Davich. "He was also a Chief Engineer. He fell in love with the Captain's daughter who was on board at the time. For some reason he wanted to escape from the situation. I don't know what the details were, if she rejected him, but he jumped overboard when the ship was off the Azores. It was only three miles to the shore, but the ship was making speed. He must have been a hell of a swimmer to make it with the current and swell around the islands. The police found him in a bar, sitting at a table with a bottle of wine. The company brought him back to Sweden and he ended up in a machine shop inland, as far away from the sea as was possible, according to the owner."

Tomas and Davich leant on the rail, looking wistfully down at the water. I crept away and went back to the swimming pool.

Off the coast of Brazil

A few days later as we were approaching the Brazilian coast, Tomas told me that he was going to show me something special and to be prepared to be up on the bridge in an hour.

"What is it?" I asked him.

"The Finger of God," he said.

Three hundred and sixty kilometres north east of Cabo de Sao Roque off the coast of Brazil, there is a volcanic island called Ilha Fernando Noronha, which rises three hundred and thirty two metres above sea level. As the island is only eleven miles wide by four miles long, it's an astonishing pinnacle rising up from the sea and into the sky. I was not the only one to be staring in awe. The crew were lining the rails. It was a magnificent sight.

"We're lucky. It can be surrounded by cloud, but not today."

No, not that day. The 'Finger of God', was in clear view. A dark green spire against a dazzling blue sea and sky. Unbelievable. Unforgettable.

A sailor's life may have changed in many ways but there were still wonderful things to see, and in another six or seven days of travelling down the east coast of South America, we would be in port.

In another six or seven days we would be in San Antonio Este.

San Antonio Este is a tiny town and nowhere near where the grapes, apples or pears are grown.

The fruit comes from far away, and if you travel any distance through the Rio Negro district to the town, you wonder where it is grown at all, the land is so arid and bare.

The answer is the truck. Dozens of trucks, which were waiting at the dockside. Many more were parked in lines at the back of the town, and more roared to and fro on the highroad leading in. Truck drivers from long distances and sailors from far away lands need some company when the work is done and there were plenty of ladies in San Antonio Este. We were to be there for several days, and there was much animated talk and raucous laughter in the bar as the men teased each other about their prospects.

Stanley came to us with a romantic story. He wanted two thousand dollars to go ashore for two days.

This was a fortune to him. Stanley was the steward, the lowest paid on the ship. He had a girlfriend coming from Chile and he needed to pay her fare. It was the weekend and Stanley had not had a day off for months. He had also saved, not drawing any advances either. Tomas tried to warn him that he would need the money when he went on leave. Stanley had also spoken about one or two ladies at home in Guyana. Paying for a ticket from Chile was a huge expense for him, but who were we to make judgements. We often spent money for air tickets we couldn't afford, so we could be together. Stanley was given the money in cash and cook was asked if he could manage without Stanley for the weekend. Sunday lunch could be cancelled for example, as anyone who didn't have to be on the ship would certainly be ashore. Cook would take that day off as well.

Wafts of aftershave floated down the passageways and men I had only seen wearing oily boiler suits emerged like butterflies, unrecognisable in floral shirts and natty chinos. The loading had been partial but now there were no more trucks on the dockside and none were expected until Monday. Work would not begin until then. I took photographs of several of the crew in their smart clothes, smiling from ear to ear, including Stanley. Later I sent copies to the ship titled 'Photographs taken after crew had had the 'sad' news that they would be delayed in San Antonio Este for another two days.'

It was suddenly very quiet on the ship. One or two of the more married men on board, who preferred not to go ashore, stayed on duty to keep things running and secure. We were there and Tomas could relax a little. Agents and chandlers and loading masters ceased to bother him after Saturday lunchtime and in the afternoon we went for a walk along the shore.

As it was such a small port, the ship was docked at a jetty just at the shore, rather like being on the end of Brighton Pier. We crossed the bridge and started along the beach, the ship well in sight for at least a mile before we turned a corner.

On the land side, it was scruffy sandy earth covered with sea shore plants, some in bloom. The beach was a mixture of large pebbles, gravel, and sand at low tide, like many of the beaches in the UK.

We smelt them before we saw them. "Ooof. What a smell. Must be the seaweed," I said. There was a poor dead penguin lying close to the water. Was the smell coming from him? We were walking behind sandy dunes covered in bushes when I heard a yawning roaring sound and froze. "What was that?"

Tomas went ahead a few yards. "Quick. Come and see," he whispered. Come and see?

It had sounded like a dragon.

I edged forward.

Confronting large wild animals in their natural habitat is a thrill tinged with fear and caution.

A group of about fifteen sea lions were lying close to us up on the beach. The males raised themselves up and roared a warning. They must have weighed a thousand kilos each. They were dark brown with paler yellowish bellies and sported a wild eye. Their breath and body odour alone would drive anyone away unless you were a lady sea lion. The ladies blinked their watery eyes and woffled their noses at us. The whole group really did smell like rotting fish, but they were magnificent to look at, also a bit dangerous. One of the larger males suddenly took off, lifting his giant body up on his flippers and almost galloping up the beach in our direction. "OK," said Tomas, "Time to make a retreat." We backed away, rather than taking a run, and the sea lion was satisfied. He had not been happy at our presence, who could blame him, we probably smelt as bad to him as he did to us. He must have signalled the others to go back into the sea, as with surprising agility they all slipped into the water and were gone beneath the waves in a moment.

Exhilarated by the experience, we walked for several miles. The sea was not really blue, but green, several shades of green, sending churning waves crashing up the beach and spreading foam at our feet. Not a sea for swimming and not another soul on the beach. The only sign of man were four wheel drive track marks circling the sand dunes.

Sunday afternoon Stanley returned but not for long. He was smiling broadly and bearing gifts. A box of chocolates and four miniature oil lamps. They were presents for us. He had also come back to ask for a further advance. Tomas was even firmer in his speech about not having any money left, but Stanley said his girlfriend could not get back to Chile as they had spent all the money. He took a further thousand dollars.

"It's his money." Tomas shrugged after he left.

In the bar that evening, there were several subdued crewmembers ordering one small beer each.

All alcoholic drinks on board are put down in the book. The crew had to pay for them and the total was deducted from their salary each month. They hardly raised a smile as I popped my head inside.

"You're not very jolly this evening," I said, looking around at the five gloomy faces.

"We have spent too much money," said one.

"And Davich here is feeling guilty," one of them joked.

Davich growled and took a deep drag on his cigarette. They were thinking about the more serious things they had meant to spend their money on, like the mortgage.

I thought about Stanley.

Six o'clock the next morning, Tomas was up early to be ready for a busy day.

"Here comes the millionaire," he said, as he looked out of one of our cabin windows. "Followed by the bridegrooms." Two of the crew had said they were getting married the next time they were ashore. I looked out. It was Stanley, looking almost as tired as the two following behind.

Tomas reached for his radio. "Chief? I want to see the three that are coming on board right now, in the office in two minutes. This is what happens," he said grumpily to me as if it was my fault. He felt I was too sympathetic about the men at times and this was not good for ship discipline.

"I didn't give them permission to go ashore!" I said indignantly.

"And I didn't give them permission to stay out all night. They have to work today."

He went out, fuming. I heard him out in the passageway dressing down the Chief Officer who had reported the evening before that "All were on board."

Later in the afternoon, a very tired and sad looking Stanley appeared with the vacuum cleaner.

"Oh don't bother in here Stanley. I've already cleared up. I hope you had a lovely weekend with your girlfriend."

He gave me a funny look. "I don't like to lie to you ma'am," he said. "I would like to say that she was my girlfriend."

"She came all the way from Chile didn't she? Did you have a fight?"

"No, not at all. It was someone I met in Chile. But not a girlfriend. A prostitute."

"Oh I see." It was the saddest thing to hear him say so.

"Did you know, that she was a prostitute?" I was still hoping to make a romance of it. The horror of how much money he had spent was very much in my mind. And for someone who possibly didn't care for him at all.

"She is very beautiful," was all he said.

There must be many stories about the truck drivers, the sailors and the women in San Antonio Este; dramas and sorrows, in between the partying, the laughter and the good times. Now the party was over, for our crew at least and the spectre of the possibility of Aids and less money to take home would hang over the heads of the not so careful who had been ashore, and they say the life of a sailor is one to be envied.

"What do woman at home expect?" said one of the crew, "It's not so easy to live like a monk for most of the year, is it?"

Stanley would have to spend many more months on board to earn back the money he had spent on the lady from Chile.

Chapter 14

DENMARK   LITHUANIA   RUSSIA   PANAMA CANAL
PUERTO BOLIVAR

Guayaquil   Ecuador   September 1999

My Love,

Thank you for the nice photo. I opened the envelope of course, even though it was meant for my birthday. You have such a smirky face on the photo. Well here I am and it could be worse. I am trying to keep my temper down, thinking of our newly planted trees and all our animals who depend on us. Even the foxes. There is a strong possibility that we are going to pass by Denmark to pick up some engine parts and supplies off shore, on our way to Russia.

If it is not so difficult call the agents there and maybe you can jump on and we can have Christmas and this Millennium New Year together that everyone is going on about.

We are anchored on the roads right now and have no loading time so I cannot give you any dates. However, I am sending this letter with a Swedish mechanic we have had on board who is leaving tomorrow. When I pass the Azores, I will phone you if I can get a signal.

Your Tomas

So it was that in late October I was travelling in a mini bus from Copenhagen to Kalundberg on the outer reaches of Sjaelland Denmark. I was quite sure that I would join the ship in time as travelling on the bus with me were the agent and two crew who were also joining the ship.

The weather the last few days had been very stormy and as we drove into the port of Kallundberg the evidence of the storm was all around us. Trees were uprooted and   even roofs of warehouses had caved in. The driver told us that it had been the worse storm that century and would surely hold the record now we were so close to the new one.

The Danish chandler had helped me buy a few extra supplies. One was a king sized foam mattress (I had slept on that ship's bed before) and the other was a dozen bottles of good quality olive oil. The stormy weather had given me concern that these things would now be awkward to get on board, I could see me juggling with a rolled up piece of foam and bottles of oil as I made my way up the accommodation ladder. When I saw the two crewmembers in the bus, was I relieved! Sailors are always capable and make the heaviest and most awkward thing look like a piece of cake to load onto the ship, even in rough weather.

The moment of peril that I always dreaded, joining the ship in a choppy sea, was made easy by many pairs of helping hands. My mattress and olive oil sailed over my head and up onto the deck. Tomas was on the steps to welcome us, I smiled up at him through the windows of the launch as we rolled and rocked against the ship's side.

When we crossed the Baltic Sea it was mild weather, the storms had gone elsewhere for awhile. We were to stop in Klaipeda, Lithuania, before continuing on to St Petersburg and I realised how little I knew about any of the Baltic States or how grand they had been before the Second World War.

The Grand Duchy of Lithuania, once a land of knights and dukes that included western Ukraine and Belarus, was one of the most powerful countries in Eastern Europe, particularly between the fourteenth and sixteenth centuries. It continued to be influential and powerful until the Soviet Union changed it out of all recognition and the Grand Duchy became Lithuanian Soviet Socialist Republic in 1945. Now with Estonia and Latvia, these three Baltic countries have struggled through their hardships to become independent once again.

The long years of Communist rule and neglect have left their mark. In Klaipeda, which is a resort for the rich as well as a port, you can see the grandeur of long ago in the buildings in the centre of the city where some restoration has already been completed.

In the 'Theatre Square', the statue of the Maiden of Klaipeda has been restored, standing again in the centre. Hitler made a speech from the balcony to declare Nazi Germany's supremacy. The shipping agent told me that the statue had been removed before Hitler arrived because the position she was standing in would have meant that she had her back turned towards him.

Across the square Tomas bought an amber brooch and earrings for me. The shopkeeper explained that this frozen fire was fossil tree resin. Amber is found along the shores of the Baltic more than anywhere else and can be between forty million and one hundred million years old. We chose unformed natural pieces that had not been polished. The information about amber made them all the more precious. In the same store we bought a hand-woven table cloth in flax in a traditional Lithuanian pattern and across the street in a bar we tried traditional food. We enjoyed several dishes except the 'zeppelins', named after the airship because of the shape. Zeppelins are made by covering a small piece of sausage with a great deal of shredded potato and glutinous fat, shaped and then steamed. The effect was like having a stone in your stomach for four hours.

It was then eight years since Lithuania had gained back its independence. Many thousands were sent to Siberia or killed between 1945 and 1991 and were replaced by many more thousands of Russians who were encouraged to settle in the country. I was told that the big houses along the beach were owned by Russians. I wondered if they were now learning the official language, Lithuanian.

Then we were off north and east through the Baltic Sea and the Gulf of Finland to the old cold war enemy.

In the port of St Petersburg, restrictions at the port made me wonder what it had been like before. A supervisor from the company was on board our ship and having completed his work was going over to join a sister ship that was moored nearby. There was a great deal of talk about it and a ton of paper work but in the end they would not allow him to walk the few hundred yards around the dock to board the other ship. They were so concerned that he might do this, that they actually escorted him all the way to the airport. It was said that we were docked near an old Russian Naval Base, still somewhat in use. The supervisor was very frustrated and made many angry telephone calls but the agent could not get permission.

I was very glad I had got on the ship in Denmark. It would not have been possible in that dock.

St Petersburg is visited by millions of tourists and business travellers who do not arrive however by docking near to a naval base. If they did, they would all have to go home.

After all of that I had not expected to be allowed ashore but the agents were very charming and said they could get us a pass and a driver to take us around the city for an hour or two.

Tomas had not stepped ashore for weeks and this time did not have to be persuaded.

The driver was not allowed to come to the ship's side. We walked through grim warehouses and broken down buildings to the gate where a small car that had seen better days was parked, waiting for us. The driver flashed the weak headlights as we appeared.

Our driver, Andre, had been chosen because he could speak English, which at first, he seemed reluctant to use. He switched on the radio as we drove away and after a few minutes of blaring Russian pop, the music was interrupted by an announcement.

"Der iss demonstration," said Andre, turning down another street suddenly. "In support of government," he added. Up the side street in the direction of the Winter Palace, which was our original destination, there were simply crowds of people marching purposefully along. Barricades were being erected. If they supported the government why did they need to demonstrate and in such numbers I wanted to ask.

We were now driving along the Neva River, with grand buildings either side, but not a tree in sight. Andre took us to as many golden domed cathedrals and palaces as he could but kept having to turn up side streets to avoid traffic and crowds. The buses, cars and trucks were really dirty, the office buildings furry with years of dirt. The famous palaces and cathedrals gleamed, they were all very clean. "Dis vos der year eighteen ninety two fer ixampool," said Andre as we swooped by another grand piece of architecture. The buildings on the other side off the street were black, including the windows. "Also the date the last window cleaner died," Tomas murmured in my ear.

We saw one clean car the whole drive through the city and it immediately made us laugh out loud as it was a Volvo. The only Swede in town.

But when was Andre going to stop? He seemed reluctant, but further away from the centre he found a place he thought was fine. Looking out, we saw the inevitable souvenir stalls but were happy to stretch our legs.

The stalls had beautifully crafted items, as well as the usual babushkas, and we bought three carved boxes from Siberia, made from birch bark. There was a hat stall, this was Russia, and Tomas wanted to buy himself a typical astrakhan but there wasn't one. "They wear them in Chechnya of course," Tomas said in an aside to me "not popular to sell them at the moment perhaps?" He settled on a black Russian Naval Captain's hat and I insisted he wear it as we walked back to the taxi. As we got into the car, a street artist was following and in the two minutes between putting it on his head and arriving, he had completed a very good likeness of Tomas, complete with hat. We bought the drawing. He had managed to catch Tomas' expression exactly. I had also bought an enormous hat and when we arrived back at the ship there were a few jokes and comments as we came up the gangway.

On our way, we had asked Andre to take us to a grocery shop. He had told us that a typical treat was vodka and salt pickles. The grocery shop was in a suburb and most interesting as it contained only Russian food and drink. We bought sausages, jars of salt pickles and several half bottles of vodka as there were many types. I remembered a hot pepper vodka I had enjoyed at a Russian restaurant in Los Angeles and we found one, complete with a chilli at the bottom. We loaded Andre up with vodka and salt pickles and a tip in dollars, which he changed immediately into roubles at an exchange bank before dropping us off.

Andre was not a typical Russian in looks or build, he had a sensitive face, you might have guessed he was French for example, but he had lived in St Petersburg all his life. He was probably about fifty years old.

Months after I got home, I read in the paper, about Dostoyevsky's granddaughter who was living, as her grandfather did, in St Petersburg, but who was poverty stricken. All the worldwide fame that Dostoyevsky had brought to St Petersburg, his influence on the novel, even recognised in the old USSR as one of the great writers and his granddaughter was living in one room. The article also mentioned that his grandson Andre was poor, and worked as a taxi driver in the city. If we go back again, we will try to find Andre and ask him if he is that man.

We stayed on board for the rest of the time in port and the next afternoon as the last boxes of bananas were swung ashore in a snowy blizzard, I noticed that the water around the ship was frozen. There were rivulets of water running between the large floes of ice, but you could feel the temperature dropping, and see the estuary freezing in front of your eyes.

There was a gathering urgency on the ship to get away, and as soon as the steps were up and the agent able to jump ashore, we were moving out from the dock, parting the ice, but making slow progress.

I was up on the bridge, in the dark, by the side windows, watching the snow pile up on the bridge wings where I had stood so often in the sunshine. The snow fell with astonishing speed and the wind blew it quickly into great drifts. Ice began forming over the windows. I looked behind me at the dark shapes of Tomas, the Russian Pilot, the Chief Officer and the Helmsman trying to see out through the twirling white flakes. I looked at the radar, but I knew, as Tomas had told me before. In snow, radar is almost useless.

We were out in the estuary, the pilot left, and we took off into waters where the patches of ice were few and far between. I felt relieved, but I didn't know what was ahead of us.

We moved out to sea. We were in ballast, light, with no cargo, and we tossed about in the wind. I went downstairs to bed. Chief Officer would probably take over in a little while and Tomas would be down. I left some coffee in the pot for him and went to bed.

I was thrown awake by the storm. I had been waking up every few minutes before, but choosing to ignore the increased movement of the ship. Now I was up, eyes wide and lying on the floor as everything in the bedroom tumbled on top of me.

The noise was tremendous. Everything everywhere was falling. Not only small items, but chairs and tables, things that were usually stable or attached to the floor. I grabbed my padded jacket and managed to pull trousers on and rammed boots on my feet, falling over onto my knees several times and smashing my elbows and knees on every corner.

I knew Tomas was on the bridge and would have enough to think about, so I tried to put things in their place, but the storm was increasing.

I jammed myself inside the space under the desk in the office, bracing my feet and back between the drawers. One of the half bottles of pepper vodka was rolling around under the desk. I grabbed it, unscrewed the top, and took a large swig. Tomas had bought many large plants in South America. They were in huge ceramic pots at the end of the room. The Boson had made a wooden frame around them all, nailed and lashed for stability. There were small trees and tall banana plants.

These plants in their heavy pots became dangerous flying missiles, as at a sudden great lift and surge of the ship, the frame surrounding the pots cracked and the trees went rolling and flying around the room. There were pots of giant cactus on the shelf, loose and dry in their containers, they were easy flyers and joined the mess heaving around on the floor, tumbling about with the crockery, ashtrays and food falling out from the open door of the refrigerator.

I hugged the vodka bottle to my chest and closed my eyes.

We were in the Gulf of Finland, heading toward the very place where the Estonia had gone down in September 1994. It kept coming into my mind. I had never been in a storm like this.

It was only with a great effort that I could stay crouched under the desk against the wall and not get thrown around the room. When we hit an extra large wave, which we did every minute, the opposite wall became the ceiling. It was like being on one of those old fashioned swing boats at a fair, when you think you have reached the pinnacle and will surely go right over on the next swing. The difference is that you do not believe anything really bad will happen to you at the fair, you are only on the edge of fear and it's exciting. The terrible storm was not exciting, because I could feel its serious purpose. It wanted to rip everything apart that was in its path.

I knew rough weather, gale force winds, but this was more. I waited each time for the moment when we would roll right over. I screwed up my eyes and bit my lips. I could hear the tremendous crashing of the waves breaking high over the ship, the swerving, agonising movement as the ship tried to steady herself in the deep troughs of the waves.

Tomas had slowed the ship right down but there was little else he could do, except to look for an opportunity to break away from this hurricane as soon as he could.

We were not invincible. The fear that we could actually go down, that the sea could easily take us, that waves could come crashing in at the door at any minute, invaded my mind. It won't happen, it won't. I insisted to myself, but the thought remained like a dark threat, the rational me telling the optimist, "Oh yes it can, and it can happen any minute. It will be sudden and you won't have any control over it. You think you will be able to do something but if it happens, you won't."

The things crashing around the room and the sound of breaking glass added to my tension. I could see broken jagged glass bottles and others, still whole, rushing around the room, tossing themselves against the walls. I realised in more misery, that these were the large bottles of olive oil I had brought on board. They had escaped from their box and were now spilling their contents everywhere. The horror of the dangerous glass and the waste made me venture out from my cave. Perversely, I allowed myself to be tossed about on the floor like a rag doll, determined to save at least two of the bottles.

I smashed my knees and cut my hands on the glass in many feeble attempts. I was trying to act as if what I was doing was quite normal and to retrieve the unbroken bottles would somehow make everything alright.

The office chairs rushed at me on their castors, then spun away as a table knocked them out of the way and plant pots and boxes came flying through the air. I snorted and swore my way through the mayhem and grabbed two bottles as they went by, one in each hand. Clutching my prize, one whole bottle of olive oil and a half bottle of pepper vodka, I sheltered back inside the well of the desk again, like an animal in a cave, wedging my self once more against the sides of the desk. The peppery vodka was a huge comfort. My jacket, boots, trousers and hair were now soaked in olive oil, earth, coffee and blood.

The storm raged. I was so glad to be a little drunk. It took away some of the terror.

The ship continued swerving, listing over, then mercifully righting itself again. Before you could feel relieved, another great crashing wave would roar onto the ship and it would lean over once again, repeating what you had so quickly thought was by far the worst that you could stand, the worst that the ship could stand. The storm was not going to let us free from its grasp. It wasn't going to allow us to feel safe, not for a moment. It was endless. When would it stop?

On that next morning, at dawn, I made a supreme effort to drag myself up the rolling stairs to the bridge, only to find Tomas, strapped into a swinging high chair it was true, but chatting away to the electrician who was from Ecuador and shared Tomas taste in music.

"Boleros de San Valentin, er, Nosotros et…?"

"Hola soledad?"

"Si! Si Capitain!"

The ship gave another violent lurch and they saw me. I was smothered in olive oil and earth.

"You alright?" said Tomas "What do you have all over you?"

"How do you know if I'm alright? Your plants have been flying around. I could have been killed just by one of them."

"The plants? What's happened? They're not all broken are they?"

"The plants!" I grabbed onto the chair, missed and ended up across the room.

"I have been checking on you. I sent Stanley to see. He said you were asleep," Tomas said.

"ASLEEP!?"

Carlo the electrician made his retreat.

In a minor lull, Tomas came down to the cabin to check on the damage and was furious with the mess. "Look at this! What did you bring that oil for? What kind of job did that Boson do? Everything is broken!" He raged about.

I knew he hadn't had any sleep and his nerves were understandably a bit on edge but I could have cheerfully killed him. I thought I had been brave not to complain, not to come to him in floods of tears and I was furious that he was now telling me off about things that were out of my control. We could be drowning but his banana plants must be saved.

The severe storm continued for two more days. The whole of the Gulf of Finland and most of Europe was in the grip of that storm.

That first night it had been a Force 12, Tomas told me later. He had had to leave Russia not to get frozen in, and had an idea what he might be heading for.

Sometimes there is nowhere else to go.

The weather conditions we were in that night after we left Russia were similar to those confronted by the ESTONIA on September 28th 1994. The ESTONIA, on its usual voyage from Tallinn to Stockholm, was about half way on her journey when the bow visor was torn off by the pressure from the six metre high waves. Perhaps something had released the latching mechanisms because the ramp opened slightly. Within minutes, the sea flooded into the car deck and the ship lost its stability, listing over thirty to forty degrees. There was no time to launch the lifeboats. It all happened so quickly and the ship was tilted so far over it made it impossible. Nine hundred and eight people were on the ESTONIA. Only one hundred and thirty seven people were able to be rescued from the water.

Through the Baltic, into the North Sea, along the Channel, it was my worse time ever at sea. Miraculously I wasn't seasick. This I put down to the vodka and the fact that no matter what, I can always eat. How they were making any sense of the kitchen I could not imagine, but hot food would occasionally appear. Stanley told me mournfully that the stores were in a mess. It would be his job to clear it up once we were in calmer waters.

I thought about the engine room. The Chief Engineer told me that as it was so low in the ship, it wasn't quite so bad as being up above deck where there was more movement. But all those frightful hissing steaming machines! And the giant pistons going up and down.

"You better hope they're going up and down. 'Cos if the engine stops in storms like these you're in very serious trouble." He was a Scot, and therefore liable to a bit of dourness, but his words struck home. Of course. It was only the engines that kept us stable at all. If they were to fail, we would be like a cork.

Out into the Atlantic it was only slightly better. Sometimes we heard the BBC World News and the effect of the storms on land. Flooding and trees down. At sea, we were to endure a total of eighteen days of rough weather after leaving St. Petersburg. Tomas changed course as much as possible. We had no instructions other than to head for the Panama Canal. We had no real deadline, except for fuel and fresh water. As we headed south, I realised we were getting closer to Christmas.

After surviving the storms, the concentration of keeping men safe and the ship functioning, when we were only swinging in swell from the distant weather, Tomas and the cook started to discuss the menu for Christmas and the Millennium New Year's Eve. It seemed that we would be at sea for both occasions, we had no information on the next port and a menu to suit everyone would be some compensation. The sea was still not calm enough to walk in a straight line without holding on and I was remembering a time on board one ship when we barely noticed Christmas because of the weather.

We needed the morale boost of a celebration and as we sailed through the Mona Passage between Puerto Rico and the Dominican Republic into the Caribbean Sea, the swinging began to ease. By afternoon, the occasional lift would throw you off balance, sending me running to retrieve the table decorations, but preparations were underway.

It was Christmas Eve. All hands rushed to hang balloons and to take down the sliding doors between the crew and officer's mess and open it out into one large room.

We made up a box of presents and put on an impromptu cabaret and even the most cynical joined in and contributed a joke, a trick or a song. The crew said it was the best Christmas they had had for years.

On the famous New Year's Eve we were still in the Caribbean Sea and it was warm and calm and gloriously sunny so we roasted meat on a barbecue on the stern deck as always, but with the extra kick of free bottles of champagne all round. True the champagne was Russian, but it was cold and bubbly, had survived the storms, and was not bad at all.

In the Philippines, in Guyana, in Ecuador, in Sweden, and in Scotland, when was it going to be midnight? We had become confused at just when it would be New Year's Eve, but on the ship, it was twelve midnight.

Tomas and I went up to the bridge at twelve and blasted away on the ship's siren to welcome in the new millennium.

"Take a look at this," Tomas was raising the blind. I sat up in bed and looked out. The QE2 was passing just metres away against the rising sun. A glorious sight and unusual for two huge ships to be so close to each other, but we were at anchor at the entrance to the Panama Canal. The QE2 was just about to start her journey through, like a large white swan.

293

It was my daughter Claire's birthday, January 12th and that is why I remember the date as I sent her a fax saying 'Guess what just passed our cabin window?'

We had been waiting at the entrance to the canal for nearly two weeks, but at least on calm water, looking out on other ships, either waiting orders like us, or we would see the puff of smoke from a funnel and they would up anchor and pass into the entrance.

It was a significant time for the Canal. America was handing over it's management and control to Panama after nearly one hundred years. Ceremonies were taking place not so far away in the city on the Pacific Ocean side and the new lady President of Panama had been given the keys.

This was to be a first time for me, Tomas had been through the Canal dozens of times he had lost count, but he was still enthusiastic about it. I had believed it would be a long slotted waterway, like Suez, and I was surprised when at last we went through.

I was sitting up on the sundeck, or the Monkey Island, the place where all the radar masts are on top of the bridge. Tomas' head appeared at the top of the steps.

"I have news. Guess."

"Ecuador?"

"Yes. But not Guayaquil. Puerto Bolivar!"

Puerto Bolivar. The hotel with the blue walls and the gunshots at night outside the window where we had stayed.

We were to pass through the canal at night and at first I was disappointed. The passenger ships go through in the day, but cargo ships are not meant to be sightseeing, but in the end it made it all the more marvellous, more mysterious. On the way back we did go through by day, it was beautiful, but not so other worldly as at night.

As the ship approached, you could see masses of lights on high, as if coming upon a futuristic football stadium. This was the high mast lighting at the first set of locks. The ship ahead had gone into the next lock and was towering above us, but only metres away from our bow. Rail tracks along the side and small cabooses holding the mooring lines, ran up the arching roadway like the beginning of a ride at a fair. They guide the ship along.

At intervals simply dozens of canal workers got on board and took care of the complicated moves. The Panama Canal is the only place in the world where the Captain is not in charge. The Panama Canal Pilots are fully responsible for the passage. The engineering of the canal can be read about, but to see how it all works, by gravity and water, is a marvel. It was a dream for years and cost many lives before it opened. The operation relies on rain, not sea water, which was a revelation to me. It takes 8-12 hours to go through. Tomas was up on the bridge the whole time, but I gave in to sleep and went to bed, waking up now and then to look out.

At one point we arrived in a big lake. There were lights on poles sticking out of the water to guide us through, as other huge ships passed, heading back the way we had come. I could see mountains around us and the stars. Then through a narrow cut, with orange lights set at intervals along the rocky cliff. It was a magical mystery tour from the Atlantic to the Pacific without going around Cape Horn.

Oro verde. Green gold. Bananas, a huge part of the economy in Ecuador. We were loading the entire ship with bananas which are very green when they are cut, a velvety glowing green. The supervisors and the owners from the plantation stood at small tables alongside the ship and watch as a sample one is cut from a stem and a pulp thermometer is thrust into the flesh inside. Too much 'field heat' and they would be rejected. One box of bananas starting to ripen is a nightmare in a hold. The delivery temperature is of the utmost importance. Too cold and you get UPD, or under peel discoloration, it can all amount to a great loss of money. The crop generates an average of six hundred million dollars in export revenue annually. No wonder it's called green gold.

The ship started up the refrigeration process. The holds, opened up to the hot sun, still have to be cold to receive the hundreds of boxes. Men stood in the bottom, catching the huge heavy net that the crane driver swung down to them. The boxes are palletised, on wooden slats, and a small truck whizzed about skilfully, lifting the pallets and stacking them in rows. No one was on strike, so the banana doors were not opened. Music trilled out from the many trucks and from the radio in our cabin. "Siempre que te pregunto, Que cuado como y donde, Tu siempre me respondes, quizas, quizas, quizas." There was no question. We would go ashore for the anniversary. It had been thirteen years since I had flown to Ecuador to meet the sea captain I had met on the aeroplane.

The day we arrived in Puerto Boliva, we heard that there was a huge demonstration in the capital Quito, in the north.

That evening we managed to get a shadowy reception on the ship's television and the amazing image of thousands of Otavalo and other indigenous people who had come down from the mountains and were filling the streets of the capital. Holding flaming torches aloft, they demanded that the inflationary prices of their staple foods be reduced. It was a peaceful but mass demonstration and it worked. The shipping agent told us that the ports would not be affected, but the situation was making politicians nervous, and in South American style, the army was on the streets when we drove into town the next day. Soldiers stood along the pavements, particularly outside the banks, with legs astride, guns at the ready.

The driver was completely unfazed by this and drove right into the centre, parked and opened the door for me as if it was any other day.

I bought sun cream, shampoo and aspirin with soldiers outside the window and tanks rolling by.

This was all a precaution, said the driver, to protect the port. The demonstrators had won the day in Quito, but they didn't want the idea to spread around the country.

Tomas and I were on a romantic mission, so we still continued into Machala, where the driver dropped us off at the beautiful Hotel Oro Verde, a branch of the same hotel where we had stayed when I came to Guayaquil all those years ago.

We sat out on the terrace, looking across the tropical gardens as exotic birds made whooping calls in the palm trees.

We were the only people there.

A waiter appeared.

Tomas smiled. "Dos Pisco Sour, por favor."

ISBN 141202091-3